Studien zum dänischen Strafrecht

Studies in Danish Criminal Law

Vagn Greve & Karin Cornils

Studien zum dänischen Strafrecht
Studies in Danish Criminal Law

DJØF Publishing
2011

Vagn Greve & Karin Cornils
Studien zum dänischen Strafrecht
Studies in Danish Criminal Law
First Edition 2011

DJØF Publishing is a company of the
Association of Danish Lawyers and Economists

Cover: Bo Helsted
Print: Scandinavian Book, Århus

Printed in Denmark 2011
ISBN 978-87-574-2517-8

Sold and distributed in North America by
International Specialized Book Services (ISBS)
Portland, OR 97213, USA
www.isbs.com

Sold in Scandinavia by
DJØF Publishing
Copenhagen Denmark
www.djoef-forlag.dk

Sold in all other countries by
The Oxford Publicity Partnership Ltd
Towcester NN12 6BT, UK
www.oppuk.co.uk

Vorwort/Preface

Dieses Büchlein enthält fünf Aufsätze, die ursprünglich als Beiträge zu rechtsvergleichenden Forschungsprojekten des Max-Planck-Instituts für ausländisches und internationales Strafrecht in Freiburg i.Br. geschrieben wurden. Die Projekte sollen in der Schriftenreihe des Instituts publiziert werden. Wir denken, dass die Dänemark betreffenden Landesberichte auch für sich allein von Interesse sein können, und veröffentlichen sie deshalb vorab in einer Art Sonderdruck. Dem Max-Planck-Institut danken wir für die Genehmigung. Den Beitrag "Strafrechtliche Zusammenarbeit zwischen den nordischen Ländern" haben wir gemeinsam verfasst, den Aufsatz über "Freiheitsentziehende Maßnahmen gegen gefährliche Rückfalltäter" hat Karin Cornils, die übrigen drei Beiträge hat Vagn Greve geschrieben. Der Sonderdruck gibt unsere Aufsätze in ihrer ursprünglichen Fassung wieder, obwohl die Rechtslage in der Zwischenzeit einige Änderungen erfahren hat.

This book contains five articles, originally written for comparative research projects at Max-Planck-Institute for Foreign and International Criminal Law in Freiburg i.Br. They will be published at the institute's publication series. We hope these country reports on Denmark may be of interest independently of the original projects, and we thank Max-Planck-Institute for its kind permission to print them in this form. The article "Strafrechtliche Zusammenarbeit zwischen den nordischen Ländern" is co-authored by us; the article "Freiheitsentziehende Maßnahmen gegen gefährliche Rückfalltäter" is written by Karin Cornils; the other three articles have Vagn Greve as author. The articles are printed in their original form although, in the meantime, some changes of law have taken place.

Hundige / Freiburg, November 2010

Vagn Greve Karin Cornils

Inhaltsverzeichnis/Contents

The Criminal Justice System in Denmark*

I. Basic Country Characteristics

A. Statistical Data

- *Geography and Population*

The Kingdom of Denmark is situated in the Northern Hemisphere. It consists of Denmark *(Danmark)*, the Faroe Islands *(Færoyjar)* and Greenland *(Kalaallit Nunaat)*. The information in this report refers only to Denmark unless otherwise stated.

The area of Denmark is 43,560 km^2, of the Faroe Islands 1,399 km^2 and of Greenland 2,166,086 km^2 (410,449 km^2 presently free of inland ice). The population of Denmark is 5,411,000, of the Faroe Islands 48,000 and of Greenland 57,000.[1]

The average population density for Denmark is 126 inhabitants per km^2.[2] In 2006 there were 270,000 foreigners living in Denmark, this being 5% of the population; the largest groups are from Turkey (29,491), Iraq (18,721) and Norway (13,928).[3]

- *Economy*

The gross national product for 2004 is estimated at DKK 1,467,311 million (€196,793 million). This is equivalent to approximately 272,000 DKK (€ 36,480) GNP per inhabitant.[4] This ranks Denmark high internationally, yet

* Translated by Malene Frese Jensen who is thanked cordially. Quotations are also translated from Danish. Stand vom 1 April 2007.

1. Statistisk Årbog 2006, table 1.
2. Statistisk Årbog 2006, table 1.
3. Statistisk Årbog 2006, table 20.
4. Statistisk Årbog 2006, table 404.

still lower than countries such as Luxembourg, Norway, Switzerland, and New Zealand.[5]

Of the population, 37% are employed in industry, 14% in trade and 10% in agriculture.[6] Danish business is dominated by small and medium-sized companies.

The average family income is DKK 360,000 (€48,280).[7] The taxation of income is one of the highest in the world – 50.1% in 2006.[8]

Denmark is a welfare state. Schools, high schools and universities are free. Medical and hospital treatment is free. Everybody is entitled to a state pension.

- *Crime*

The number of Criminal Code offences reported to the police in 2004 was 474,419. This represented a 2.4% decrease compared to 2003. The 2004 figure is equivalent to 10,822 offences per 100,000 inhabitants 15 years and older. Divided into types of offences, the breakdown per 100,000 inhabitants is 71 for sexual offences; 412 for violent crimes; 10,144 for property offences; and 195 for other offences.[9] In comparative European statistics, the numbers are computed differently which results in minor discrepancies between the two sets. There, the Danish figure is 9,013 criminal offences per 100,000 inhabitants (the European mean being 4,736); intentional homicide is 1.2 (2.7); assault 202 (267); rape 9 (10); robbery 59 (79); theft 5,323 (2,404); drug offences 269 (166) and drug trafficking 20 (40).[10]

A total of 195,000 decisions were rendered in the criminal justice system in 2004. Of these, 114,800 (59%) concerned the Road Traffic Act; 56,400 (29%) the Criminal Code; and 23,800 (12%) special laws.[11] It should be noted that fines under DKK 1,500 (€200), and with that many road traffic fines, are not statistically registered.

Of the above-mentioned decisions, 76% were fines; 7% suspended imprisonment; 6% imprisonment; 1% acquittals; and 10% other decisions. The frequency of sentences (suspended imprisonment and imprisonment) was 541 per 100,000 inhabitants. The average custodial sentence was 1.6 months for

5. Statistisk Årbog 2006, table 491.
6. Statistisk Årbog 2006, table 111.
7. Statistisk Årbog 2006, table 213.
8. Statistisk Årbog 2006, table 437.
9. Kriminalitet 2004, pp. 11–12.
10. European Sourcebook 2003, pp. 37, 40, 42–45, 49–50.
11. Kriminalitet 2004, p. 19.

suspended imprisonment and 6.1 months for imprisonment.[12] The European statistics for 2003 are also based on different figures here. There, the number of persons convicted of criminal offences in Denmark is 2,630 per 100,000 inhabitants (the European mean being 913).[13]

Of the 40,600 persons who were convicted of Criminal Code violations in 2004, 83% were Danish citizens; 9% were from other European countries; 4% were from Asia; 3% were from Africa and 1% was of other origins (incl. stateless). Among the foreigners, 70% were illegal residents; 16% were tourists and foreigners with visitor visas; 9% were asylum applicants and 5% held residence permits.[14]

In 2004, 9,602 persons were sentenced to prison after conviction. The average number of prisoners was 3,769, including 1,089 in detention or custody awaiting trial.[15] The Danish prison population was 67 per 100,000 inhabitants in 2003. This is on par with the other Nordic countries, but under half of the European mean of 141.[16]

- *Criminal Justice Institutions*

The *police* in Denmark, the Faroe Islands, and Greenland constitute one national force employed directly by the State. The Minister of Justice, who is the chief police authority, exercises his or her powers through the National Commissioner *(rigspolitichefen)* and the chief constables *(politidirektørerne)*. The National Commissioner supervises the chief constables. The average number of employees was 13,655 in 2003. The figure can be broken down into 580 lawyers; 10,343 police officers and 2,732 clerical staff, civilian staff and trainees.[17] The number of police officers is equivalent to 192 per 100,000 inhabitants; the European mean being 357.[18] The *Prisons and Probation Service* employed 4,337 individuals in 2004; of these 2,556 guards.[19]

The *prosecution service* is placed under the authority of the Minister of Justice, who supervises the public prosecutors. The prosecution service is comprised of the Director of Public Prosecution, regional public prosecutors and the chief constables. This personnel overlaps with that of the police to a

12. Kriminalitet 2004, pp. 19–21.
13. European Sourcebook 2003, p. 99.
14. Kriminalitet 2004, p. 27.
15. Kriminalitet 2004, pp. 121–122.
16. European Sourcebook 2003, p. 129.
17. Dansk Politi.
18. European Sourcebook 2003, p. 74.
19. Kriminalforsorgen Statistik 2004, p. 72.

great extent. The public prosecution employs slightly fewer than 700 jurists and a number of administrative assistants, etc.

The *judiciary* consists of one Supreme Court, which also functions as the constitutional court, two High Courts and 24 city courts (courts of first instance). Certain cases are heard in the Maritime and Commercial Court of Copenhagen. There are 364 judges; 284 other jurists; 1,159 administrative assistants and 81 others (officers of the courts etc.). The numbers include all levels of the court system; there is no information available on the number of persons working specifically on criminal cases. Denmark has 4,635 practising lawyers; i.e. 86 per 100,000 inhabitants; this positions Denmark in the middle among the Nordic countries (Finland 33, Sweden 48, Norway 125 and Iceland 237).[20]

The *net cost* of the police in 2006 was DKK 7,565 million (€1,014 million); DKK 2,319 million (€311 million) of the prisons and probation service; and DKK 1,836 million (€246 million) of the judiciary.[21] The expenditure is approximately US$140 per capita for police; US$9 for prosecution; US$35 for courts; and US$35 for prisons. This means that Denmark is on average in all four categories compared to other countries with large gross national products.[22]

B. General Organisation of State Structure

Denmark has been an independent kingdom since the early Viking period and is thus one of the oldest monarchies in the world. From 1660 to 1849, the king held absolute power. The first democratic constitution *(Grundloven)* was adopted in 1849. One of the prominent features of the constitution is the separation of the legislature, the executive and the judiciary. The country is now based on parliamentary democracy. The king or queen reigns, but does not rule. The one-chamber parliament *(Folketinget)* holds the superior power. The executive power is exercised by a number of ministers.

The three regions of the kingdom – Denmark, the Faroe Islands and Greenland – have different legislations, including different criminal codes and administration of justice acts. The codes and acts of Denmark and the Faroe Islands are essentially identical, whereas the Greenlandic codes and acts to a great extent reflect a fundamentally different treatment ideology. The police, prosecution service and courts, as well as the prisons and probation ser-

20. European judicial systems, overview on p. 12.
21. Statistisk Årbog 2006, table 411.
22. *Farrell/Clark*, What does the World spend, pp. 16–17.

vice, are common institutions for all three parts of the kingdom. Denmark is a member of the European Union, but the Faroe Islands and Greenland are not.

C. Framework of the Criminal Justice System

1. Legislation

In accordance with the *Rechtsstaat* principles, only acts punishable by means of a statute passed by the parliament shall be punished (Section 1 Criminal Code). The demand for statutory legislation is also fulfilled, however, if a minister passes regulations, etc. using power delegated to him or her by a parliamentary statute. The courts control conformity with the enabling statute, sometimes overruling the regulation.

Internal regulations regarding administrative matters in the police or prosecution service do not necessarily need to be founded in an act passed by parliament. Before they are issued, they are often presented to the law committee in Parliament. In this informal way, the parliament often supplies a sort of political recognition.

Formally, the legislative powers are held by the parliament and the king. However, the king cannot act without the approval of a minister, so, in reality, the legislative powers lie with the parliament and the government. Any member of parliament can introduce a bill. Yet, in practice, the vast majority of bills are prepared in the ministries and introduced by the respective ministers; this is especially the case for extensive changes. The ministries prepare the bills within their subject areas, but receive technical assistance from the Ministry of Justice. This is also the procedure for substantive criminal law in their areas, e.g. concerning foodstuffs, fishing and the environment. The area of the Ministry of Justice includes the police, prosecution service, courts, prisons and probation service. Bills concerning these institutions, including bills related to the national budget, thus belong to this ministry.

The Faroe Islands and Greenland have certain capabilities to implement their own rules; otherwise everything in Denmark is centralised. The local police and gaols were integrated into the state police and state prison system in 1938.

2. Judiciary

Prior to 1999, the Ministry of Justice was responsible for the administration of the judiciary. A Court Administration was founded on 1 July 1999 pursuant to the Court Administration Act of 1998. As a result, the administration of the judiciary is separated from the executive and the legislature. The Court Administration is headed by a Board of Governors composed of one Supreme Court Judge, two High Court judges, two city court judges, one practising lawyer and two persons with special managerial experience. The governors are appointed by the Minister of Justice upon recommendation of a number of organisations.

3. Minister of Justice

The Minister of Justice is the head of the police, prosecution service and the prisons and probation service (see *supra* about the judiciary). The Minister is politically responsible to the parliament for her or his administration. This is the only manner in which there is a direct political influence upon the judicial system (see, however, *infra* about the police district boards). The three institutions – police, prosecution service and prisons and probation service – have different administrative structures.

4. Police

Since January 1st 2007, Denmark has been divided into twelve police districts. The Minister of Justice is the superior of the National Commissioner and police constables (Section 108 AJA). The National Commissioner is responsible for national police operations and supervises the chief police constables (Section 109 AJA; see also circular 10093/2006). The National Commissioner's office covers a number of departments, several of which have operational functions, and provides assistance to the police districts, e.g. the Data Department, Traffic Department and the Danish Security Intelligence Service.

Each police district is headed by a chief police constable, who is responsible for the police activities in his or her district (Section 110 (2) AJA). He or she has a separate budget and responsibility for the way the district is run. There is a deputy police constable. There are two pillars under the chief police constable and the deputy police constable: one is responsible for police tasks, another for prosecution.

Independent crime investigations occur within the different administrative sectors, such as the taxation authorities and the occupational safety and health authorities. Some of these authorities can impose fines, yet, if the fines are not paid voluntarily, the cases are submitted to the police. The police also have several functions in the area of crime prevention, e.g. collaborating with schools and social authorities.

5. Prosecution

The Administration of Justice Act from 1916 (AJA), with its numerous later amendments, regulates in detail the administration of justice and also contains provisions concerning the basic features of the prosecution service. The prosecution service is subordinate to the Minister of Justice. The service is structured as a hierarchy of three levels headed by the Director of Public Prosecution. The second level comprises six regional public prosecutors, while there are 12 chief prosecutors at the local level. The service includes two special units with nationwide powers: the Special Prosecutor for Serious Economic Crime and the Special International Crimes Office for handling war crimes, crimes against humanity, etc. The two special units are assigned their own criminal investigators and undertake the investigation of their own cases.

There is a large overlap between the prosecution service and the police. The traditional clear separation of duties where the police independently investigate and then turn the investigation results over to a prosecutor, who, in turn, decides on the bringing of charges, does not exist in Denmark. Only in rare cases is there a possibility for private criminal cases to be tried (see *infra* under B.3).

6. Corrections

The Prisons and Probation Service that administers both the prisons and probation services (relating to recipients of suspended sentences, parolees, etc.) is also under the Ministry of Justice.

7. Underlying Principles Related to the Criminal Justice System

The key task of the police, prosecution service, courts and the prisons and probation service is to ensure enforcement of the law in pursuance of constitutional rights, human rights and other rights, e.g. as specified in the Administration of Justice Act. The overall principle for the police is described in the Section 1 of the Police Act:

> The police shall serve to maintain safety, security, peace and order in society. The police shall further this purpose by means of prevention, assistance and law enforcement.

Section 743 of the Administration of Justice Act lays down the following concerning investigations:

> The purpose of the investigation is to clarify if the conditions for imposing criminal liability or other criminal legal consequence exist, and to procure information for the disposition of the case, as well as to prepare the case for trial proceedings.

The duty of the prosecutor is described in Section 96 of the Administration of Justice Act:

(1) The duty of the public prosecutors is, in connection with the police, to pursue crime pursuant to the rules of this law.
(2) The public prosecutors shall proceed with every case at the speed permitted by the nature of the case thereby ensuring that those liable to punishment are prosecuted while the innocent are not prosecuted.

In short, the prosecutor's duty is to uphold the law in accordance with the pursuit of truth and human rights.

The Danish legal system is, of course, to a very large degree similar to other European systems. However, there are differences with regard to the acceptance and application of some of the common principles. The following two examples may show that Denmark is stricter in implementing the principle of equality of arms and the principle of objectivity than some other countries.

Secret investigative measures, such as telephone tapping, bugging, camera observation and home searches without informing the owner, are subject to court order (Sections 783, 791 a, 799 AJA). If the suspect has not been informed, he or she cannot defend his or her own interests in court when the police present its case. In order to compensate this disadvantage and restore the equality of arms, the Danish law provides for a specific procedure: before the court decides on such an investigative measure, a lawyer has to be appointed ex officio to attend to the interests of the person concerned. The lawyer receives access to police files, is summoned to all court meetings and is entitled to comment the action itself, as well as file for a possible extension of the permit (Sections 784, 785, 791 a(6), 799(2) AJA).[23]

The second example is taken from a real case: a prosecutor was not convinced of the accused person's guilt during examination of a witness in court. He did not mention this doubt in his final remarks to the court, but only later did so – outside the court – to his superior prosecutor. Due to this omission, the convicted person was granted a retrial by the Special Court of Indictment and Revision as the prosecutor had not been fully objective. The prosecutor receives access to police files and is summoned to the court when the police present its case (Sections 784 and 785 AJA). The same rules apply if the police ask the court for permission to search a place without informing the owner (Section 799 AJA). A number of other principles will be mentioned in the following.

23. See further *Cornils/Greve,* Rechtliche Initiativen gegen organisierte Kriminalität, pp. 44 et seq.

II. Actors in Criminal Proceedings

A. Police

1. Introduction

The overall principles for the role of the police are laid down in the Police Act, Section 1:

> The police shall serve to maintain safety, security, peace and order in society. The police shall further this purpose by means of prevention, assistance and law enforcement.

The Administration of Justice Act, Section 743 lays down the following concerning investigations:

> The purpose of the investigation is to clarify if the conditions for imposing criminal liability or other criminal legal consequence exist, and to procure information for the disposition of the case, as well as to prepare the case for trial proceedings.

It is characteristic for the Danish legal system that the police are also responsible for prosecutorial tasks at the local level.

The duties of the police are in particular

- to prevent criminal offences, breaches of public peace and order, and danger to the safety of individuals and public security;
- to avert any danger of breaches of public peace and order, and any danger to the safety of individuals and public security;
- to put an end to criminal activities and to investigate criminal offences;
- to prosecute criminal offences;
- to assist citizens in other dangerous situations;
- to carry out checks, controls and supervision measures in accordance with applicable law;
- to assist other authorities in accordance with applicable law;
- to issue weapons licenses, etc.;
- to participate in crime prevention efforts, for example, by giving presentations to children in schools and daycare facilities;
- to advise citizens on technical measures against burglaries, etc.; and
- to perform other duties as specified in applicable law or otherwise naturally associated with police activities.

It is apparent that the Danish police have both repressive and preventive duties, but this distinction is used neither in police law nor in administrative practice. Although the distinction as such is not used, problems and solutions similar to those found in German law exist.[24] For instance, the principle of legality and court control differ according to the actual task. In this connection, it is important to note that a vast area of preparatory acts in Danish law can be punished as attempt (Section 21 Criminal Code). Therefore, the police in Denmark often operate within the repressive area, whereas the police in most other countries operate within the preventive area. However, the police may choose to define a task as recreating an order instead of pursuing minor infractions as crimes.[25]

2. Organisation

a) General Police Forces

Up to 1938, the municipalities had local police forces and gaols. Since then, the State has held the responsibility for the entire police force and there is only one police corps (compare *supra*, Section I.C about the roles of the Minister of Justice and the National Commissioner).

A chief constable heads the police force of a district and, as such, he or she is responsible for the work of the police. The chief constable is assisted by a deputy chief constable, police officers, police prosecutors, etc.

The police prosecutor is the public prosecutor in the district court. The relationship between the police and the prosecution service is described *infra*, in Sections II.B.3. and III.A.

The uniform branch and the criminal investigation department in the police district are each headed by chief superintendents who are police-trained leaders. The administrative personnel is headed by a section leader.

b) Special Units within the Police Structure

Alongside the local police, additional national units are in place, for example in the areas of road traffic and child pornography. Crimes detected by these units are pursued by the local police (see *supra*, Section I.C about further special national units for economic crimes, international crimes, etc.).

The Danish Security Intelligence Service *(Politiets efterretningstjeneste,* PET*)* is part of the regular police force and, as such, regulated by the ordinary Police Act and Administration of Justice Act. There is no special act regulating PET activities. The PET is set up to prevent, investigate and counter operations and activities that pose or may pose a threat to the preservation of Denmark as a free, democratic and safe country. The PET's actions are essen-

24. See *Henricson*, Politiret, pp. 35 ff., 56 f., 320 ff.
25. See further *Cornils/Verch*, Justitielle Einbindung, pp. 22 f., 26.

tially preventive. By gathering and processing information, the PET prepares risk analyses that, in turn, provide the basis for an evaluation of which action must be implemented to prevent any threats from developing further. Thus, the actions of the PET differ from most investigations carried out by the rest of police. It is a characteristic of most of the matters the PET deals with that they do not develop into actual criminal cases. This situation may change slightly as new legislation on terrorism expands the scope of its investigations and may thus provide the basis for actual criminal cases. Information obtained by the PET may be sent on to the regular police for use in its standard cases.[26]

c) Organisation in Relation to other Administrative Bodies

The Minister of Justice is the head of the police and he or she is politically responsible to the parliament for its administration. In every police district, there is a district board composed of the chief constable and the mayors of the municipalities that the police district comprises. The district board discusses general matters concerning the police functions and organisation as well as matters concerning the development of crime and cooperation between the police and local community, including a local plan of collaboration. The chief constable annually submits a written report to the district board concerning police operations in the district, including crime prevention collaborations. Any member of the district board can request a board review of matters that are of common interest to the police and the municipalities. The district board can recommend to the chief constable that the police focus on solving certain tasks for a limited period of time. Each year the chief constable prepares a plan for the collaboration between the police and the municipalities, other public authorities, interest organisations and associations, etc. in the police district (see further Sections 111–113 AJA and Order No. 1426 of 13 December 2006).

The local police complaints board consists of one private attorney as chair and two laymen appointed by the Ministry of Justice. The attorney is appointed by nomination by the Council of the Danish Bar and Law Society *(Advokatrådet)* and the laymen by nomination by the Local Authority Interest Association *(Kommunernes Landsforening)*, (Section 1021 AJA). The regional public prosecutors review complaints on the conduct of police officers on duty (conduct complaints), e.g. rudeness, as well as reports on criminal offences committed by police officers on duty (Sections 1019 and 1020 AJA).

26. See further Politiets efterretningstjeneste.

The regional public prosecutor immediately notifies the police complaints board about complaints and reports. The police complaints board can request that the regional public prosecutor conduct certain inquiries or investigative measures. The police complaints board notifies the regional public prosecutor on how cases should be decided in the opinion of the board (Sections 1021 a, 1021 c and 1021 e AJA). The Director of Public Prosecutions submits an annual report to the parliament about the processing of these cases (Section 1021 h AJA). The Minister of Justice recently appointed an expert committee for the purpose of a possible revision of these rules.

3. Powers

The purpose of police investigation is to clarify whether the conditions for conviction exist and to procure necessary information (Section 743 AJA). The police initiate investigations on the basis of a complaint or *ex officio* (Section 742 AJA).

The investigation procedure is, to a certain extent, regulated by the Administration of Justice Act. The guiding principle is that compulsory means must be specifically provided by law. Compulsory means are defined as acts that would be punishable unless specially authorised. Deprivation of liberty is, for example, penalised by Section 261 in the Criminal Code, justifying arrest and detention only when authorised by an act of parliament. In recent years, a clear tendency has developed toward extending the concept of compulsory means and, with that, the requisite legal basis. Since 1999, observation and the taking of photographs within a closed area, the showing of photographs to witnesses, confrontation, and public advertisement have been regulated (Sections 812–819 AJA).

As a "relic" of the inquisitorial system, Denmark used to have a preliminary judicial investigation *(forundersøgelse)*, whereby the suspect and witnesses were interrogated in court before the decision to prosecute and then once more during the trial proper. The preliminary judicial investigation was abolished in 1978. Since then, the investigation has been the domain of the police. Denmark has no *juge d'instruction*. The role of the court is restricted to:

- the application of certain, but not all, means of compulsion – above all detention, but not arrest;
- the ruling on disputes between the prosecution and the defense, Section 746 AJA; and
- the recording of evidence for use during trial when such evidence is not expected to be directly available at the time of the trial, especially state-

ments from witnesses expected to be absent at the time of the trial; a court hearing to record evidence can also be held if a detainee on remand is placed in isolation and the securing of evidence is of relevance to the question of revoking the isolation (Section 747 AJA).

The following compulsory means exist:

- arrest, Sections 755–781 AJA;
- detention, Sections 762–778 AJA and Section 71 of the Constitution;
- interception of communication, observation, and the taking of photographs, Sections 780–791c AJA and Section 72 of the Constitution;
- inspection of the body, Sections 792–792 f AJA;
- search, Sections 793–800 AJA and Section 72 of the Constitution;
- seizure and orders of edition, Sections 801–807 d AJA; and
- the showing of photographs to witnesses, confrontation, and public advertisement (so-called "other means of investigation"), Sections 812–819 AJA.

The following measures also exist alongside the above-mentioned compulsive means:

- interrogation, Sections 750–754 AJA; and
- so-called "special means of investigation", e.g. the use of undercover agents, Sections 754 a–754 e AJA.

The investigation is closed with a decision to dismiss the case, place it on hold awaiting new information, or bring charges (see *infra*, Section III.A for further information).

4. Individual Agents

a) Recruitment

District prosecutors are recruited from among individuals who have a university degree in law. At present, all chief constables are also law graduates, although this is principally no longer a requirement.

Uniformed police officers are recruited from among individuals who have reached the age of 21, are Danish nationals, in good health, have a driver's license, etc. Basic police training starts with a nine-month course at the Police College, followed by 18 months of inservice training in a police district. The police officer then completes another nine-month course at the Police College. In the years following basic training, all police officers are offered or, in some areas, required to take further courses, including special courses covering matters such as environmental crime, computer crime, and international relations. All employees are appointed for life.

b) Personal Dependencies

Recruitment to positions at the highest level is carried out by the Minister of Justice. The chief constable takes care of recruitment to other positions locally.

c) Self-Perception

The police view itself as the backbone of public administration. It is the police who have initial contact with citizens when something goes wrong. It is also the police who, in the field, make the first decisions that are crucial for subsequent processing of a case. They apply the most invasive measures. It is the police who must step in when other authorities cannot handle a situation or when their offices are closed. It is also the police who must provide all citizens with legal protection.[27] Based on such legal notions, a strong *esprit de corps* is built, which, on the one hand, is extremely positive for the police with regard to ensuring peace and maintaining order in critical situations, but, on the other hand, can make the police very difficult to penetrate for the purpose of external control. International studies of public opinion place trust in the Danish police at the top;[28] corruption is practically non-existent in the police corps.

5. Further Investigative Agencies

Considerable parts of the public administration are occupied with monitoring compliance with regulations concerning their respective sectors, e.g. tax and customs. In connection hereto, these authorities often have the right to take physical control of rooms, bookkeeping, etc., even if there is no reason to suspect the company or individual in question of having committed a crime. The authorities can further often require the company or individual to disclose information concerning the company or individual that is subject to criminal liability. In this way, they differ from the police who usually do not have such powers – with the exception of certain areas, such as road traffic. It has been a cause of uncertainty and debate to what extent these powers can be used to generate material for inclusion in the criminal prosecution of a com-

27. See further *Henricson*, Politiret, p. 51.
28. For example *Balvig*, (2001) 83 Juristen, pp. 270–271.

pany or individual. It is, for example, of great importance whether the human right prohibition of self-incrimination applies here. These matters are now thoroughly regulated in the Civil Rights Act of 2004.[29] The main rules in the Act are the following:

> Section 9 (1): If an individual or legal person on reasonable grounds is suspected of a criminal offence, coercive measures against the suspect for the purposes of gathering information about the matter or matters in question can only be carried out pursuant to the criminal procedural rules in the Administration of Justice Act.
>
> Section 9 (2): The provision in Subsection 1 does not apply if a coercive measure is used for the purposes of gathering information for a decision other than the imposition of a sanction.
>
> Section 10 (1): If there is a specific suspicion that an individual or legal person has committed an offence that can result in punishment, the provisions in the legislation etc., about duties of disclosure to the authority, do not apply to the suspect unless it can be precluded that the sought information can have significance for the judgment of the presumed offence.
>
> Section 10 (3): An authority shall inform the suspect that the individual does not have a duty to disclose information that can have significance for the judgment of the presumed offence ...

If the police and the prosecution service during the investigation are in contact, e.g. with the taxation authorities in a tax case, the exchange of letters form part of the case documents that the defense is entitled to see, pursuant to, among other regulations, the European Human Rights Convention Article 6. There may, however, also be correspondence, e.g. about petitioned punishment, which is of a different nature. In practice, these documents are handed over to the defense as well. At times, the police retain the services of an accountant to review bookkeeping; the accounting report is part of the case documents and must be shared with the defense.

B. Prosecution

1. Introduction

The Danish prosecution service was created in 1919 as part of the great judicial reform of 1916. The comprehensive Administration of Justice Act *(Retsplejeloven)* comprises the procedures in both the civil and criminal justice systems. Its first book regulates the organisation of the courts, prosecution service, police and attorneys. The second book contains rules common to both civil and criminal justice, e.g. a chapter on witnesses. The third book con-

29. See, further, rules of guidance of 22 December 2004 on the Civil Rights Act related to the public administration's use of coercive measures and duties of disclosure.

cerns civil justice and the fourth one criminal justice. The current criminal justice system in Denmark is based upon a separation of accusation and adjudication (see *supra*, Section I.C about the structure and tasks of the prosecution service).

2. Organisation

a) General Prosecution Service

See *supra*, Section I.C.

b) Specialised Units within the Service Structure

See *supra*, Section I.C.

c) Organisation in Relation to other Administrative Bodies

See *infra*, under 3 (Powers) about the relationship between the Minister of Justice and the prosecution service; see also *supra*, Section A.2.c) about the police district boards.

3. Powers

a) Hierarchical Distribution

The highest authority in the prosecution service is, in practice, the Director of Public Prosecution but, in theory, it is the Minister of Justice *(justitsministeren)*. The Minister handles the supervision of the service, appoints prosecutors, issues general orders concerning the service and reviews specific complaints regarding decisions made by the Director of Public Prosecution. The Minister of Justice also has the legal power to intervene in each and every case, to initiate or terminate it, even against the wishes of the prosecution service. Although this power is exercised extremely rarely, the possibility for political interference in the concrete criminal justice system has been the subject of harsh critique. It is therefore now a requirement that an order to initiate, continue, abstain from or terminate prosecution shall be put in writing and be substantiated. In addition, the Speaker of Parliament must be informed of the order in writing. (Section 98 (3) AJA). In some cases, for instance cases concerning the safety of the State, including terrorism, an indictment can only be filed by order of the Minister of Justice (Section 118 a Criminal Code).

The non-political head of the hierarchic prosecution service is the Director of Public Prosecution *(rigsadvokaten)*. He or she represents the crown in the Supreme Court. The Director is superior to the other prosecutors and may issue instructions to them of a general nature and with regard to specific cases. A very significant part of his or her job is to make sure that the prosecution service is working efficiently and that disparities do not occur within the criminal justice system. His or her general communications and circular letters to all the prosecutors are of paramount practical importance. They include, for example, information about the standard amounts of fines so that proposals to accept fines as well as petitions in court cases become homogeneous. He or she further gathers information about case law, for example with respect to sentencing in rape cases, and conveys summaries to both the parliament and all prosecutors. There are regular meetings of all the higher-level prosecutors as well as among prosecutors specialised in certain sorts of crime.

The six regional prosecutors *(statsadvokaterne)* conduct appeal criminal cases before the high courts and jury cases for the city courts. They are responsible for all questions of appeal, including the decision of whether or not to appeal a judgment to the high courts (whereas the police are empowered to appeal simple court orders, e.g. a refusal to detain or so-called complaint *(kære)*). In addition, the regional prosecutors supervise the local prosecutors' handling of criminal cases and they review citizens' complaints (as for the latter see *supra*, Section A.2.c). The regional prosecutors further ensure that persons who are sentenced to treatment for an indefinite period, e.g. due to insanity or dangerousness, are not confined longer than necessary. The determination of the area of the prosecutors' tasks is based on districts. There are also two prosecutors who cover the whole kingdom for serious economic crimes and international crimes, respectively. The Administration of Justice Act has been amended several hundred times. In regard to the prosecution service, the most important changes are the gradual retreat of the middle tier, i.e. the regional prosecutors, from day-to-day prosecution in courts of first instance and the corresponding extension of the competence of the lower tier, i.e. the police district prosecutors.

The police district prosecutor's power to decide whether to prosecute in court or not, which originally applied to petty cases only, has now been extended to almost all cases. A very small number of so-called private penal cases concerning libel, slander and certain other areas are prosecuted personally by the victim in the civil courts (Section 275 Criminal Code). A similar possibility exists, e.g. requests for sanctions against a company's marketing practices that are deemed unfair to another company (Section 30 Marketing Practises Act). As will be seen below, other administrative departments can merely make suggestions and possibly complain to a higher-ranking prosecutor, but cannot prosecute on their own, and the same applies to private victims or complainants.

b) Dismissing a Case without Prosecution

The criteria for dismissing a case without prosecution *(påtaleopgivelse)* are (Section 721 AJA):

1) that the complaint is manifestly ill-founded, in which case not only the prosecution service, but also the police, can dismiss the case (see also Section 749 AJA);
2) that further action cannot be expected to bring about a conviction; or
3) that costs, the expected length of proceedings, or amount of work are out of proportion to the importance of the case or the expected penalty.

The most interesting critierion is the last one, which is often used to curtail the case by dismissing single counts, leaving out potential co-defendants, etc. Partial charges are brought, e.g. in cases of crimes committed as part of a business operation, by only prosecuting the business, the management or the individuals in the business, who exercised particularly aggravated behaviour. Charges are not brought against low-level personnel, even if, in principle, the case could have been pursued against them as well. Charges against an individual suspected of having committed a large number of similar offences, such as fraud, can be limited to some of them. Charges against an individual suspected of having committed similar offences, e.g. tax fraud over many years, can be limited to recent years. As a result, the police, prosecution and court resources are freed up, allowing for the processing of criminal cases against a greater number of people than there would otherwise be capacity for. In short, it is better for society to convict four subjects to two years of imprisonment each than one subject to five years of imprisonment. A decision not to prosecute is regarded as an administrative decision which sets in motion a duty to provide justification in writing (Sections 22–24 Public Administration Act), and the affected party – the complainant or the victim – must be informed about his or her right to file a complaint about the decision with a higher-ranking official.

The Act and its general instructions regulate only the decision to drop the case, but not the situation in which the police receive a complaint and then file it without taking further action and without formally dismissing the case. This is not permissible in cases of assault or in cases where the suspect is held in pre-trial detention. Otherwise, prioritising of this kind take place regularly. The prosecution service has implemented procedures in recent years to ensure that such prioritisations take place fairly. In addition, rules have been implemented which make it an obligation to report to the superior prosecutor when cases reach a certain date, so that it may be monitored whether it is due to the nature of the case or to dawdling. Similar prioritisation is also utilised by other investigating administrative agencies, of which many have adopted a practise of only reporting repeated offences or offences exceeding a certain threshold (defined by the agency itself) to the police.

c) Waiving Prosecution

The Danish prosecution service is not statutorily obligated to prosecute every crime brought to its notice, but can also waive prosecution and exercise discretion to a certain extent. Traditionally, it is considered being under the *principle of opportunity*. The Administration of Justice Act does not specifically formulate a principle of legality or opportunity. However, by listing in detail the cases where discretion is permitted, the act presupposes a duty to prosecute when the evidence so warrants it and grounds for discretion do not apply. Thus, a modified principle of opportunity exists.

Waiver of prosecution *(tiltalefrafald)* is permitted (Section 722 AJA):

1) where only a fine is applicable and the offence is of a minimal nature;
2 & 3) where social service measures are to be applied, e.g. to a young person;
4) if the accused has already been sentenced abroad or sentenced after the offence for other, more serious crimes and it is presumed that no or only a nominal supplementary penalty would be imposed;
5) where the expected costs are out of proportion. (If the accused confesses and the confession is strengthened by prima facie evidence, an abbreviated procedure is possible (Section 831 AJA) before a single judge without lay assessors and without witnesses. When, in such cases, the prosecution tenders several counts, and the accused confesses to some, but not all, counts, the prosecution may decide to ask for conviction for only the admitted counts. According to Circular No. 216 of 29 September 1919, the prosecutor in court is empowered to reduce the charges in order to attain judgment upon confession without obtaining consent from the otherwise competent prosecutor);
6) where a special statute legitimises a waiver; and
7) according to general rules issued by the Minister or the Director of Public Prosecutions (see, for example, Order No. 621 of 25 June 2001 on minor cases of assault, indecency, possession of drugs, asylum seekers entering the country on forged papers, etc.). It is further applied to offences committed in Denmark, where the prosecution is assumed by a foreign authority.

Section 722 (2) AJA concerns cases, "where there are particularly mitigating circumstances or other special conditions, and prosecution is not considered necessary based on public interest". With such vague legal authority, it can be argued that, in reality, the law embodies a principle of opportunity. This authority is employed, for example, as follows:

- when the accused is an alien who has already left the country, and proceedings abroad would be unduly cumbersome;
- when the accused is already undergoing the same treatment as would be the probable outcome of a new case, e.g. psychiatric treatment;
- when the accused is mentally deviant and no special treatment seems necessary;
- when the accused, by negligence, has caused a road traffic accident causing death or very serious bodily harm to somebody very close to him- or herself, or very serious bodily harm to him- or herself; this does not apply, however, if the accused was driving under the influence of alcohol; and
- cases of sexual intercourse between a person aged 14 (i.e. younger than the minimal age of 15) and a person under the age of 18.

d) Compound Fines

In cases where the prosecution does not call for a penalty higher than a fine, an "indictment" is often mailed to the accused, describing the alleged offence and adding that the case may be settled by payment of the fine stipulated in the letter (Section 832 AJA). Payment of the fine is usually, in itself, a sufficient manifestation of guilt.

In fiscal cases, as well as in cases concerning subsidy fraud, the respective administrative departments have the authority to propose a compound fine on their own. The offer of a compound fine is a "take it or leave it" offer. If the fine is not paid, the case proceeds to the court in the normal way and, in almost all cases, the judgment contains a fine of the same amount as initially proposed by the prosecuting authority. Thus, the process of proposing fines out-of-court is not of a plea bargaining nature.

4. Individual Agents

a) Recruitment

Public prosecutors are appointed by the State in a public career system. Most are appointed directly by the Minister of Justice, but the higher echelons are appointed by the Queen on the advice of the Minister of Justice. Although the politically responsible Minister of Justice is directly and, in fact, solely responsible for the appointment of public prosecutors, politically motivated appointments are unheard of in Denmark. Alongside the legally trained prosecutors in the police and the higher levels of independent prosecution, there are also police officers who, without having law degrees, act as prosecutors. In petty cases, especially concerning violations of the Road Traffic Act, a police sergeant often represents the prosecution service in court.

b) Personal Dependencies

All prosecutors are employed in permanent positions that they can hold until they reach the age of 70. They thus enjoy very good job security. The common hierarchical system applies to official orders of a general or concrete nature.

c) Self-Perception

The prosecution service perceives itself as an authority that makes professionally sound and correct decisions on objective and factual bases while observing formal and material rules. It contributes to ensuring stability and homogeneity in the application of law so that rules are enforced in the clearest and most uniform manner possible and the response pattern is characterised by the highest degree of predictability. The prosecution service utilises its resources effectively, with the necessary promptness and thoroughness and for the purpose of providing citizens with the best possible legal protection.[30]

The prosecution service is obligated to seek the objective truth as opposed to the defense counsel, whose duty it is to assist the defendant within the rule of law. There is hardly any doubt that the prosecutors make an effort to fulfil the objectivity requirement and that they themselves believe they actually do so. From the perspective of outsiders, including that of defendants, it is probably similarly certain that representatives of the prosecution service are marked by the prosecutor role in that they are not seen as completely fulfilling the task of being objective servants of the truth. Some conflict may exist in relation to other administrative authorities as these authorities, in the view of the prosecution service, may be too dominated by the interests of their respective areas, resulting, for example, in a call for penalties that are out of proportion with decisions in similar cases in other areas.

30. Notice from the Director of Public Prosecution of 21 December 2004 on ensuring the quality of the supervision of criminal case processing in the police districts.

5. Further Prosecutorial Agencies

a) Military

The most important special prosecutors are the corps of military prosecutors *(auditørkorpset)*. Military penal cases are entrusted to them.

b) Specialised Administrative Agencies

If a case concerns an offence that does not fall under the Criminal Code or the Road Traffic Act, the crime will often have been uncovered by some specialised administrative agency, e.g. the fisheries inspection agency or the work environment inspection agency. Some or even most of the relevant investigations here may very well be carried out within the orbit of the specialised agent. Some administrative bodies, e.g. the customs and tax agency and the administrative department in charge of European Union subsidies, have the authority to impose a fine on an individual or legal person. However, if the fine is not accepted or if imprisonment of a physical person is called for, the case must be handed over to the general police for further processing of charges, etc. In such cases, there is close co-operation between the police and the agency concerned. If the police and the administrative agency disagree on the decision to prosecute, the police must refer the case to the regional prosecutor, and the administrative agency is then given the opportunity to argue its opinion before the question of prosecution is decided by the regional prosecutor.

C. Courts

1. Introduction

In an article[31] the Danish courts were compared to those of other countries in the following way:

> In common law systems, the judge has a more passive role as an arbiter between the factions, each presenting its case in a partisan manner for final determination by the trier of facts. Today, Denmark falls into this camp. Danish criminal trials resemble those in Britain, the Commonwealth, and the United States more than they do those in France or Spain and their former colonies.
>
> Instead of hammering out truth on the anvil of adversarial confrontation, inquisitorial systems are distinguished by a greater use of judicial inquiry in camera to elicit facts. A *juge d'instruction* (German: *Untersuchungsrichter*) has the primary responsibility for finding out what happened and presenting the dossier to a higher judge.

31. *Anderson*, (1992) 64 Scandinavian Studies, p. 197.

Lay participation entails open and oral procedures, again distinguishing Denmark from the inquisitorial mode in which the final (and public) judgment of the trial court is based upon the written record as provided by an investigatory judge.

The extensive use of lay judges places Denmark in the center of a circle of north and central European countries which rely on this mode of popular participation, while the utilisation of juries, albeit modest, makes Denmark the chief example of their use outside of the traditional common law countries.

A civil service judiciary – contrasting with the common law practise and mid-career appointment of practicing lawyers – puts Denmark, on the other hand, partly in the continental or civil law camp as does the heavier weight given to statutory law, when compared to the extensive reports of court cases which play a somewhat greater role under the common law.

Compared with many foreign legal systems, the procedures of Danish courts are characterised by simplicity and they are not strictly governed by formalities. Formalities are frequently handled in a practical manner in order to reach a reasonable result. As for criminal cases, Sections 925 and 936 AJA expressly provide that a city court's procedural error shall result in reversal of the judgment only if the proper observance of the rule in question might have led to another outcome.

2. Organisation

a) General Court Service

The Supreme Court *(Højesteret)* covers the whole state. It covers all types of cases from civil cases, criminal cases and public administration cases to constitutional cases. There is also no division into chambers handling certain types of cases. Only cases of general public importance can be brought before the Supreme Court. A verdict in a criminal case can only be appealed to the Supreme Court on questions of law and sentence, whereas questions of fact are not subject to review here. The leave to appeal is granted by a special body, The Appeals Permission Board. The board is chaired by a Supreme Court judge and includes two city court judges, a practising lawyer and a professor of law.

There are two high courts: the Eastern High Court *(Østre Landsret)* located in Copenhagen and the Western High Court *(Vestre Landsret)* located in Viborg on the Jutlandic peninsula. In criminal cases, they function as appellate courts. As a rule, all cases may be appealed only once. However, this does not apply to minor cases involving penalties in the form of fines or confiscation equal to less than DKK10,000 (€1,300); in such cases, a special leave to appeal is required from the Appeals Permission Board. The limitation of the right to appeal in smaller cases has caused a Danish reservation to the International Covenant Art. 14, Para. 5 and to Protocol No. 7 to the European Convention on Human Rights, Art. 2, Sec. 1. Following the objectivity principle, the prosecution is entitled to appeal in favour of the convicted person.

There are 24 city courts *(byretter)* in Denmark. Denmark has 6.8 professional full-time judges per 100,000 inhabitants; Norway has 16.0 and Sweden 17.9 in comparison.[32] Lay assessors participate in many cases, though never in those of the Supreme Court (compare *infra*, Section 3).

b) Specialised Units within the Court Structure

Just as there is no functional division between the investigating judge and the trial judge, the Danish system of criminal courts is simple and unitary. There are no separate police courts, correctional courts, etc. alongside the maritime and commercial court of Copenhagen and the court for the trial of ministers.

c) Organisation in Relation to Other Administrative Bodies

As mentioned (*supra*, II.C.1 and *infra*, 4.b) the courts are independent of the administration (see further details below under III.B and III.C about the relationship to the police and the prosecution service). The formation of the independent Court Administration was characterised as representing the most extensive degree of independence of the administrative and authoritative conditions held by courts in Western Europe.[33]

3. Powers

The separation of powers is stipulated in Section 3 of the Constitution, according to which "Judicial authority shall be vested in the courts of justice". The courts are hence an independent state power. Today, the courts consider themselves empowered to reject an act of legislation as unconstitutional and to declare decisions made by the administration (the government) invalid. It is generally recognised that it follows from the separation of powers that criminal cases must be decided by the courts. Still, it is accepted that individuals consent to fines and confiscations out of court. Fines may also be agreed to in court; in such cases, a ruling is not declared.

The prosecuting service lodges applications with the city court to obtain warrants, which allow the police and prosecution to undertake certain measures during investigation (see *supra*, Section A.3). These applications are re-

32. European Judicial Systems 2006.

33. *Christensen*, Domstolene.

viewed by a city court judge and the defendant is provided with legal representation.

If a defendant is expected to plead guilty, a formal charge is send to the city court in the jurisdiction of the defendant's habitual residence. The court summons the defendant and, if he or she in fact pleads guilty in court and the plea is sustained by corroborating evidence, the presiding city court judge passes conviction and sentence (abbreviated procedure).

If the defendant pleads or is expected to plead not guilty, a formal indictment is drawn up and lodged with the city court in the jurisdiction where the alleged crime was committed. The defendant and the witnesses are then summoned by the prosecution.

The case is tried by a single city court judge if the prosecution does not request a sanction more severe than a fine. In other cases, the judge sits with two lay assessors and together they decide on both the question of guilt and the sentence to be imposed. Witnesses may be examined by the prosecution, the defense and the court.

More serious cases, i.e. cases in which the prosecuting service calls for a punishment of imprisonment for four years or more, and where the defendant pleads not guilty, are tried before a jury in the city court. The court is composed of three judges and six jurors. The jurors participate in the determination of both guilt and sentence, but not in other court proceedings or decisions during the trial. The court is not empowered to dismiss the case immediately due to lack of *prima facie* evidence. The case can only be summarily dismissed for formal reasons, including limitation (Sections 846 and 862 AJA). The rules governing appeals are omitted here.

The judge in the Danish legal system can play – and often does play – a relatively active role if it is considered necessary in order to elicit sufficient information to judge the case. For example, he or she may question witnesses for information that the prosecution or the defense has not asked for (see *infra* III.C.1). The limitations of this discretionary power are rarely debated. The judge is also not bound by the prosecution's petition for sanction; it is possible to impose a sentence more severely than what was requested, although it seldom occurs.

4. Individual Agents

a) Recruitment

Judges are appointed by the Queen on recommendation of the Minister of Justice and as advised by the Judicial Appointments Council. The Judicial Appointments Council, established in 1999 by a unanimous parliament, is expected to facilitate that judges are recruited from all branches of the legal profession: trainee lawyers, civil servants, academics and practising lawyers, among others. The Judicial Appointments Council is composed of one Supreme Court Judge, one High Court Judge, one city court judge, one practising lawyer and two members appointed by organisations representing a broad spectrum of interests in Danish society. It is envisaged that the recommendations of the Judicial Appointments Council are followed by the Minister.

The introduction of the Judicial Appointments Council was not an indication of appointments previously being perceived as politically motivated. Political considerations, the political views of the candidates, etc. have probably never played a role in relation to the appointment of judges; at least not in the last 100 years. Rather, the creation of the new body represented a wish for a better pool of candidates from which to recruit; previously, a disproportional large number of the judges had been former civil servants in the Ministry of Justice. The parliament wanted to eliminate the theoretical possibility that the independence of the courts might be brought into question.

Trainee lawyers *(dommerfuldmægtige, retsassessorer)*, who are not appointed judges, are employed in the courts and allowed to preside over smaller trials. The protection of trainee lawyers against arbitrary dismissal and transfer has been strengthened in order to ensure that they have the degree of independence required by the Constitution and the European Convention on Human Rights Art. 6, respectively.

Lay assessors *(domsmænd)* and jurors *(nævninge)* have to be Danish subjects, between the age of 18 and 66 years at the time of their appointment, of good character, physically and mentally capable and have sufficient knowledge of the Danish language. Employees of the central state administration, courts, police, etc. are excluded (Sections 69 and 70 AJA). The basic lists are created by selection, not drawn by lot; the lists are compiled by local council members.

b) Personal Dependencies

The Danish Constitution guarantees judges absolute independence from the government and the parliament. Section 64 of the Constitution provides that judges, in the execution of their duties, are to be governed by the law only, including secondary legislation issued by the administration under statutory authority (functional independence). Further, judges cannot be removed against their will and may be dismissed only by order of the Special Court of Indictment and Revision *(Den Særlige Klageret)* in case of gross misconduct or lasting illness (personal independence). The majority of the members of the Special Court of Indictment and Revision are judges themselves. All judges must retire from their positions by the end of the month in which they turn 70 (see *supra*, under a) about trainee lawyers).

c) Self-Perception

The visions of the courts[34] of Denmark are:

- The courts of Denmark make up a highly respected and confidence-building organisation that performs its tasks with the highest degree of quality, service and efficiency.
- The courts of Denmark protect the community governed by law and are the modern and primary fora for the solution of conflicts.

In 2001, the Court Administration Board conducted a large survey of the performance of the courts in the opinion of users. 90% were satisfied or very satisfied with performance. The percentage is also high among persons convicted in a criminal case or ruled against in a civil case (79% in the city courts and 91% in the high courts).[35]

5. Further Judicial Agencies

Apart from the Special Court of Indictment and Revision, which rules on petitions to resume criminal cases due to errors or new information, there are hardly any other judicial agencies. Military cases are also heard in the conventional courts.

D. Defence

1. Introduction

Practising law is more than a trade – it is an integral part of the judicial and legal system. This is not tantamount to the attorneys being part of the public authorities. Danish attorneys are private and work independently of the state and public authorities. This is also true for defense attorneys; there is no special corps of publicly employed defense counsels. In all jurisdictions; the Ministry of Justice appoints a number of private *pro bono* counsels upon recommendation by the court and after consultation with the local and national bar society (Section 733 AJA) (see immediately below about duties). *Pro bono* does not mean that they work for free; they are paid by the State (see *infra* 2).

34. Courts of Denmark, p. 14.
35. *Melchior*, The Danish Judiciary, p. 127.

2. Scope of Action

a) Appointment of Defense Counsel

At all stages, the accused is permitted to be represented or assisted by a counsel paid by himself, no matter how diminutive the case. (Sections 729 a and 730 AJA). In practice, privately retained counsels are extremely rare. The system of court-appointed *pro bono* counsels applies to rich and poor alike; there is a free choice within the group and the quality is very high, making the need for assistance from other lawyers to both be and appear very small.

The court may appoint a counsel in all cases and at all stages at its discretion. (Section 732 AJA). This happens, for instance, in the earlier stages of large economic cases and in cases concerning serious sexual offences.

Circumstances under which counsel is mandatory for the accused and for the court to appoint include:

- when a question of pre-trial detention arises,
- when the case will involve the participation of lay assessors or jury, and
- when the public is excluded during the examination of the accused (Section 731 AJA) (see *supra* I.C on telephone tapping and searches). The appointment of defense counsel is mandatory for the court upon request from the accused as follows:
  - in an abbreviated procedure (Section 831 AJA),
  - when there is a petition for imprisonment, and
  - in cases involving the loss of a driver's license (Section 731 AJA).

Unless the accused requests a specific lawyer, one of the *pro bono* counsels is appointed by rotation. However, another lawyer, *pro bono* or not, may be appointed later at the request of the accused. A *pro bono* counsel cannot refuse the appointment.

If the accused requests defense counsel with office far from the pertinent judicial district, the appointment can be conditioned upon the accused personally compensating for the additional cost of travel.

The court decides on the fee for appointed counsels. The convicted – but not the acquitted – defendant is obligated to reimburse to the public purse all costs, including the fees of court-appointed counsels.[36]

36. See further *Cornils/Verch.*

b) Duties of the Defense Counsel

The defense counsel has the right to be present during police questioning of the accused and in court. If the accused is detained in isolation, questioning may not take place without the defense counsel present unless both the accused and the counsel consent hereto (Section 745 c AJA).

The defense counsel has the right of disclosure, normally including copies of all evidence. The defense counsel is allowed to discuss the evidence with the accused but not to hand over the evidence or copies thereof to him or her (Section 729 a AJA). In Denmark, citizens have wide access to information about the affairs of the public administration. The access is particularly wide in cases that directly concern the individuals themselves. The Public Information Act does not, however, apply to the area of criminal justice (see Public Information Act, especially Section 2(1)). At all stages, the defense counsel has the right to unrestricted access to a detained client. (Sections 771 and 772 AJA). The police and the prosecution are bound by the principle of objectivity (Section 96 AJA), whereas the defense counsel is only prohibited from actively counteracting the investigation (Section 739 AJA).

3. Agents and Institutions

a) Independent Lawyers

Practising lawyers need to have a university law degree and three years of practical training with a law firm. Before qualifying, they must pass a legal practice exam. The right to appear before the High Court is acquired by satisfactorily trying two High Court cases. Admittance to the Supreme Court presupposes five years of practice as a lawyer and a statement from the High Court that the lawyer is experienced in procedure (Sections 119, 133 and 134 AJA).

- *Self-Perception of Lawyers:*
- to be the most competent in law and the most qualified to see through and solve complex problems for citizens;
- to be independent of all but their clients' interests;
- to act and conduct themselves responsibly and conscientiously; and
- to be productive.

b) Private Professional Associations

The Danish Bar and Law Society *(Advokatsamfundet)* conjoins lawyers holding the Danish title "Advokat" and authorised to practise law, whether in Denmark or abroad. Membership to the Society is mandatory (Section 143 AJA). It can be characterised as a semi-private professional association.

By law, it is vested in the Society to ensure that lawyers adhere to the legal and ethical rules regulating the legal profession. The Board of the Society has in that capacity adopted a professional code of conduct with guidelines stating the rights and duties of lawyers. Further, the Society acts to promote justice and protect constitutional and human rights. The Society exerts influence upon the law-making process by participating in the governmental hearings of prospective law proposals as well as by appointing members to governmental committees.

The Disciplinary Board (Advokatnævnet) is part of the Danish Law and Bar Society. The Board handles complaints against lawyers. The Board is chaired by a judge and the members are representatives of the public and legal professions. The chairman and vice-chairmen are appointed by the Ministry of Justice. Complaints regarding fees chartered by lawyers are handled by the local complaint boards of the eleven constituencies, the decisions of which may be appealed to the Disciplinary Board (see further Sections 144–147 h AJA).

c) State Agencies
See *supra*.

E. Other Institutions

The Danish *Parliamentary Ombudsman* is of enormous importance for the affairs of the public administrations. The functions of the ombudsman do not, however, include the area of the courts (Section 7 Ombudsman Act).

See also *supra*, II.A.5.

III. Vertical Co-operation in Criminal Matters

A. The Relationship between the Police and the Prosecution Service

1. Instructing Competence

On the local level, the police and the prosecution service are amalgamated in so far as the chief constable of each of the 12 police districts is both the chief of the local police and head of the local prosecution service. He or she is thus ultimately responsible for both a proper criminal investigation and an effective running of the prosecution service. Likewise, the chief constable's staff of jurists carries out both police and prosecution tasks.

The main duties of the prosecution service are summarised in Section 96 AJA. In particular, prosecutors are required to ensure not only that guilty persons are held responsible, but also that innocent ones are not prosecuted – the so-called principle of objectivity. Throughout every criminal investigation, the chief constable is responsible for the police observing all statutory rules and procedures. Supervisory authority over the decisions of the police constables is held by the regional prosecutors (Section 101(2) AJA). The police are not obligated to consult with the prosecution service in matters of investigation; still, there are exceptions based on either legislation or general orders issued by the Director of Public Prosecution.

The staff of jurists in the police district is involved when a court order is necessary as the police cannot act on its own in this regard. This is particularly relevant when the police or prosecution service wish to employ a special means of coercion. The Director of Public Prosecution also requires that a police jurist is consulted in large-scale and complicated cases, especially in cases where there may be a request to curtail it instead of pressing all theoretically possible charges. Other general instructions from the Director of Public Prosecution stipulate that a police jurist be included early on in the investigation, for instance in cases against medical caregivers and in serious environmental cases.

The police jurist may give detailed instructions to the police concerning investigative activities. When a file has been passed on to a prosecutor for the purpose of possible indictment, it is, for example, not uncommon for him or her to send the file back to the police asking for additional investigation, such as the questioning of an additional witness mentioned by other persons who have already given statements to the police.

In cases conducted by the special prosecutor for serious economic crimes, or the prosecutor for special international crimes, plain-clothes detectives and staff jurists co-operate in the investigation from the beginning. The regional prosecutor must be consulted or at least kept informed prior to the use of very costly means of investigation and in cases in which an accused has lodged a complaint against the use of special means of coercion, such as interception of communication or the use of an undercover agent. The local prosecution service may apply for a general psychiatric examination of the accused *(mentalundersøgelse)* at its own discretion, but an application for admission of the accused to a mental hospital for examination – which entails a delay of at least several months and a corresponding lengthening of pre-trial detention – can only be filed after consultation with the regional prosecutor.

Certain other matters must be reviewed by the Director of Public Prosecution. For instance, the police cannot request the court to extend a detention on remand in isolation beyond eight weeks (four weeks, if the individual is under the age of 18) without first having obtained the approval of the Director of Public Prosecution. (Sections 770 c and 770 d AJA).

Most offences fall within the competence of the chief constable, but in some very serious and rare cases, the decision whether to prosecute or not is left to the regional prosecutor, the Director of Public Prosecution, or even the Minister of Justice. Examples of cases outside the competence of the chief constable are also those involving a risk of bias because the victim is a policeman or, in cases of perjury, in court. Politically very sensitive cases against a person for insulting a group of people because of race, colour, national or ethnic origin, religion, or sexual inclination similarly fall within the competence of the regional prosecution. Blasphemy can only be prosecuted by order of the Director of Public Prosecution. Prosecution for some terrorist acts and other crimes against the State can only take place by order of the Minister of Justice. The same is true if jurisdiction is based on the principle of universality and a duty to prosecute according to a convention.

The Director of Public Prosecution is notified if a court, during the investigation or trial proper, has found that the conditions for the police use of an investigative measure were not fulfilled or if a court directly criticised the conduct of the police. The chief constable may at any time set priorities on when and when not to initiate investigations, and he often does so (see Proclamation No. 10681 of 12 April 1995 about the case and task distribution and Notice No. 10 of 22 December 2006 from the Director of Public Prosecution about legality and quality assurance as well as supervision of criminal case processing in the police districts). The regional public prosecutors attend to complaints against the police.

2. Sharing of Information

See directly above, Section 1.

3. Common Decisions

See *supra*, Section II.B.3 and directly above, Section 1.

B. The Relationship between the Police and the Courts

1. Instructing Competence

Since investigative courts do not exist in Denmark, there is no situation in which the courts directly instruct the police. Certain inquiries and measures by the prosecuting service and the police presuppose approval from the courts prior to or following their execution (see *supra*, under Section II.A.3 for further details).

2. Sharing of Information

See directly above, Section 1.

3. Common Decisions
This is not relevant (see directly above, Section 1).

C. The Relationship between the Prosecution Service and the Courts
1. Instructing Competence
Danish criminal procedure is based on the accusatorial principle. The scope of a case is determined by the public prosecutor. The subject matter of the trial is the indictment; the accused cannot be convicted of a crime that is not mentioned in the indictment. In practice, the evidence provided by the prosecutor is the decisive material in the trial, and the prosecutor examines the accused and witnesses first. The trial is, of course, conducted under the direction of a judge. However, the judge is not a mere supervisor of how the prosecution service and defense counsel act (thus see, Section 867 AJA: The person presiding over the court is entitled and obligated to pose questions to the person, who is giving testimony, whenever it is necessary in the interest of the truth." and Section 874(3) AJA: "The court may, when it is considered necessary for the full elucidation of a case, decide that evidence, which none of the parties have wanted to present or which the person, who has submitted the evidence, has declared to withdraw, shall be presented. The court may postpone the case for this purpose. The arrangements necessary for presenting the evidence are made by the court or by the prosecution service as ordered by the court.") In practice, the powers authorised in Section 867 are used daily, whereas the far-reaching rights inherent in Section 874 are only indirectly applied.

Even when there is sufficient evidence to press charges for a more serious crime, the prosecutor is entitled to lower the charges to a less serious offence and commonly does so (as mentioned above, Denmark follows mainly the principle of opportunity). This happens most often when there is a possibility of an abbreviated procedure on the basis of a confession (Section 831 AJA). This can, for example, come about if the accused – as regards a certain object – is willing to plead guilty to receiving stolen property, but not to theft. Also, if the accused admits to seven out of ten similar counts, the prosecutor may well consider that a penalty for all counts will at most result in a small supplementary penalty on top of the expected penalty for the admitted counts. If the amount of work necessary to produce the evidence for the remaining three counts is considerable, a rational prosecutor may give in and lower the charges.

If deemed necessary, the prosecutor may reduce the charge during a court session, for instance if it turns out that the original charge is untenable. During trial, the prosecution service may, with the consent of the court, extend the charge to counts other than those mentioned in the indictment if the accused consents hereto or if the additional count has been committed during the trial. The same applies to major corrections that the prosecution service wishes to make in the indictment during trial. If the accused does not consent to the extension, the prosecution service must then bring additional new charges against the accused (Section 836 AJA). In the latter case, a sentence is imposed in the form of a supplementary punishment so that the total imposed punishment is equivalent to the punishment that would have been imposed had the counts been considered together (Section 89 Criminal Code).

The court may change the statutory name of the charge, e.g. convict for embezzlement, although the charge is fraud, or change trivial details, e.g. the date of the crime (Tuesday instead of Wednesday). Traditionally, the court is entitled to convict for a lesser crime than the one being charged, e.g. for attempt, even though the charge is a completed crime. However, the court is not entitled to convict on the grounds of facts not mentioned in the indictment. The parties, especially the accused, must be given opportunity to conduct their part of the case in any new light, e.g. producing an alibi for Tuesday instead of for Wednesday.

The prosecutor may recommend a sentence, but the court is not bound by the request. In practice, the judge nearly always refrains from imposing a stiffer penalty than requested by the prosecutor.

2. *Sharing of Information*

The Administration of Justice Act sets out a wide range of detailed rules aimed at facilitating a fair trial for the defendant and protecting the rights of victims and witnesses. The aim is also to strike a fair balance between the rights of the individual and the interests of society, including the necessary efficiency of the criminal justice system.

Basic principles include the presumption of innocence, the burden of proof placed on the prosecution service, application of *in dubio pro reo,* the free assessment of evidence, the right of the defendant to remain silent, that an accused is not liable to punishment for his or her perjury (Section 159(1) Criminal Code) and equality of arms between prosecution and defense.

3. *Common Decisions*

A case typically ends with a verdict, conviction or acquittal. Acquittal must take place, when:

- the act is not subject to prosecution by the State,
- the count is withdrawn by the prosecution service,

- the act is not punishable due to limitation, or
- the accused is found not guilty.

The court cannot convict for something that is not included in the indictment as it appears after any changes during the case (Section 883 AJA) (see directly above, Section 2 for further information). A case may also be decided in court by the accused accepting a fine or confiscation. However, this also requires the consent of the prosecution service (Section 899 AJA). Finally, a case can be closed by the issuance of a warning. This does not require the consent of the prosecution service (Section 900 AJA).

D. The Relationship of Other Agencies with the Criminal Justice System

The other relevant agencies are described *supra*, in Section II.A.5. In the criminal justice system, they are considered reporters of criminal offences. As reporters of criminal offences, they can provide the police, prosecution service and courts with information to be used as evidence.

Furthermore, as specialists within their respective areas of public administration, the agencies can explain to the police, prosecution service and, possibly, the court, factual circumstances, for example, methods for measuring pollution.

E. Involvement and Notification of the Defence

1. Interaction with Investigatory Agencies

The defense counsel has the right to be present during police questioning of the accused and in court. If the accused is detained in isolation, he or she can only be questioned in the presence of the counsel unless both the accused and the counsel waive the right. (Section 745 c AJA). Defense counsel has the right of disclosure, normally including copies of all evidence. Counsel is allowed to discuss the evidence with the accused but not to hand over the evidence or the copies to him or her. (Section 729 a AJA).

When an interrogation, confrontation, the showing of photos or other investigative measures of similar importance can be presumed to be used as evidence during trial, the police notify the defense counsel beforehand in order that the counsel has the opportunity to be present. The defense counsel is allowed to make suggestions regarding the conduction of the investigative measure in question (Section 745 d AJA). The defense counsel has the right to unrestricted access to his or her detained client at all stages (Sections 771 and 772 AJA). The police and the prosecution are bound by the principle of objectivity (Section 96 AJA), whereas the defense counsel is only prohibited from actively counteracting the investigation (Section 739 AJA).

The defense has certain opportunities by which to influence the direction of the investigation, for instance to ensure that leads against other potential suspects are followed up on. The defense can file an application for a court order to force certain actions. Cases of disputes between the prosecution and defense during the investigation are settled by the court; as for police investigative measures, only their legality is reviewed by the court, whereas requests, acts, etc., on the part of the defense also are judged with consideration to expediency (Section 746 AJA). Practitioners argue that there is a slight tendency toward *favor defensionis*. For example, a request from the defense counsel for a probation report will only be refused if it is totally frivolous.

Typically, only one expert witness is called upon in a Danish court of law, not expert witnesses from both sides. And this one expert is usually consulted in writing only. If, for example, there is a need for an opinion from the Medico-Legal Council *(Retslægerådet)* about a cause of death or the mental state of the accused, the defense counsel is entitled to add comments to the questions posed by the prosecution service and to pose additional questions.

The most debated point is the right of the defense counsel to conduct a parallel investigation of her or his own. Most attorneys are passive, perhaps only asking for supplementary investigation from the police, adducing the observation of the principle of objectivity by the police and prosecution, or, when met with refusal, by the court. However, a few attorneys wish to conduct a more active defense, e.g. questioning witnesses instead of merely supplying witnesses' names to the police for the purpose of investigation. On the one hand, the defense is entitled to be active. On the other hand, the Supreme Court has held[37] that a defense counsel acted improperly in approaching a witness who had already been questioned by the police and summoned to court in order to confirm his statement. In theory[38] it has been suggested that defense counsel should not be censured as long as his or her actions do not tamper with the evidence according to Section 739 AJA. This opinion inspired a long debate. It has been held that a defense counsel did not act improperly by posing supplementary questions to a publicly appointed medical officer, who had given a statement to the prosecution earlier, as the defense counsel had notified the prosecution of his steps at the same time.[39]

Two different types of defense counsels are depicted in the literature: the "hired gun" (called "the subjective theory" in Danish law) and "the guide" (called "the objective theory" in Danish law). The hired gun takes on any

37. UfR 1982.800.
38. *Gammeltoft-Hansen*, (1983) Juristen 53.
39. UfR 1999.556 Ø.

kind of client and fights for the clients' beliefs to the utmost limits of the law. The guide takes his or her own moral beliefs into account, declines cases involving certain kinds of crimes, and takes the interests of society and consideration of the victim into account. The guide thus, to some extent, submits him- or herself or to a principle of objectivity of the kind which undoubtedly applies to the police, prosecution service and courts. He or she is comparable to a doctor who refuses to treat hideous diseases. Such an attorney should not be a defense lawyer. The "hired gun" has become the increasingly acceptable role for Danish defense counsels. Among other things, this means that a defense counsel cannot resign using the argument that the crime in question is reprehensible. Still, this does not imply that it is purely the role of "hired gun" which is accepted. The defense counsel may not, for instance, knowingly bring forth false evidence or false witness statements. It is further questionable whether a defense counsel must accept that his or her client falsely pleads guilty.[40]

2. Interaction with the Prosecution Service

Given that police and prosecution in Denmark are amalgamated at the local level, this subject is covered by Section 1 (see above).

3. Interaction with the Court

The defense counsel interacts with the court during the process of receiving the appointment; compare, *supra*, Section II.D.2.

The defense counsel plays a role during the investigation, as described earlier in Section 1. If a dispute arises between the defense counsel and the police during the investigation, the matter is brought before the court pursuant to Section 746 AJA. The same applies if the defense counsel or the accused asserts that the police have acted illegally during the investigation. Even if the court finds that rules have been violated, this does not automatically exclude any possible new evidence from being considered. Often, the court will leave this matter to be decided by the court subsequently processing the actual trial.

It follows from the fundamental principle of the substantial truth that formal rules must be given less importance for the evaluation of the evidence. This means that evidence, as a rule, can be considered even if it has been obtained in an illegal manner. The courts, however, have in recent years started to attach greater importance to compliance with the formal rules. The com-

40. See further *Rørdam*, (2003) Advokaten.

mon notion in Danish law has been that compliance with the rules must be forced through the application of disciplinary rules and criminal liability for those police officers who violate the rules (compare Sections 754 c and 783 AJA), not by substantially incorrect acquittals of notorious guilty parties. The role of the defense counsel during trial has been omitted here.

F. The Role of Safe-guarding Principles and Rights for Vertical Co-operation

The key task of the police, prosecution service, courts and the prison and probation service is to ensure enforcement of the law in pursuance of constitutional rights, human rights and other rights, such as those stipulated in the Administration of Justice Act.

The purpose of the investigation is to clarify whether the conditions for imposing criminal liability or other criminal legal consequences exist and to procure information for the disposition of the case, as well as to prepare the case for trial proceedings. The task of the prosecutor is to pursue crimes in collaboration with the police. The public prosecutors proceed with every case at the speed permitted by the nature of the case, thereby ensuring that those liable to punishment are prosecuted while the innocent are not. This can also be perceived to be the task of the courts.

Altogether, the task for all authorities is to uphold the law while respecting the pursuit of truth and human rights. Basic principles in relation hereto include those of objectivity, the presumption of innocence, the burden of proof placed on the prosecution service, the application of *in dubio pro reo*, the free assessment of evidence, the right of the defendant to remain silent and to lie and equality of arms between prosecution and defense.

As the Danish courts do not comprise special courts for administrative or constitutional matters, it is the ordinary courts that must safeguard the rights of the accused and society throughout the course of a case. Still, the control is initially implicit in the hierarchical administrative systems of the police and prosecution service, both of which are headed by the Minister of Justice. The Parliamentary Ombudsman monitors this part of the apparatus, but not the courts.

IV. National Horizontal Co-operation in Criminal Matters

A. Police

1. Co-operation between Non-central Police Agencies

In the following, only Denmark is covered. Co-operation between Denmark, the Faroe Islands and Greenland has been treated in an article on Nordic Co-operation (Section E) by Cornils and Greve.

The legal regulation of the Danish police changed radically on January 1st, 2007. Up until then, the police had been decentralised, so that the competence concerning the investigation was placed with the individual chief constable, who was, in principle, ranked directly under the Minister of Justice pursuant to the former Administration of Justice Act, Section 114. Starting January 1st, 2007, the executive management of the police has been turned over to the National Commissioner of Police pursuant to Sections 108–109 AJA. Collaborations between police districts previously relied on agreements between the respective chief constables; as with all such systems, this was able to function well and be flexible, yet was also subject to friction of various degrees, depending on the circumstances. As part of the new structure, it is expected that common rules will be issued for such collaborations and that a centralised management will take place in those areas where such rules have not been issued.

The Danish administrative system is generally very pragmatic and informal. This is shown in this area as well. If, for instance, a case officer from the criminal police in one district needs information from another district, contact with the relevant person in the other district will be taken up directly; superiors still may, depending on the nature of the case, be notified or consulted beforehand.

All charges and decisions are centrally registered in an electronic data base to which the citizen's civil registration (CPR) number is the key. All employees in the police and prosecution service have access to this register. It is therefore quite simple to ascertain whether there is an ongoing investigation or if charges have been filed against an individual by the same agency or somewhere else in the country.

In cases of serious crimes, which are presumed to have been committed by the same individuals across several police districts, joint investigation units with representatives from all involved districts are established as needed. This has, for example, occurred in investigations of criminal activities within motorcycle gangs and in investigations of major robberies. Such co-operation has, among other things, made it easy to compare information and coordinate searches.

2. Co-operation between Central (federal) and Non-central Police Agencies
This question does not apply as Denmark is a unitary state.

3. Co-operation between Police Agencies and other Agencies in other jurisdictions
In areas of priority, there are task forces that operate on a nationwide basis. Such task forces exist, for instance, in the areas of taxation and illegal employment. It is expected that another task force will be formed in regard to investigating trafficking in women. When a task force has obtained information that amounts to a criminal case, the case is transferred to the relevant police district for further pursuance.

If, in an area without a special task force, such as a local work environment agency, an authority wishes to obtain information from the police, such a request is governed by the same rules, regardless of whether it is made to the police in its own district or to the police in another part of the country. The main rule here is that the police may, and exclusively so, give information to the respective authority when it is permitted pursuant to the Public Administration Act Sections 28–31 (cf. the Ministry of Justice's guide about the law No. 174–192). In practice, the most important legal basis is the Public Administration Act Section 28(2) No. 3, pursuant to which even information regarding an individuals' strictly private circumstances can be disclosed if the disclosure takes place in protection of private or public interests which clearly outweigh consideration of the interests that are the reason for confidentiality. In addition, ibid. No. 4, pursuant to which disclosure can take place if it is a necessary part of the processing of the case or is necessary in order for an authority to carry out supervisory or control duties, applies.

Coercive measures by public authorities outside the area of criminal justice are regulated by the Civil Rights Act. Pursuant to that Act's Section 9, coercive measures against an individual or legal person, who on reasonable grounds is suspected of a criminal offence, can only be carried out pursuant to the criminal procedural rules in the Administration of Justice Act. In practice, this means that the respective authority must file a police report and that the case then is pursued as other police cases.

4. Special Problems Relating to Co-operation with other Agencies
See directly above, Section 3.

B. Prosecution Service

1. Co-operation between Non-central Prosecution Services

As described above, the police and prosecution service are amalgamated at the local level. Consequently, the comments under section A also apply here. There is, however, the practical difference that the prosecution service has had a hierarchical structure since 1919, so that any disagreements between two local authorities can be brought before and decided by the superior prosecution service (a similar hierarchical structure has now been introduced in the police).

The Administration of Justice Act does not regulate which of several equivalent prosecution authorities is the competent one. A case will normally be pursued by the law enforcement agency that has carried out the investigation. A decisive factor in this regard is the jurisdiction rules in Sections 694–709 AJA. Still, it frequently occurs that a police district prosecutes a criminal case which has been investigated by a different police district, for example in confession cases, which are normally heard at the accused's home court under Section 694(3) AJA. If a case comprises several counts committed in different police districts, they can all be pursued together as provided by Section 700 AJA. A case can be moved to a different jurisdiction, for instance due to lack of resources or in order to guarantee a proper hearing of the case, if there are strong sentiments against the accused in one part of the country (Section 702 AJA).

2. Co-operation between Central (federal) and Non-central Prosecution Services

Since such a division does not exist in Denmark the question does not apply. Nonetheless, similar questions do arise because of the nationwide competence of the Public Prosecutor for Serious Economic Crime and the Director for Special International Crimes. Disputes between one of these services and the regional prosecutors must be resolved by the Director of Public Prosecution (see Order No 1146 of 13 December 2002, Sections 2(2) and 3(2)).

The procedure in cases of EU fraud illustrates the interaction. If an administrative national or EU authority discovers grounds for filing a police report, it is submitted to the Public Prosecutor for Serious Economic Crime; if the case calls for immediate investigative measures, the respective police district may be contacted directly. The police notify the Public Prosecutor for Serious Economic Crime if they become aware of possible EU fraud. The Public Prosecutor for Serious Economic Crime refers the case to the police district that, pursuant to the general rules, shall process the report and at the same time notifies the regional public prosecutor. The Public Prosecutor for Serious Economic Crime also assists the police districts with advice and guidance concerning the pursuance of the cases, including sanctions and relevant case law; the same is true as for more general information, e.g. the fight against fraud within the EU. If the chief constable recommends that an indictment should not be filed, the case is then brought before the regional public prosecutor for decision; the regional public prosecutor confers with the Public Prosecutor for Serious Economic Crime before a decision is made in such a case. If the case is prosecuted locally, notification about the outcome is given to both the regional public prosecutor and to the Public Prosecutor for Serious Economic Crime. The regional public prosecutor makes the decision on possible appeal after consulting the Public Prosecutor for Serious Economic Crime. The Public Prosecutor for Serious Economic Crime notifies EU and national administrative authorities about the final outcome of the case (Notice No. 4/98 from the Director of Public Prosecution).

3. Co-operation between Prosecution Services and Police Agencies in other Jurisdictions

See *supra*, under Section A.1.

4. Co-operation between Prosecution Services and Courts in other Jurisdictions

Court hearings during the investigation are held upon request by the police in any district in which information about the case can be presumed to be obtainable (cf. Section 694 AJA).

5. Co-operation between Prosecution Services and other Agencies in other Jurisdictions

See *supra*, under Section A.3.

6. Special Problems Relating to Co-operation with other Agencies

See *supra*, under Section A.3. and 4.

C. Courts

1. Co-operation between Non-central Courts

The non-central courts are authorised to carry out certain acts outside their own jurisdictions without involving the local court; this includes serving court documents and arranging for the execution of arrest orders, orders of imprisonment and orders to bring witnesses or experts before the court by use of force. In other cases, as deemed expedient, a court may carry out official acts in another jurisdiction with the consent of the court in the respective jurisdiction or of a higher court and, in urgent cases, even without such consent. Notification of the court in the respective jurisdiction must then be done as soon as possible (Section 709 AJA).

This process can be illustrated by a case in which a city court issued an order authorising the local police to carry out a search for IT material in a different part of the country. The accused argued that the order was illegal in that it was issued in the wrong jurisdiction. The high court stated, among other things, that the law intended to allow the police considerable freedom in deciding the jurisdiction in which to hold the court meeting. (UfR 2001.1640 Ø). Section 704(2) AJA further stipulates that the fact that a few isolated acts of the court, separate from trial, did not take place in the "proper" jurisdiction, does not invalidate their legitimacy. This also applies if the accused was not present. If there is disagreement among parallel courts about the proper jurisdiction in a case, the question is decided by a superior court according to Section 704(3) AJA.

2. Co-operation between Central (federal) and Non-central Courts

This question does not apply as Denmark has a monochordal court system.

3. Co-operation between Courts and other Actors in other Jurisdictions

There are hardly any interactions other than those mentioned (see *supra*, under Section II). Specifically, it can be noted that the crime victim does not have a special status in Danish criminal procedure. The victim is, in principle, treated as any other witness. In certain cases, e.g. rape cases, an attorney is appointed to help the victim; other measures are also in place. In addition, public authorities who control an area are treated according to the normal rules for victims. Still, public officials and others who act in an official capacity cannot normally, without consent from the authority in question, be required to testify regarding circumstances about which they, in the interest of the public, have a duty of confidentiality (Section 169 AJA).

D. Involvement and Notification of the Defence

1. Interaction with Investigatory Agencies

See *supra*, Section II.D.2 and III.E.1.

2. Interaction with the Prosecution Service (or equivalent)

See *supra*, Section II.D.2.

3. Interaction with the Court

See *supra*, Section II.D.2.

E. The Role of Safe-guarding Principles and Rights for Co-operation

The most essential guarantee for compliance with the rules of the system lies in the culture and self-perception of the authorities. The Danish authorities – police, prosecution service and courts – have enormous respect for the law and corruption is practically non-existent. The second and very important guarantee lies in the hierarchical structure of the police, prosecution service and courts, all of which ensure an ongoing control at the different levels. Together with the fact that the country is comparatively small, this maintains a high degree of social control within the different bodies of law. The Parliamentary Ombudsman is perceived by the public as an important control factor, and he is indeed; numerous principles of public administration have become commonly recognised through the work of the Ombudsman and critique from the Ombudsman has resulted in a great number of changes to administrative practices, e.g. in the area of corrections.[41] The entire administration is further subject to control by the courts (Section 63 Constitution). Finally, the European Court of Human Rights is widely known and respected by the people; there have only been a small number of Danish cases before it, but these and cases concerning other countries have resulted in several important changes to the Danish legal system, e.g. concerning the circumstances under which judges are disqualified to hear a case.

Basic principles include the presumption of innocence, the burden of proof placed on the prosecution service, the application of *in dubio pro reo*, the free assessment of evidence, the right of the defendant to remain silent, and the equality of arms between prosecution and defense. With regard to which principles may cause problems or act as a hindrance or even barrier to co-operation, the point of all legal guarantees is that they shall impose constraints on the administration and courts. Viewed in this way, all procedural principles can cause problems for the police, prosecution service and courts and thus limit their possibilities to function in the manner they desire. If one listens to the debate, the principles most criticised by the police and prosecution service seem to be the principles that hinder the free exchange of information between authorities.

41. He reviewed 204 complaints involving the prisons and probation services in 2005 and expressed criticism in 35 of them, according to a reply from the Ministry of Justice to question No. 112 of 5 December 2006 from the Parliamentary Law Commission.

V. Fundamental Principles as they Play out in Matters of Organisation and Cooperation

The key task of the police, prosecution service, courts and the prisons and probation service is to ensure enforcement of the law in pursuance of constitutional rights, human rights and other rights, e.g. in the Administration of Justice Act. In short, the task is to uphold the law while respecting the pursuit of truth and human rights.

The criminal justice system is characterised by the State having very far-reaching powers over its citizens. Conversely, it has been deemed necessary to implement a number of constraints on the State's use of these powers. Through these constraints, the aim is to achieve a rule of law under which citizens are treated fairly. The implementation of constraints is furthermore necessary to ensure that the truth prevails. Alleviating the citizen's legal protection would, in numerous areas, increase the risk of an innocent person being prosecuted and convicted.

Historically, the constraints in Danish law have had several milestones that can be regarded as representing still higher levels of a *Rechtsstaat*. When democracy was implemented in 1849, a number of criminal justice guarantees became part of the Constitution. Later, in 1919, several principles took effect with the implementation of the Administration of Justice Act. After the Second World War, with the European Convention on Human Rights and the dynamic interpretations by the European Court of Human Rights, still more principles have become part of the rule of law. In other areas – in the big picture – the past 150 years have been marked by an abundance of additions to a Danish *Rechtsstaat*. During the most recent decades, however, there have been a number of changes to the law that, to the contrary, must be characterised as being anti-*rechtsstaatlich*.[42] It is emphasised in the jurisprudential literature that Denmark is far from being a police state, but that a major tendency in the past fifteen years of lawmaking is clearly a move in this direction. This is evident in the parliamentarian lawmaking process in that a referral to increased police efficiency has become the altogether primary argument, whereas it used to be the consideration to ensuring the citizen a fair trial (see also, *infra*, under section VI).

42. See, for example, the review in *Greve*, (2006) European Journal of Crime, Criminal Law and Criminal Justice.

VI. Evaluation and Recommendations

- *Point of Reference*

This project primarily aims at changing the existing rules and factual application of the rules so that the European justice system is improved. In relation hereto, it is important to note that a qualitative evaluation of the rules and practice is something different and more than a quantitative evaluation based on the number of processed cases, etc. Within the EU, there have always been two completely different views, with one accentuating the desirability of a rapid and very extensive common regulation, while the other points to the negative elements of this fundamental view. These underlying positions will undoubtedly also become apparent in the contributions to this project. Before the arguments for the two fundamental views are given, it is important to emphasise that there is no disagreement on the fact that the European justice system must be fair, respect basic human rights, and be efficient in prosecuting violators of the law. The disagreement relates only to how this goal shall be attained and how to weigh the opposing considerations when conceiving the system.

- *Democracy and Legitimation – Legitimate Sources of Law*

It is an altogether central part of a *Rechtsstaat* that measures against the citizens require parliamentary approval. It is only elected officials who can legitimise measures against the freedom of their citizens. Traditionally, and ever since Montesqieu, this consideration has been used in the Continental theory as the key argument to reduce the weight given to case law and to underline the necessity of parlamentary authority and legitimation. Recently, within the EU, it has become significant with regard to the rejection of measures that do not have the support of the Parliament. A considerable part of the criticism of EU is precisely caused by the fact that the Commission does not have a popular mandate and that the Council has only an indirect popular mandate. It is the same fundamental concern that lies behind a broad criticism of the dynamic interpretations stemming from both the European Court of Human Rights and the European Court of Justice. In Denmark, this critique has reached such a level that the otherwise highly regarded European Human Rights Court is about to lose its authority; such criticism has, for instance, been expressed by a number of leading jurists.[43]

43. See, e.g., *Bryde Andersen* 2005.

- *Criminal Law: A Technical Tool or Cultural Manifestation*

In close connection to the above stands the fundamental question of the role and legitimacy of the criminal justice system in general. The development within EU has been criticised for one-sidedly regarding the criminal justice system as a technical tool, without appreciating that the legal systems of the different countries are significant parts of their national culture.[44] These are not just political arguments. International law requires that consideration is taken of pluralism and cultural diversity.[45]

- *Fundamental Rights*

In the harmonisation process so far, the culturally conditioned limitations have commonly been dealt with by referring to the fact that all EU countries recognise the European Human Rights Convention. With this recognition, however, the human rights level is considered a norm, not a lowest norm. All criminal justice systems of the European countries are characterised by how they, in numerous areas, but far from the same areas, afford citizens a protection better than that which results from the Convention and the precedents from the European Court of Human Rights. A harmonisation based on this particular level would therefore be a clear step backward.

- *Rules or Reality*

Harmonization is not just a matter of common rules. In connection with the implementation of the European Arrest Warrant it has, for example, been pointed out in the Danish debate that several South-European justice systems had very long case processing periods and that prison conditions in several East-European countries were considerably lower than the North-European standard. The concentration on the common, formal set of rules in the form of the European Human Rights Convention means, in reality, that extradition to other EU countries can expose citizens to treatments which are substandard compared to the norm in their native justice system.

- *Level of Harmonisation*

The issue of choosing the level of harmonisation is a wider concern. Within the criminal justice policies of the Nordic countries, and those of many other countries as well, it has been a firm principle over many years that unnecessary punishment is unethical punishment. This meant, among other things,

44. See, e.g., *Greve*, Technical Tool or Cultural Manifestation.
45. See, e.g., *Sieber*, JZ 52 (1997) 373 and 375.

that if it could be demonstrated that one country did not have a need for a criminalisation or used a lower punishment level, it was a strong argument for the own country not to have a need for such a criminalisation or high punishment level either. Within the EU, the argumentation seems to be predominantly the other way around.[46]

- *Documentation*

Finally, it may be pointed out that a large share of the discussion is carried out based on arguments of the kind that more severe punishment is more effective than milder punishment and that similarity between the countries increases the legislation's efficacy. Both arguments are very popular, but far from documented. To the contrary, there are many reasons to believe that they only are valid in far more limited areas than those in which they are applied.[47]

- *Closing Remarks*

It is the common Nordic observation that the key conditions for reaching a durable, unified criminal justice system are that there be an open and objective foundation and that the composition of the conformal rules takes place with great consideration to the diverse opinions that always exist. The scientific debate is crucial in both regards. We see here how an objective analysis and debate can lead to harmonisations, yet also how different perceptions can result in different legislations, even within the otherwise generally homogeneous Nordic countries. The close and trusting relationship between these countries and the awareness of the fact that the systems and societies in most regards – legally and factually – are already very much alike, has resulted in the observation that the well-known concerns associated with a close international collaboration in the criminal justice area and the relinquishment of parts of the traditional sovereign way of thinking have not had much effect in the intra-Nordic collaboration. Agreements about important issues have hence been made with contents which would have been unthinkable in relation to other states.[48] These experiences are worth building on.

46. See further *Elholm*.
47. See, e.g., *Greve*, European Criminal Policy.
48. See further *Cornils/Greve*, Die nordische Zusammenarbeit in Strafsachen.

Bibliography

Anderson, Stanley, The Transition from Inquisitorial to Adversarial Criminal Procedure in Denmark. (1992) 64 Scandinavian Studies in Law 181–198.

Balvig, Flemming, Kriminaliteten i Danmark – i europæisk perspektiv [Crime in Denmark – In a European Perspective]. (2001) 83 Juristen 263–283.

Bryde Andersen, Mads, Opgør med menneskeretstænkningen [Confronting the Human Rights Thinking]. Berlingske Tidende (Danish newspaper) 13 March 2005.

Christensen, Jens Peter, Domstolene – den tredje statsmagt. [The Courts – the third power of the state]. Århus 2003.

Courts of Denmark – an organisation in development. Copenhagen [Unknown year, 2005?].

Cornils, Karin/Verch, Ulrike, Dänemark. In: Sabine Gleß/Rainer Grote/Günter Heine (Hrsg.). Justitielle Einbindung und Kontrolle von Europol, Freiburg i.Br. 2001, pp. 9–74.

Cornils, Karin/Greve, Vagn, Dänemark. In: Walter Gropp & Barbara Huber (Hrsg.): Rechtliche Initiativen gegen organisierte Kriminalität. Freiburg i.Br. 2001, pp. 3–68.

– Strafrechtliche Zusammenarbeit zwischen den nordischen Ländern. [The Nordic Collaboration in Criminal Cases] In this book p. 67 ff.

Dansk Politi. www.politi.dk/en/finance/.

Elholm, Thomas, Does EU Criminal Cooperation necessarily mean increased repression? (in print).

European Sourcebook on Crime and Criminal Justice Statistics 2003. www.europeansourcebook.org/

Farrell, Graham /Clark, Ken, What does the world spend on criminal justice? Helsinki 2004.

Frese Jensen, Malene/Greve, Vagn/Høyer, Gitte/Spencer, Martin, The Principal Danish Criminal Acts. 3rd ed. Copenhagen 2006.

Gammeltoft-Hansen, Hans, Ligestilling mellem forsvarer og anklagemyndighed [Equality for Defense and Prosecution]. (1983) 65 Juristen 43–57.

Garde, Peter, www.eurojustice.org/member_states/denmark/country_report/-2735

Gomard, Bernhard/Møller, Jens/Talevski, Oliver (eds), Kommenteret retsplejelov [Annotated Administration of Justice Act]. 7th ed. Copenhagen 2004.

Greve, Vagn, European Criminal Policy. Towards Universal Laws? In: Nils Jareborg (Ed.): De lege, Towards Universal Laws, Trends in National, European and International Lawmaking. Uppsala 1995, 91–116.

– Criminal Law: A Technical Tool or a Cultural Manifestation. A Danish Point of View on Uniformity and Subsidiarity. In: Bahri Öztürk & Walter Gropp (Hrsg.): Maßnahmen gegen Organisierte Kriminalität im Rechtsstaat – Möglichkeiten und Grenzen. Ankara 2003, 163–175.

– Sheep or Wolves. (2006) 13 European Journal of Crime, Criminal Law and Criminal Justice 515–532.

Greve, Vagn/Elholm, Thomas, Introduction to criminal procedure in Denmark. Copenhagen 2005.

Henricson, Ib, Politiret [Police Law]. 3rd ed. Copenhagen 2004.

– Politiloven [Annotated Police Act]. Copenhagen 2005.

Kriminalforsorgen Statistik 2004. [Statistics from the Danish Prisons and Probation Service]. www.kriminalforsorgen.dk/publika/Statistik%202004-/html/default.htm

Kriminalitet 2004 [Criminality 2004]. Danmarks Statistik Copenhagen 2005.

Langsted, Lars Bo/Garde, Peter/Greve, Vagn, Criminal Law Denmark. 2nd ed. Copenhagen 2004.

Melchior, Torben, The Danish Judiciary. In: Børge Dahl et al. (eds), Danish Law in a European Perspective. 2nd ed. Copenhagen 2002, 109–129.

Politiets Efterretningstjeneste, PET, Årsberetning 2004–2005.

Report on European judicial systems – Edition 2006 (2004 data). www.coe.int/t/dgl/legalcooperation/cepej/evaluation/default_en.asp.

Rørdam, Thomas, Anmeldelse af Lena Ebervall: Försvararens roll [Review of Lena Ebervall: The Role of the Defense Counsel]. (2003) Advokaten (Danish periodical) 72–82.

Sieber, Ulrich, Memorandum für ein Europäisches Modellstrafgesetzbuch. (1997) 52 JuristenZeitung, 369–381.

– Bekämpfung des EG-Betrugs und Perspektiven der europäischen Amts- und Rechtshilfe. (2000) ZRP 186–192.

Smith, Eva/Jochimsen, Jørgen/Kistrup, Michael/Lund Poulsen, Jakob, Straffeprocessen [The Criminal Procedure]. Copenhagen 2005.

Statistisk Årbog 2006 [Statistical Yearbook]. www.dst.dk/HomeDK/Statistik/ags/Statistiskaarbog.aspx

Stokholm, Jon/Bitsch, Henrik, Law Practising in Denmark. In: Børge Dahl et al. (eds), Danish Law in a European Perspective. 2nd ed. Copenhagen 2002, 131–144.

Toftegaard Nielsen, Gorm, Straffesagens gang [The Course of the Criminal Case]. 3rd ed. Copenhagen 2004.

Abbreviations

Administration of Justice Act	*Retsplejeloven*, Consolidated Act No. 1001 of 5 October 2006.
AJA	Administration of Justice Act.
Civil Rights Act	*Retssikkerhedsloven/lov om retssikkerhed ved forvaltningens anvendelse af tvangsindgreb og oplysningspligter,* Law No. 442 of 9 June 2004.
The Constitution	*Grundloven* Law No. 169 of 5 June 1953.
Court Administration Act	*Lov om domstolsstyrelsen*, Law No. 401 of 26 June 1998.
Criminal Code	*Straffeloven*, Consolidated Act No. 1000 of 5 October 2006.
JZ	JuristenZeitung.
Marketing Practices Act	*Markedsføringsloven*, Law No. 1389 of 21 December 2005.
Ombudsman Act	*Lov om Folketingets Ombudsmand*, Law No. 473 of 12 June 1996.
PET	Politiets efterretningstjeneste/Danish Security Intelligence Service
Police Act	*Politiloven/Lov om politiets virksomhed,* Law No. 444 of 9 June 2004.
Public Administration Act	*Forvaltningsloven*, Law No. 571 of 19 December 1985.
Public Information Act	*Offentlighedsloven*, Law No. 572 of 19 December 1985.
Road Traffic Act	*Færdselsloven*, Consolidated Law No. 1100 of 8 November 2006.
UfR	*Ugeskrift for Retsvæsen,* Danish periodical.
Ø	Judgment or decision from the Eastern High Court.

Strafrechtliche Zusammenarbeit zwischen den nordischen Ländern

Ein rechtsvergleichendes Projekt des Max-Planck-Instituts für ausländisches und internationales Strafrecht.

A. Einleitung[1]

Die nordischen Länder sind Dänemark, Finnland, Island, Norwegen und Schweden. Innerhalb des dänischen Königreichs bilden die Färöer und Grönland autonome Landesteile; das Gleiche gilt für die Åland-Inseln innerhalb Finnlands.[2] Im Rahmen allgemeiner internationaler Zusammenarbeit sowie vor allem innerhalb der Europäischen Union und der Europäischen Wirtschaftszone pflegen die fünf nordischen Staaten enge Beziehungen mit anderen Ländern. Sie sind unter anderem den meisten völkerrechtlichen Übereinkommen zur Verbrechensbekämpfung und Rechtshilfe in Strafsachen beigetreten. Die folgende Darstellung konzentriert sich jedoch auf die besondere innernordische Kooperation, das heißt auf die Zusammenarbeit zwischen allen oder den meisten nordischen Ländern. Daneben bestehen bilaterale Beziehungen auf zahlreichen Gebieten, auf die hier im Einzelnen nicht eingegangen wird.[3]

1. Dieser Landesbericht gibt die Rechtslage vom 1. April 2007 (Bearbeitungsstand) wieder.
2. Zu den Besonderheiten, die sich aus der autonomen Stellung dieser Landesteile ergeben, siehe unten E.
3. Mit Ausnahme der polizeilichen Zusammenarbeit zwischen Dänemark und Schweden im Bereich der Öresundbrücke; siehe dazu D.9.

B. Allgemeiner historischer Hintergrund

In der Wikingerzeit bildeten die drei nordischen Reiche Dänemark, Norwegen und Schweden einen gemeinsamen Sprach- und Kulturraum. 1397 gingen sie miteinander die Kalmarische Union ein, aus der sich Schweden mit der Provinz Finnland später wieder befreite. So entstand im 16. Jahrhundert eine Aufteilung in einerseits Dänemark-Norwegen, zwei Königreiche unter demselben König, und andererseits Schweden mit Finnland, das zunächst schwedische Provinz und ab 1556 ein Herzogtum innerhalb des schwedischen Reiches war. In diesem Zusammenhang ist besonders erwähnenswert, dass die alten Landschaftsgesetze in der Folgezeit durch Reichsrecht abgelöst wurden. Die nordischen Länder waren die ersten in Europa, die *umfassende nationale Gesetzbücher* zum Privat-, Straf- und Prozessrecht erließen. Das *Danske Lov* von 1683 und das *Norske Lov* von 1687 waren weitgehend identisch. Für Schweden und Finnland trat 1734 ein entsprechendes Reichsgesetzbuch, das *Sveriges rikes lag*, in Kraft. Infolge eines russisch-schwedischen Krieges fiel Finnland 1809 an den russischen Zaren, und zwar als autonomes Großfürstentum unter weitgehender Bewahrung des eigenen Rechts. Dänemark musste nach der Niederlage Napoleons, mit dem es verbündet war, im Kieler Frieden von 1814 Norwegen an Schweden abtreten. Doch auch Norwegen konnte seine bisherige Rechtsordnung und seine eigenen Gesetzgebungsorgane beibehalten, bis es 1905 die volle Unabhängigkeit erlangte. Finnland wurde 1917 ein selbstständiger Staat; Island löste sich 1944 als unabhängige Republik von Dänemark.

Während die nordische Geschichte bis zum Ende des 18. Jahrhunderts im wesentlichen von Kriegen innerhalb des Nordens geprägt war, kamen die Gefahren nach dieser Zeit eher von außen, aus südlicher und östlicher Richtung. Dies hat dazu beigetragen, dass sich ein Gefühl der Schicksalsgemeinschaft bildete, obwohl die Bedrohung der einzelnen Länder nicht vergleichbar war und ihre Geschichte insoweit einen sehr unterschiedlichen Verlauf nahm.

Die Nationalromantik zu Beginn des 19. Jahrhunderts mit ihrer Rückbesinnung auf die historischen Wurzeln führte zu einer Wiederbelebung des gemeinsamen altnordischen Volksgeistes und der volkstümlichen Kultur. Die Universitäten beispielsweise veranstalteten ab 1839 skandinavische Forschertreffen. Doch die Bewegung beschränkte sich nicht etwa auf den akademischen Bereich, sondern fand breite Anhängerschaft auch in der übrigen Bevölkerung, nicht zuletzt durch die Volkshochschulen. Seit 1919 setzt sich die Vereinigung *Der Norden* aktiv dafür ein „die Zusammenarbeit der nordischen Völker auf allen Gebieten zu stärken und zu entwickeln" (§ 1 der Satzung); die Vereinigung hat heute rund 72.000 Mitglieder.

Ausgehend von der Dichtung eroberte der skandinavische Gedanke gegen Mitte des 19. Jahrhunderts auch den politischen Bereich. Hier führten die Bestrebungen unter anderem zu einer vorübergehenden skandinavischen Münzunion (1873–1924) sowie – in neuerer Zeit – zu dem gesamtnordischen Arbeitsmarkt (seit 1954), der nordischen Passunion (seit 1954) und dem Recht aller nordischen Staatsbürger, mit den Behörden der jeweiligen Nachbarländer in der eigenen Sprache zu korrespondieren (seit 1981). Die Ideologie des Skandinavismus tauchte auch in einigen Diskussionen auf, die nach 1945 über Alternativen zur NATO und später zur EU geführt wurden.

C. Annäherungen im Bereich des Rechts

Zu Beginn des 19. Jahrhunderts gab es also zwei nordische Rechtskreise, den dänisch-norwegischen und den schwedisch-finnischen, zwischen denen große Ähnlichkeiten bestanden. Im Rahmen der skandinavischen Bewegung war es naheliegend, eine noch weitergehende Rechtsgemeinschaft zu schaffen. Seit 1872 finden in dreijährigem Intervall nordische Juristentreffen statt, in denen breit gefächerte Themen, darunter auch strafrechtliche, behandelt werden. Es werden mehrere gesamtnordische rechtswissenschaftliche Zeitschriften herausgegeben, teilweise alle Rechtsgebiete umfassend wie die *Tidsskrift for Rettsvitenskap*, teilweise spezialisiert wie etwa die strafrechtliche und kriminologische *Nordisk Tidsskrift for Kriminalvidenskab*.

Auf bestimmten Gebieten des Zivilrechts besteht heute eine nordische Rechtsgemeinschaft. Sie ist zumeist durch den Erlass einheitlicher Gesetze in den einzelnen Ländern zustande gekommen. Die übereinstimmenden Entwürfe wurden gewöhnlich von Experten, nicht von Verwaltungsbeamten oder Politikern erarbeitet. Auf diese Weise erhielten die nordischen Länder im Lauf der letzten 100 Jahre eine Reihe nahezu identischer Gesetze in den Bereichen des Kaufrechts, des Vertragsrechts, des Versicherungsvertragsrechts, des Schuldverschreibungsrechts, des Wechselrechts, des Warenzeichenrechts, des Seerechts, des Kinderrechts und des Eherechts; aus neuerer Zeit ist das Verbraucherschutzrecht zu nennen. Vorübergehend wurde die Einführung eines gemeinsamen nordischen Gesetzbuchs erwogen, ein Gedanke, den man jedoch wieder fallen ließ. Das nordische Urteilsübereinkommen von 1932 schuf jedoch die Grundlage für die Anerkennung und Vollstreckung von Urteilen der jeweiligen Nachbarländer. Selbst wenn die Aktivitäten innerhalb der EU in letzter Zeit die nordische Zusammenarbeit überschatten, hat doch die nordische rechtliche Gemeinschaft auf den genannten Gebieten weiterhin Bestand.

Im Vergleich zum Zivilrecht waren die Bedingungen für eine Kooperation im öffentlichen Recht wesentlich schwieriger.[4] Doch gab es auch hier bereits frühzeitige Initiativen, etwa im Staatsangehörigkeitsrecht und im Strafrecht. Im Folgenden wird ausschließlich der Bereich des Strafrechts behandelt.

D. Die strafrechtliche Zusammenarbeit

1. Theoretische Grundlagen

Nach den Erfahrungen der nordischen Länder bestehen die wichtigsten Voraussetzungen für die Bildung einer tragfähigen Rechtsgemeinschaft darin, dass die Arbeit auf einer offenen und sachlichen Grundlage erfolgt und dass bei der Ausformung übereinstimmender Regelungen weitgehend Rücksicht genommen wird auf Meinungsunterschiede, die stets vorhanden sind. In beiden Hinsichten ist die fachliche Diskussion ganz entscheidend.

Im Jahr 1878 erschien erstmals eine „Nordische Zeitschrift für das Gefängniswesen“ *(Nordisk Tidsskrift for Fængselsvæsen)*. Nach mehrmaliger Namensänderung heißt sie heute „Nordische Zeitschrift für Kriminalwissenschaft“ *(Nordisk Tidsskrift for Kriminalvidenskab)* und ist das Mitgliedsorgan der fünf nordischen Strafrechtsvereinigungen mit ca. 1.200 Mitgliedern. Diese Vereinigungen gaben in den Jahren 1936–1963 ein gemeinsames Jahrbuch heraus: *De nordiska kriminalistföreningarnas Årsbok – Annuaire des associations de criminalistes nordiques*. Ihre heutige Zeitschrift enthält unter anderem regelmäßige Übersichten zur Rechtsentwicklung in den einzelnen nordischen Ländern. Entsprechende Berichte werden seit 1962 vom Nordischen Forschungsrat für Kriminologie *(Nordisk Samarbejdsråd for Kriminologi)* in dem gemeinsamen Mitteilungsblatt *Nordisk Kriminologi*[5] veröffentlicht. Durch diese Publikationen erhalten die nordischen Strafrechtler laufend ausführliche Informationen über die rechtlichen und rechtstatsächlichen Verhältnisse in den Nachbarländern, einschließlich Gesetzgebung, Rechtsprechung, Reformvorhaben, öffentlicher Debatte in den Medien usw.

Ebenso wichtig für die Rechtsentwicklung sind Kongresse, die Theoretiker und Praktiker zusammenführen. Auf dem Gebiet des Strafrechts gibt es eine lange und lebendige Tradition gesamtnordischer Fachtagungen. Während des Zeitraums 1878–1951 wurden mit wechselnden Intervallen gemeinsame Gefängniskonferenzen abgehalten.[6] Seit 1937 findet alle vier oder fünf Jahre die Nordische Strafrechtstagung *(Nordisk Kriminalistmöte)* mit turnusmäßig zirkulierendem Veranstaltungsort statt. Die Hauptthemen der letzten

4. Vgl. u.a. *Herlitz*, Festskrift till Birger Ekeberg, S. 267 ff.
5. www.nsfk.org/publications/newsletter.shtml
6. Zu den heutigen Treffen von Vertretern des Strafvollzugswesens siehe unten D.10.

Tagung dieser Art waren die Entwicklung der Kriminalität und der Sanktionspraxis in den einzelnen Ländern sowie der Terrorismus. Der Nordische Forschungsrat für Kriminologie, der von den fünf Justizministerien eingesetzt wurde, veranstaltet seit 1962 regelmäßig jährliche Forscherseminare und mit zweijährigem Abstand sogenannte Kontaktseminare, bei denen Wissenschaftler mit Praktikern eines bestimmten Fachgebietes zusammentreffen. Das letzte Kontaktseminar fand beispielsweise mit Vertretern der Anklagebehörden statt.

Auch zwischen den Universitäten bestehen enge Kontakte. So finden etwa seit 1976 institutionalisierte Treffen zwischen den Strafrechtswissenschaftlern der Universitäten Uppsala und Helsinki statt. Zu der jährlichen dänischen Strafrechtslehrertagung, die zu Beginn der 1970er Jahre eingeführt wurde, werden stets Gäste aus Island, Norwegen und Schweden eingeladen. Seit 1997 wird ein jährliches Doktorandenseminar für alle promovierenden Strafrechtler aus den nordischen Ländern durchgeführt, an dem zugleich auch die meisten Lehrstuhlinhaber des Nordens im Strafrecht und Strafprozessrecht teilnehmen. Beim letzten Seminar bildeten die Themen Korruption und Rechtsökonomie je einen Schwerpunkt. Auf dem Gebiet des Strafprozessrechts tagen die Universitätsprofessoren jedes dritte Jahr, zuletzt zu den Themen DNA und Beweiswürdigung.

2. Das Nordische Strafrechtskomitee

Nachdem die nordische Zusammenarbeit im Bereich der zivilrechtlichen Gesetzgebung recht umfassend und erfolgreich war, startete das schwedische Justizministerium 1948 eine Initiative zur Ausdehnung der Zusammenarbeit auf das Gebiet des Strafrechts.[7] Es wurden jährliche Treffen zur Behandlung von besonders bedeutsamen Themen vereinbart. Diese sogenannten *nordischen Kriminalrechtskonferenzen* fanden während des Zeitraums 1948–1956 insgesamt zehnmal statt.

Das gleiche Verfahren zur Harmonisierung der nationalen Rechtsordnungen, das mit so großem Erfolg auf dem Gebiet des Zivilrechts eingesetzt worden war, nämlich Erlass einheitlicher oder nahezu einheitlicher Gesetze auf der Grundlage eines gemeinsamen Sachverständigenentwurfs, wurde 1960 auch für das Strafrecht eingeführt, als die Justizminister das *Nordische Strafrechtskomitee (Den nordiske Strafferetskomité)* einsetzten. Es kann als eine straffer organisierte Fortsetzung der nordischen Kriminalrechtskonferenzen betrachtet werden. Dem Komitee gehörte ein Mitglied aus jedem Land

7. Vgl. *Hurwitz*, NTfK 1949, 74 f.

an; außerdem wurden zu einzelnen Projekten weitere Personen mit jeweils besonderer fachlicher Qualifikation hinzugezogen. In dieser teilweise wechselnden Besetzung erarbeitete das Komitee eine Reihe von Reformgutachten zu verschiedenen Themen: Konfiskation (1963),[8] Verjährung (1966),[9] bedingte Strafrestaussetzung (1969),[10] Anrechnung von Untersuchungshaftzeiten (1971),[11] Geldstrafe (1975),[12] Alternativen zur Freiheitsstrafe (1980),[13] Strafzumessung (1983),[14] Unternehmensstrafbarkeit (1986)[15] und internationales Strafrecht (1992).[16]

Auf der Grundlage dieser Reformgutachten wurden harmonisierende Änderungen in den nationalen Strafgesetzen vorgenommen. So basieren seither beispielsweise die allgemeinen Konfiskationsregeln und Verjährungsvorschriften in allen nordischen Ländern auf demselben gemeinsamen Grundprinzip. Früher hatte etwa in Dänemark die konkret verwirkte Strafe als maßgebendes Kriterium für die Unterscheidung von Verjährungsfristen gegolten, während die Strafrechtsordnungen der Nachbarländer auf den gesetzlichen Strafrahmen abstellten. Nachdem man sich im Strafrechtskomitee auf Letzteres geeinigt hatte, wurde das dänische Recht entsprechend angepasst. In ähnlicher Weise erfolgte eine weitgehende Harmonisierung der Verjährungsfristen selbst. Lediglich in der Frage der Verjährung bestimmter schwerster Verbrechen sind nicht alle nationalen Gesetzgeber dem Strafrechtskomitee gefolgt. Entgegen dessen Empfehlung entschied sich beispielsweise Dänemark – anders als Schweden – für die generelle Unverjährbarkeit von Straftaten, die mit lebenslanger Gefängnisstrafe bedroht sind. Dieses Beispiel zeigt, wie einerseits eine sachliche Analyse und Diskussion zu Harmonisierungen führen kann, und wie andererseits eine unterschiedliche Beurteilung bestimmter Fragen selbst unter den sonst in vielen Bereichen übereinstimmenden nordischen Ländern sich in abweichender Gesetzgebung niederschlagen kann.

Das Nordische Strafrechtskomitee ist niemals formell abgeschafft worden, jedoch werden ihm seit vielen Jahren keine neuen Aufgaben mehr erteilt, und

8. Abgedruckt in: Straffelovrådets betænkning nr. 355/1964 om konfiskation, S. 91–103.
9. NU 15/1967, Om forældelse i nordisk strafferet; auch abgedruckt in Straffelovrådets betænkning nr. 433/1966 om strafferetlig forældelse m.v., S. 42–50.
10. NU 3/70, Prøveløsladelse; auch abgedruckt in: NTfK 1970, 61 ff.
11. NU 1971:9, Avräkning av häktningstid m.m.
12. NU 1975:5, Bötesstraffet.
13. NU A 1980:13, Alternativer til frihedsstraf.
14. NU 1984:2, Straffutmåling.
15. NU 1986:2, Företagsböter.
16. NORD 1992:17, Straffrättslig jurisdiktion i Norden.

es werden auch keine neuen Mitglieder mehr berufen. Stattdessen verwenden die Justizminister heute eine interne Gruppe als informelles Organ der Zusammenarbeit.[17] Der Wechsel von dem einen zu dem anderen Modell ist kein Zufall, sondern spiegelt einen allgemeinen Trend wider. Früher hatten externe Sachverständige entscheidenden Einfluss auf die nordische Zusammenarbeit im Bereich der Strafgesetzgebung; heute ist sie in die allgemeine Verwaltungsarbeit integriert und dadurch enger mit der allgemeinen politischen Steuerung der Rechtsentwicklung verknüpft. Diese Entwicklung, die sich seit Längerem abzeichnet, wurde bereits Mitte der 1970er Jahre wie folgt beschrieben:

> Kennzeichnend für die heutige Situation ist, dass die nordische rechtliche Zusammenarbeit zwar ein breiteres Spektrum an Aufgaben als je zuvor umfasst, man sich aber gleichzeitig in einem gewissen Spannungsfeld befindet zwischen der traditionellen Gesetzesharmonisierung auf rechtswissenschaftlicher Basis und der heutigen Gesetzgebung, die immer mehr als ein wichtiges politisches Instrument zur Verwirklichung auch bestimmter parteipolitischer Ziele benutzt wird.[18]

3. Der Nordische Rat

1952 wurde der Nordische Rat *(Nordisk Råd)* als ein offizielles Kooperationsorgan der nordischen Parlamente und Regierungen errichtet; heute stützt er sich auf das „Übereinkommen zur nordischen Zusammenarbeit" (den sogenannten Helsinki-Vertrag) von 1962. Art. 1 des Helsinki-Vertrags in der geänderten Fassung vom 18. März 1993 lautet:[19]

> Die vertragschließenden Parteien sind bestrebt, die Zusammenarbeit zwischen den Ländern auf rechtlichem, kulturellem, sozialem und wirtschaftlichem Gebiet [...] zu bewahren und weiterzuentwickeln.

Der Nordische Rat, der sich aus Mitgliedern der nationalen Parlamente und Regierungen zusammensetzt, tritt einmal im Jahr zusammen. Er kann beratend und initiativ tätig werden, hat aber keine staatsübergreifenden Befugnisse. Während die Bedeutung des Rates und seiner Einrichtungen inzwischen vorwiegend auf kulturellem Gebiet liegt, ist sein unmittelbarer Einfluss im Bereich des Strafrechts seit vielen Jahren sehr begrenzt. Innerhalb dieses ein-

17. Zur Nordischen Strafrechtsexpertengruppe siehe unten D.3.
18. NU 1976:32, S. 16; vgl. dazu auch *Lidbom*, SvJT 1973, 273 ff.
19. Das folgende sowie alle weiteren Zitate sind hier in deutscher Übersetzung wiedergegeben.

geschränkten Rahmens spielt jedoch die strafrechtliche Zusammenarbeit eine zunehmende Rolle.

Im Jahr 2005 hat der Nordische Rat ein „Programm und Grundsätze für die nordische Zusammenarbeit der Justiz"[20] aufgestellt. In dessen Einleitung (I) heißt es:

> In Bezug auf den Helsinki-Vertrag gilt Folgendes: Bei der Abfassung von Gesetzen und anderen Rechtsvorschriften in den nordischen Ländern sind Staatsbürger der übrigen nordischen Länder den eigenen Staatsbürgern gleichzustellen. Ferner haben die nordischen Länder sich darum zu bemühen, dass [...] die Rechtseinheit in der Gesetzgebung über strafbare Handlungen und strafrechtliche Sanktionen gefördert wird, und eine Rechtsangleichung darüber hinaus anzustreben, wo es zweckdienlich ist.
>
> Die rechtliche Zusammenarbeit hat außerdem zum Ziel, eine einheitliche Implementierung von EU/EWR-Recht sowie die Erfüllung anderer internationaler Verpflichtungen im Justizbereich zu fördern.

Als Grundsätze für die rechtliche Zusammenarbeit (II) werden unter anderem genannt:

> Die nordische rechtliche Zusammenarbeit soll die demokratischen Entscheidungsprozesse in den nordischen Ländern stärken und die Rechtssicherheit [...] fördern. [...] Gemeinsame historische Traditionen und Werte erleichtern die Arbeit zur Förderung der Rechtseinheit [...]. Zugleich besteht Raum für abweichende Lösungen, wo tatsächliche Unterschiede, unterschiedliche Wertvorstellungen oder ein Bedarf an neuen Erkenntnissen sich geltend machen.
>
> [...]
>
> Das Erfordernis eines „nordischen Nutzens" bedeutet nicht, dass die Zusammenarbeit notwendig auf identische Regeln in den nordischen Ländern zielen muss. Eine klar festgelegte und ausgebaute Kooperationsroutine kann auch „nordischen Nutzen" bringen. Die rechtliche Zusammenarbeit besteht somit teilweise im Austausch von Wissen und Tatsacheninformationen, unter anderem über bestehendes Recht und gesetzliche Reformvorhaben in den nordischen Ländern. [...]
>
> [...]
>
> Die Zusammenarbeit in der Gesetzgebung zielt auf eine nordische Rechtseinheit. Dies bedeutet wie oben erwähnt nicht, dass die Regelungen notwendig identisch sein müssen. Nordische Rechtseinheit umfasst auch den Fall, dass eine einheitliche Struktur des Rechts erreicht wird und dass Einigkeit über die tragenden Prinzipien innerhalb eines Rechtsgebietes besteht.
>
> Umfang, Bedarf und Charakter der nordischen rechtlichen Zusammenarbeit können auf verschiedenen Rechtsgebieten unterschiedlich sein. [...] Es besteht [...] ein zunehmender Bedarf an nordischer Zusammenarbeit im Strafrecht und im Strafverfahren. Selbst in Bereichen, in denen man eine Rechtsvereinheitlichung nicht erwarten kann – weil etwa die

20. Program og principper for det nordiske justitssamarbejde.

moralischen Wertvorstellungen oder die institutionellen Rahmenbedingungen unterschiedlich sind –, kann dennoch ein Informations- und Erfahrungsaustausch zweckdienlich sein.

[...]

In der nordischen rechtlichen Zusammenarbeit muss stets klargestellt werden, welcher Zweck verfolgt werden soll.

[...]

Zur internationalen Rechtsentwicklung (IV) wird in dem Programm unter anderem ausgeführt:

Die nordische rechtliche Zusammenarbeit soll einen schlagkräftigen Beitrag zur Entwicklung von Regelungen in internationalen Foren leisten. Nordische Zusammenarbeit während der Vorarbeiten zu einem neuen internationalen Regelwerk soll dazu beitragen, die Qualität neuer Regelungen zu erhöhen. Nordische Rechtseinheit wird in einigen Fällen den Einfluss nordischer rechtspolitischer Werte in Europa steigern können. Eine gut funktionierende rechtliche Zusammenarbeit im Norden wird generell die Zusammenarbeit in Europa stärken. Die nordische rechtliche Zusammenarbeit soll darauf zielen, im Hinblick auf die Weiterentwicklung der nordischen Rechtseinheit neue internationale Verpflichtungen, die die nordischen Länder eingehen, effektiv in deren Recht zu implementieren.

[...]

Von wesentlicher Bedeutung ist die Zusammenarbeit, wenn es darum geht, die Konsequenzen von EU/EWR-Rechtsakten so früh wie möglich einzuschätzen. [...] Auch generell gilt es, auf die Möglichkeiten zu achten, vor dem Hintergrund nordischer Erfahrungen und Einschätzungen eine gemeinsame nordische Initiative für neue EU/EWR-Rechtsakte oder für Änderungen bestehender EU/EWR-Rechtsakte zu ergreifen.

[...]

Es ist nicht erforderlich, die gleichen gesetzgeberischen Lösungen in sämtlichen nordischen Ländern zu wählen. Allein die Einigkeit im Verständnis und in der Auslegung der betreffenden Gemeinschaftsrechtsakte ist von erheblicher selbstständiger Bedeutung.

[...]

Zur nordischen rechtlichen Zusammenarbeit gehört es, innernordische Kontakte und Diskussionen zu fördern sowie nach Bedarf im Zusammenhang mit Verhandlungen in anderen internationalen Foren, beispielsweise dem Europarat und den Vereinten Nationen (UN), eine Gleichschaltung auf Beamtenebene und auf politischer Ebene zu schaffen.

Außerhalb der Regie des Nordischen Ministerrates beteiligen sich die nordischen Länder auch an anderen regionalen Kooperationen auf Beamtenebene, beispielsweise an der Baltic Sea Task Force on Organised Crime, die unter anderem polizeiliche Zusammenarbeit umfasst und in die auch andere Anrainerstaaten der Ostsee einbezogen sind.

1971 wurde der *Nordische Ministerrat (Nordisk Ministerråd)* geschaffen, in dem sich die Justizminister ebenso wie die übrigen Fachminister regelmäßig zu Beratungen gemeinsamer Angelegenheiten treffen. Entsprechende Treffen finden zwischen den jeweiligen Staatssekretären, den Abteilungsleitern der Justizministerien, den Leitern des Strafvollzugswesens, den Leitern der Obersten Anklagebehörden und den Leitern der Obersten Polizeibehörden statt. Der Nordische Ministerrat kann einstimmige Entscheidungen mit bindender Wirkung für die Regierungen treffen. Für die strafrechtliche Zusammenarbeit ist diese Einrichtung jedoch ohne besondere Bedeutung geblieben.

Dem Nordischen Ministerrat angegliedert ist das *Komitee für Gesetzgebungsfragen (Embedsmandskomiteen for lovgivningsspørgsmål)*, dem die Leiter der Gesetzesabteilungen in den Justizministerien angehören. Eine Art Unterarbeitsgruppe dieses Komitees bildet die *Nordische Strafrechtsexpertengruppe (Den nordiske strafferetsekspertgruppe)*. Dabei handelt es sich um ein informelles Kooperationsorgan der Justizministerien, das unabhängig vom Ministerrat fungiert. Die Expertengruppe, die gewöhnlich zwei- bis viermal pro Jahr zusammentritt, erhält ihre Instruktionen unmittelbar von den Justizministern. Sie hat unter anderem den Entwurf eines Übereinkommens zum „Nordischen Haftbefehl" erarbeitet, das gegenwärtig von den nationalen Gesetzgebern umgesetzt wird.[21] Zurzeit berät die Expertengruppe über nordische Regelungen zum Strafvollzug und zur Überstellung von Verurteilten.

4. Rechtsvergleichende Gesetzesvorarbeiten

Selbst wenn ein bestimmter Regelungsgegenstand nicht in einem gesamtnordischen Organ behandelt worden ist, bezieht jeder nordische Gesetzgeber bei nationalen Reformvorhaben routinemäßig eine vergleichende Studie zur entsprechenden Rechtslage in den nordischen Nachbarländern mit ein. Ohne einen solchen Überblick würden die Vorarbeiten zu einem Gesetz als unvollständig angesehen. Gelegentlich werden die Regelungen eines anderen nordischen Landes unmittelbar als Vorbild für die eigene Gesetzgebung verwendet. So wurden im Anschluss an den Zweiten Weltkrieg die dänischen Strafbestimmungen über Kriegsverbrechen nach schwedischem Muster geändert. Dem norwegischen Strafrecht unmittelbar nachgebildet sind die dänischen Vorschriften über die Strafbarkeit juristischer Personen und der Hehlereitatbestand des Verbrauchs von Diebesbeute durch den Ehegatten des Täters. Es ließen sich vielfältige weitere Beispiele anführen. Auch bei der in jüngerer Zeit erfolgten Novellierung der Strafzumessungsregeln in Finnland, Schweden und Dänemark ist die gegenseitige Inspiration unverkennbar. Häufig wird bei der parlamentarischen Beratung von Strafrechtsänderungen als Argument für einen bestimmten Vorschlag angeführt, dass seine Umsetzung zu einer besseren Übereinstimmung des eigenen Rechts mit dem des übrigen Nordens führen würde. Dies war beispielsweise ein Motiv für die Anhebung des Strafmündigkeitsalters in Norwegen von 14 auf 15 Jahre, mit der eine Anpassung an die Rechtslage in den Nachbarländern vollzogen wurde. Bei einer solchen Vorgehensweise können bestehende Unterschiede sowohl kriminologisch als auch rechtspolitisch als „natürliche Experimente" genutzt

21. Siehe näher dazu unten D.11.

werden; auf der Grundlage tatsächlicher Erfahrungen in einem Land, das dem eigenen sehr ähnlich ist, können Vermutungen über die praktische Bedeutung – oder häufig fehlende Bedeutung – einer Vorschrift durch konkretes Wissen ersetzt werden. Neben der oben beschriebenen institutionalisierten Zusammenarbeit zwischen den nordischen Justizministerien bestehen allgemeine kollegiale Kontakte, in deren Rahmen man sich unter anderem gegenseitig über die Rechtslage im jeweils eigenen Land informiert. Solche informellen, häufig telefonischen Kontakte spielen in der Praxis eine bedeutende Rolle.

5. *Rechtsgrundlagen der nordischen Zusammenarbeit in Strafsachen*

Die engen und vertrauensvollen Beziehungen zwischen den Ländern und das Bewusstsein einer grundsätzlich bereits bestehenden rechtlichen und tatsächlichen Ähnlichkeit ihrer Systeme und Gesellschaften haben dazu beigetragen, dass in der nordischen Zusammenarbeit die sonst üblichen Bedenken gegenüber einer engen internationalen Zusammenarbeit auf strafrechtlichem Gebiet und gegenüber dem Verzicht auf traditionelles Souveränitätsdenken keine große Rolle spielen. Nach allgemeiner Ansicht besteht eine weitgehende Übereinstimmung hinsichtlich grundlegender Werte und Rechtsprinzipien im Zusammenhang mit Fragen der Kriminalisierung, Strafverfolgung, Strafzumessung und Strafvollstreckung. Deshalb konnten die nordischen Länder untereinander völkerrechtliche Absprachen treffen, die im Verhältnis zu anderen Staaten undenkbar gewesen wären. Im Folgenden werden die wichtigsten der in diesem Rahmen geschlossenen Vereinbarungen angeführt:

Auf der Grundlage eines am 26.6.1957 unterzeichneten Protokolls zwischen Dänemark, Norwegen und Schweden wurde im Verhältnis dieser Länder das Verfahren der Übersendung von *Rechtshilfeersuchen* vereinfacht. Gerichte und Anklagebehörden konnten nunmehr ihre Anträge auf *Zustellung* oder *Beweisaufnahme* in einem der Nachbarländer unmittelbar an diejenige Behörde senden, welche dort zuständig ist, die beantragte Amtshandlung vorzunehmen. Diese zwischenstaatliche Vereinbarung wurde später durch das *Nordische Rechtshilfe-Übereinkommen* vom 26.4.1974 abgelöst, dem sich auch Finnland und Island anschlossen.

Rechtsanwälte erhielten gegen Ende der 1950er Jahre die Möglichkeit einer *Zulassung* als Verteidiger in einzelnen Strafsachen auch vor den Gerichten der jeweils anderen nordischen Länder.[22]

22. Dänemark: lov nr. 125 af 10.5.1958; Norwegen: lov nr. 1 av 11.4.1958; Schweden: lag SFS 1956:230.

Zu Beginn der 1960er Jahre wurde das *Auslieferungsverfahren* zwischen den nordischen Ländern wesentlich erleichtert: In den einzelnen Rechtsordnungen wurde die gesetzliche Grundlage für die Auslieferung eigener Staatsbürger geschaffen – was zu jener Zeit sonst völlig indiskutabel war und erst 2002 im Verhältnis zwischen den Mitgliedstaaten der EU akzeptiert wurde. Auf das Erfordernis der beiderseitigen Strafbarkeit wurde in den nordischen Auslieferungsgesetzen bereits damals verzichtet.[23] Die Auslieferung war selbst in Fällen minder schwerer Kriminalität zulässig. Ferner bestand eine erhebliche Vereinfachung darin, dass die Auslieferungsersuchen nicht mehr den klassischen Amtsweg über die Außen- und Justizministerien nehmen mussten, sondern unmittelbar zwischen den betroffenen Behörden versendet werden konnten. Damit entsprach und entspricht das Verfahren noch heute in gewisser Weise dem der nationalen Amtshilfe zwischen verschiedenen Behörden eines Landes.[24]

Ein Übereinkommen zwischen Dänemark, Norwegen und Schweden aus dem Jahr 1948 über die gegenseitige *Anerkennung und Vollstreckung von Strafurteilen* wurde 1963 abgelöst durch einheitliche Gesetze in sämtlichen nordischen Ländern über die gegenseitige *Übertragung der Vollstreckung* von Freiheitsstrafen, bedingten Urteilen, Geldstrafen, Konfiskationen u.Ä.[25] Nach diesen Regelungen kann die Vollstreckung auch ohne Zustimmung des Verurteilten übertragen werden. 1986 wurde der gesetzliche Anwendungsbereich auf die Vollstreckung bestimmter Geldbußen und 1996 auf die der gemeinnützigen Arbeit ausgedehnt. Die Einführung der Gesetze wurde teilweise mit humanitären Erwägungen (unter anderem Aufrechterhaltung von Familienkontakten, Verständigung mit dem Anstaltspersonal in der eigenen Sprache) und teilweise mit kriminalpolitischen Argumenten (räumliche Nähe zu der Umgebung, in der der Verurteilte nach der Strafverbüßung seine Lebensgrundlage suchen wird) begründet.[26] Die Gesetze gelten – mit zwischenzeitlichen Änderungen – noch heute, das heißt auch nach der Ratifizierung und Implementierung des Europäischen Übereinkommens vom 21.3.1983 über die Überstellung verurteilter Personen.

Im Jahr 1970 erließen die nordischen Länder übereinstimmende Regelungen über die gegenseitige *Auslieferung* von Personen zur Vollstreckung der

23. Mit Ausnahme von Strafsachen wegen politischer Delikte.
24. Dänemark: lov nr. 27 af 3.2.1960; Finnland: lag 3.6.1960/270; Island: lög nr. 7 14.3.1962; Norwegen: lov nr. 1 av 3.3.1961; Schweden lag SFS 1959:254.
25. Dänemark: lov nr. 214 af 31.5.1963; Finnland: lag 20.6.1963/326; Island: lög nr. 69 12.12.1963; Norwegen: lov av 15.11.1963; Schweden: lag SFS 1963:193.
26. Siehe *Horned*, NTfK 1994, S. 183 ff.

angeordneten Zwangsunterbringung in einer Einrichtung der Kinder- und Jugendfürsorge, der psychiatrischen Zwangspflege oder der Suchtfürsorge.[27]

Seit 1973 werden aufgrund einheitlicher Bestimmungen jeweils *Zeiten der Untersuchungshaft*, die ein Angeklagter in einem nordischen Land erlitten hat, auf die in derselben Sache in einem der Nachbarländer zu verhängende Strafe *angerechnet*.[28]

Die *Zeugnispflicht* vor den Gerichten wurde Mitte der 1970er Jahre in der Weise ausgedehnt, dass jeder, der in einem der nordischen Länder ansässig ist oder sich dort aufhält und damit der nationalen Gerichtsgewalt untersteht, gleichermaßen verpflichtet ist, als Zeuge auch vor den Gerichten der Nachbarländer zu erscheinen und auszusagen.[29] Ausgenommen von der erweiterten Zeugnispflicht sind Personen, die sich in Untersuchungshaft oder im Strafvollzug befinden. Im Übrigen wird berücksichtigt, ob dem Zeugen aufgrund großer Entfernung erhebliche Nachteile entstehen. Diese Regelungen gelten auch nach der Ratifikation und Implementierung des Europäischen Übereinkommens vom 29.5.2000 über die gegenseitige Rechtshilfe in Strafsachen zwischen den Mitgliedstaaten der EU fort.

Die nationalen Vorschriften der nordischen Länder über staatliche *Entschädigung für Verbrechensopfer* enthalten besonders weitgehende Vorschriften im Hinblick auf Straftaten, die während einer Gefangenenflucht begangen werden. Entsprechend einer Empfehlung des Nordischen Rates kann bei der Opferentschädigung die Flucht aus einem Gefängnis eines nordischen Nachbarlandes der Flucht aus einem landeseigenen Gefängnis gleichgestellt werden.[30] Die Empfehlung kam vor dem Hintergrund eines Falles zustande, in dem ein schwedischer Strafgefangener aus dem Vollzug entflohen war und auf der Flucht in Norwegen einen Mord begangen hatte.

Angeregt durch die Einführung des Europäischen Haftbefehls schlossen die Regierungen von Dänemark, Finnland, Island, Norwegen und Schweden am 15.12.2005 ein Übereinkommen zur *Übergabe zwischen den nordischen Ländern wegen Straftaten* (Nordischer Haftbefehl).[31] Inhaltlich gehen die

27. Dänemark: lov nr. 498 af 23.12.1970; Finnland: lag 11.12.1970/761; Norwegen: lov nr. 35 av 5.6.1970; Schweden: lag SFS 1970:375.
28. Dänemark: lov nr. 320 af 26.1.1973; Finnland: lag 2.7.1973/578; Norwegen: lov nr. 29 av 1.6.1973; Schweden: lag SFS 1974:202.
29. Dänemark: lov nr. 182 af 7.5.1975; Finnland: lag 23.5.1975/349; Island: lög nr. 82 31.5.1976; Norwegen: lov nr. 9 av 21.3.1975; Schweden: lag SFS 1974:752.
30. Dänemark: lov nr. 277 af 26.5.1976; Finnland lag 20.1.1984/63; Island: lög nr. 69 10.3.1995; Schweden: lag SFS 1990:59.
31. Konvention om overgivelse for strafbare forhold mellem de nordiske lande *(Nordisk arrestordre)*.

Vereinbarungen in mehrfacher Hinsicht über den EU-Rahmenbeschluss zum Europäischen Haftbefehl hinaus.[32] In Dänemark und Norwegen liegen bereits entsprechende Gesetzentwürfe zur Umsetzung des Übereinkommens auf nationaler Ebene vor; in Finnland wird nach Auskunft des Justizministeriums ein Gesetzentwurf vorbereitet.[33]

6. Das Kooperationsabkommen der obersten Anklagebehörden

Am 6.2.1970 schlossen die Leiter der nordischen Obersten Anklagebehörden ein Kooperationsabkommen *(De nordiske rigsadvokaters samarbejdsaftale)*. Formal erfüllt es nicht die Voraussetzungen eines völkerrechtlichen Vertrags, da die Unterzeichner zum Abschluss eines solchen nicht ermächtigt waren. Deshalb ist das Abkommen von einigen Theoretikern unter Hinweis darauf kritisiert worden, dass es völkerrechtlich nicht bindend sei. Doch hat sich der nordische Pragmatismus über diese theoretischen Einwände hinweggesetzt, und ungeachtet der Lehrmeinungen bewährt sich das Abkommen in der Praxis hervorragend. Nach zwischenzeitlichen geringfügigen Änderungen hat es in seiner aktuellen Fassung folgenden Wortlaut:

> § 1 Die rechtliche Verfolgung einer Straftat, die in einem nordischen Land (Tatortstaat) begangen worden ist, kann in einem anderen nordischen Land erfolgen, wenn der Verdächtigte in diesem anderen Land ansässig und die Tat auch nach dem dort geltenden Recht strafbar ist.
>
> Das gleiche gilt, sofern der Verdächtigte sich in dem anderen Land aufhält und es aus besonderen Gründen für zweckdienlich erachtet wird, die Strafverfolgung dort vorzunehmen, und der Sachverhalt in die Strafgewalt dieses Landes fällt.
>
> Die Strafverfolgung erfolgt nach den Strafbestimmungen und Prozessregeln des Landes, welches die Sache übernimmt (der ersuchte Staat).
>
> § 2 Bei der Entscheidung darüber, ob ein Ersuchen auf Strafverfolgung in einem anderen Land als dem Tatortstaat gestellt und einem solchen Ersuchen stattgegeben werden soll, sind die Interessen des Verdächtigten sowie die Durchführung eines effektiven Verfahrens als maßgebliche Gesichtspunkte zu berücksichtigen.
>
> Ein Ersuchen darf daher nicht abgelehnt werden,

32. Siehe näher dazu unten D.11.
33. Dänemark: Gesetzentwurf L 72 2006–07 vom 15.11.2006; Norwegen: Forslag til lov om pågripelse og overlevering mellom de nordiske stater på grunn av straffbare forhold (lov om nordisk arrestordre), høringsnotat vom 12.9.2006. Zu Finnland siehe http://www.om.fi/32818.htm.

a) wenn eine Auslieferung an den Tatortstaat aus rechtlichen Gründen ausgeschlossen ist oder aus anderen Gründen nicht durchführbar erscheint,
b) wenn der Verdächtigte in dem anderen Land wegen einer weiteren Straftat zur Verantwortung gezogen werden soll und die Strafsachen miteinander verbunden werden müssen.

Ein Ersuchen kann jedoch abgelehnt werden, wenn anzunehmen ist, dass die Beweisführung in der Strafsache vor den Gerichten des anderen Landes nicht möglich ist oder die Durchführung des Prozesses in dem anderen Land zu unverhältnismäßig großem Aufwand führen würde.

§ 3 Ein Ersuchen auf Strafverfolgung in einem anderen Land als dem Tatortstaat muss so frühzeitig wie möglich gestellt werden. Nachdem ein erstinstanzliches Urteil ergangen ist, kann ein solches Ersuchen nicht mehr gestellt werden.

§ 4 Das Ersuchen muss Angaben über Namen, Alter, Staatsangehörigkeit und Wohn- oder Aufenthaltsort des Verdächtigten, über die Art der Straftat, Zeit und Ort der Tatbegehung sowie die im Tatortstaat auf den Sachverhalt anwendbaren Strafbestimmungen enthalten.

Wird das Ersuchen telefonisch, telegrafisch oder per Telex gestellt, so ist es alsbald schriftlich zu bestätigen.

Dem Ersuchen sind alle zugänglichen Verfahrensakten beizufügen. Auf Wunsch des ersuchten Staates sind weitere Angaben unverzüglich nachzureichen.

Das Ersuchen und die Verfahrensakten sind nach Dänemark auf Dänisch, Norwegisch oder Schwedisch, nach Finnland auf Finnisch oder Schwedisch, nach Island auf Isländisch, Dänisch, Norwegisch oder Schwedisch, nach Norwegen auf Norwegisch, Dänisch oder Schwedisch und nach Schweden auf Schwedisch, Dänisch oder Norwegisch zu übersenden. Sind die Akten nicht in einer der hier angeführten Sprachen verfasst, so ist eine Übersetzung in eine dieser Sprachen beizufügen.

§ 5 Das Ersuchen wird in Dänemark von dem zuständigen Polizeipräsidenten, in Finnland von dem zuständigen Ankläger, in Island von der Obersten Anklagebehörde, in Norwegen von dem zuständigen Staatsanwalt und in Schweden von dem zuständigen Ankläger ausgefertigt.

Ein an Dänemark oder Norwegen gerichtetes Ersuchen wird an den Polizeipräsidenten desjenigen Polizeibezirks gesendet, in dem der Verdächtigte wohnt oder sich aufhält. Ist nicht bekannt, um welchen Polizeibezirk es sich handelt, so wird das Ersuchen an die Oberste Anklagebehörde gesendet.

Ein an Finnland gerichtetes Ersuchen wird an die Zentrale Kriminalpolizei in Helsinki zur Weiterleitung an den zuständigen Ankläger gesendet.

Ein an Island gerichtetes Ersuchen wird an die Oberste Anklagebehörde gesendet.

Ein an Schweden gerichtetes Ersuchen wird an die Anklagebehörde desjenigen Bezirks gesendet, in dem der Verdächtigte wohnt oder sich aufhält. Ist nicht bekannt, um welchen Bezirk es sich handelt, so wird das Ersuchen an die Oberste Anklagebehörde gesendet.

§ 6 Die Behörden des ersuchten Staates sind von den Behörden des Tatortstaates alsbald über die dort getroffenen oder zu treffenden prozessualen Maßnahmen zu unterrichten.

Die Behörden des ersuchten Staates haben unverzüglich bekannt zu geben, inwieweit dem Ersuchen stattgegeben wird.

Die Behörden des ersuchten Staates können später, sofern veränderte Umstände hierzu Anlass geben, um eine Freistellung von weiterer Strafverfolgung in der Sache bitten. Auf

Absprache zwischen den Behörden der beteiligten Länder kann auch in anderen Fällen ein Beschluss zur Strafverfolgung in dem ersuchten Land zurückgenommen werden.

§ 7 Sieht eine der in § 5 genannten Behörden Anlass, im eigenen Land eine Strafverfolgung gegen eine Person wegen einer in einem anderen nordischen Land begangenen strafbaren Handlung einzuleiten, so muss die betreffende Behörde die entsprechende Behörde des Tatortstaates hierüber unterrichten.

§ 8 Fragen über die praktische Durchführung dieses Kooperationsabkommens müssen die Behörden der beteiligten Länder durch gemeinsame Beratungen und gegenseitiges Verständnis zu lösen versuchen.

Es stellt eine offensichtliche Vereinfachung dar, dass die Behörden der beteiligten Länder unmittelbar miteinander kommunizieren können und nicht auf die diplomatischen Kanäle angewiesen sind. In diesem Zusammenhang wird hervorgehoben, dass die Ähnlichkeit zwischen der dänischen, der norwegischen und der schwedischen Sprache sich als eine große Hilfe in der grenzüberschreitenden Behördenarbeit erweist.

Insoweit sahen es die nordischen Praktiker als einen Rückschritt an, dass aufgrund des Europäischen Übereinkommens von 1972 über die Übertragung der Strafverfolgung zwischen den EU-Mitgliedstaaten Dänemark, Finnland und Schweden ein vergleichsweise umständliches Verfahren eingeführt werden sollte. Die Leiter der nordischen obersten Anklagebehörden beschlossen deshalb am 19.11.1973 folgende Ergänzung zu ihrem Kooperationsabkommen:

A. Das Kooperationsabkommen gilt in vollem Umfang zwischen nordischen Ländern, sofern nicht beide beteiligten Staaten dem [Europäischen] Übereinkommen beigetreten sind.

B. Die §§ 4, 5, 7 und 8 des Kooperationsabkommens gelten über das [Europäische] Übereinkommen hinaus und an dessen Stelle zwischen nordischen Ländern, die dem [Europäischen] Übereinkommen beigetreten sind.

Eine prinzipiell interessante und praktische bedeutsame Frage ist, zu welchem Zeitpunkt der Ankläger im Tatortland, nachdem er ein Ersuchen um Übernahme der Strafverfolgung gestellt hat, die Sache bei sich als abgeschlossen betrachten kann. Dies ist insbesondere relevant in Ländern wie Finnland und Schweden, in denen das Strafprozessrecht eine absolute Verfolgungspflicht nach dem Legalitätsprinzip vorsieht. Die schwedischen Ankläger sind darauf hingewiesen worden, dass für sie eine Sache als abgeschlossen gilt, sobald der Bescheid erfolgt, dass die Strafverfolgung von den Behörden des ersuchten Landes übernommen worden ist.[34] Es braucht also

34. Vgl. *Romander*, Festskrift til Rolv Ryssdal, S. 375 f.

nicht der Abschluss des Verfahrens in dem ersuchten Land abgewartet zu werden.

Selbst im Rahmen der Geltung des nordischen Kooperationsabkommens können rechtliche oder praktische Hindernisse bestehen. Die Straftatbestände des Urteilslandes können in ihrem Regelungsumfang territorial begrenzt sein, sodass beispielsweise eine Strafverfolgung wegen Gewalt gegen einen Beamten im Dienst nicht übertragen werden kann. Auch Steuerdelikte sind häufig nicht geeignet, außerhalb des eigenen Landes verfolgt zu werden. In der Praxis ergaben sich früher aus der territorialen Begrenzung besonders oft Probleme im Bereich des Straßenverkehrsrechts; sie sind jedoch mittlerweile durch harmonisierende Änderungen der nordischen Straßenverkehrsgesetze gelöst worden.[35]

7. *Die polizeiliche Zusammenarbeit*

Die Entwicklung der polizeilichen Zusammenarbeit zwischen den nordischen Ländern wird als ein Prozess beschrieben,[36] der hauptsächlich von den Polizeibehörden selbst vorangetrieben wurde. Dabei hat traditionell ein gewisser Abstand gegenüber der Justiz und der Strafrechtswissenschaft bestanden. Weder die Juristen noch die Polizeibeamten scheinen besonderen Wert auf Kontakte oder gar eine Koordinierung ihrer Arbeit gelegt zu haben. Die Juristen haben für ihren Bereich Konventionen erarbeitet und sich auf eher grundlegende Fragen konzentriert. Für sie war die praktische Seite der Kriminalitätsbekämpfung von untergeordnetem Interesse. Folglich mussten sich die Polizeibeamten mit diesen Problemen allein auseinandersetzen, wobei sie sich auf die Anforderungen des täglichen Dienstes konzentrierten.

Die nordische polizeiliche Zusammenarbeit ist daher teilweise geprägt von außerrechtlichen und informellen Formen der Kooperation. Dies gilt insbesondere für Maßnahmen der Observation und der Nacheile über die Landesgrenzen zwischen Finnland, Norwegen und Schweden. Aufgrund der großen geografischen Entfernungen und der geringen Polizeidichte in den Grenzgebieten sind solche Formen der Dienstausübung praktisch unverzichtbar. Rechtlich wird die Befugnis zur grenzüberschreitenden Nacheile auf Gesichtspunkte der Gefahr im Verzug und des Notstands gestützt. Anders als im Rahmen der Schengen-Zusammenarbeit ist hier nicht festgelegt, wie weit ein Beamter sich in das Nachbarland hinein begeben darf.[37]

35. Vgl. *Romander*, S. 376; *Greve*, Færdselsstrafferet, S. 11 ff.
36. Siehe *Auglend u.a.*, Politirett, S. 1036 f.; *Ulrich*, NTfK 1994, 162 f.
37. Vgl. *Auglend u.a.*, S. 1039.

8. Das Kooperationsabkommen der nordischen Polizeichefs

Zahlreiche andere Formen der nordischen polizeilichen Zusammenarbeit sind stärker formalisiert, und zwar in erster Linie durch ein Kooperationsabkommen zwischen den Leitern der jeweiligen Obersten Polizeibehörden *(Den nordiske politisamarbejdsaftale)* vom 2.9.2002. Dieses Abkommen, das frühere Vereinbarungen aus den Jahren 1968 und 1972 ersetzt hat, umfasst polizeiliche Vernehmungen, Identitätsfeststellungen, die Ausstellung von polizeilichen Führungszeugnissen, Registrierungen, Fahndungen, Fahrzeugkontrollen, Beweissicherung und Beweisaufnahme, Hausdurchsuchung und Beschlagnahme, Zustellungen, Ladungen, die Auslieferung von Straftätern, die Übertragung von Strafsachen, die Beitreibung von Geldstrafen und die Überstellung von Verurteilten zum Zwecke des Strafvollzugs. In allen diesen Bereichen dient das Abkommen einer dezentralisierten und von umständlichen Prozeduren befreiten internationalen Kooperation zwischen den nordischen Strafverfolgungsbehörden. Die vereinbarten Formen der Zusammenarbeit bestehen vor allem darin, dass die einzelne Polizeibehörde direkt mit der zuständigen Polizeibehörde des anderen Landes in Kontakt treten kann. Dies stellt einen erheblichen praktischen Vorteil dar und garantiert ein weitaus geschmeidigeres und schnelleres Verfahren als dasjenige nach den Regeln des Europäischen Übereinkommens über die gegenseitige Rechtshilfe in Strafsachen vom 20.4.1959, die den Dienstweg über die vorgesetzten Behörden vorsehen.

Für den Fall, dass eine Kontaktaufnahme auf lokaler Ebene, das heißt zwischen den unmittelbar betroffenen Polizeibehörden, nicht vorgesehen oder nicht zweckmäßig ist, legt das Abkommen für jedes beteiligte Land einen *nationalen Kontaktpunkt* fest, und zwar in Dänemark das Kommunikationszentrum beim Reichspolizeichef, in Finnland die Zentrale Kriminalpolizei, in Island die Oberste Polizeibehörde, in Norwegen die Zentrale der Kriminalpolizei und in Schweden das nationale Verbindungsbüro der Reichskriminalpolizei. In diesem Zusammenhang gelten unter anderem folgende Bestimmungen (Kapitel 1):

> Für die Frage, ob auf zentraler oder lokaler Ebene oder vielleicht auf beiden Ebenen korrespondiert werden soll, sind jeweils die Art des Auftrags und die örtlichen Verhältnisse entscheidend. Nach Island ist die Korrespondenz stets über den nationalen Kontaktpunkt zu senden.
>
> Sofern Zweifel bestehen, ob eine Maßnahme in einem anderen Land durchgeführt werden kann, ist zunächst der eigene nationale Kontaktpunkt zu Rate zu ziehen – oder das Ersuchen über diesen zu senden.
>
> Sofern nichts anderes aus dem Ersuchen hervorgeht, ist eine Antwort stets an die Behörde zu senden, von der das Ersuchen stammt.
>
> [...]

Wird ein Ersuchen per E-Mail, Telefax oder Telefon übermittelt, so ist es nach Möglichkeit an diejenige Abteilung der Polizei des betreffenden Landes zu adressieren, von der anzunehmen ist, dass sie derartige Sachen bearbeitet.

[...]

Örtliche Polizeibehörden entlang der Grenzen sind aufgerufen, lokale Maßnahmen zu prüfen und eventuell zu ergreifen, um die grenzüberschreitende polizeiliche Zusammenarbeit im Rahmen dieses Abkommens weiter zu vertiefen. Eine solche Maßnahme kann unter anderem in regelmäßigen Treffen, sei es zu rein operativen Zwecken oder zu allgemeinen Informationszwecken, bestehen.

Falls ein Ersuchen aus einem anderen Land nicht innerhalb von 4 Wochen nach seinem Eingang bearbeitet werden kann, ist dies der ersuchenden Behörde so bald wie möglich mitzuteilen unter Angabe eines Zeitpunkts, zu dem mit der Durchführung der beantragten Maßnahme zu rechnen ist. Falls bis zur Ausführung des Auftrags außerordentlich lange Zeit vergehen wird, ist hierfür ein Grund anzugeben.

Für Ersuchen um polizeiliche Vernehmung ist (mit Ausnahme von Island) der direkte Behördenweg vorgesehen (Kapitel 2):

Dänemark, Finnland, Norwegen und Schweden: Ein Ersuchen um polizeiliche Vernehmung wird direkt von der lokalen Polizeibehörde an die Polizeibehörde desjenigen Bezirks übersandt, in dem der Betreffende sich aufhält oder mutmaßlich aufhält. Die Antwort wird direkt an die ersuchende Behörde übersandt. Ist der Aufenthaltsort des Betreffenden unbekannt, so wird über den nationalen Kontaktpunkt des eigenen Landes eine Fahndung beantragt. Sobald der Aufenthaltsort geklärt ist, wird das Ersuchen um polizeiliche Vernehmung in der oben angegebenen Weise gestellt.

Island: Ein Ersuchen um polizeiliche Vernehmung wird an den nationalen Kontaktpunkt übersandt.

[...]

Ein Antrag auf Anwesenheit und Teilnahme [eines Polizeibeamten aus dem ersuchenden Land] an einer Vernehmung in einem anderen nordischen Land ist rechtzeitig nach folgenden Regeln zu übersenden: In Dänemark, Finnland, Norwegen und Schweden an die Polizeibehörde in demjenigen Bezirk, in dem die Vernehmung stattfinden soll; in Island an den nationalen Kontaktpunkt.

Wenn ein Beamter aus dem ersuchenden Land bei der Vernehmung anwesend ist, muss ihm Gelegenheit gegeben werden, selbst Fragen in der Sache an den zu Vernehmenden zu stellen.

Falls aufgrund der Anwesenheit eines Beamten aus dem ersuchenden Land ein Dolmetscher beigezogen werden muss, hat das ersuchende Land die hierdurch entstehenden Kosten zu tragen.

Eine Personenfahndung in einem anderen nordischen Land kann nach folgenden Regeln beantragt werden (Kapitel 5):

Ein Ersuchen um Fahndung innerhalb des Nordens nach einer Person, die nicht im Schengen-Informationssystem (SIS) registriert werden soll, ist mit Rücksicht auf die Wichtigkeit einer zentralen Registrierung unter anderem für einen Fahndungsabbruch stets über den eigenen nationalen Kontaktpunkt zu übersenden. Nach demjenigen, der zur Fahndung in einem anderen nordischen Land ausgeschrieben ist, muss außerdem stets im eigenen Land gefahndet werden.

[...] Aus einem Ersuchen um Fahndung in einem anderen nordischen Land müssen sowohl der Grund für die Fahndung als auch Maßnahmen deutlich hervorgehen, die getroffen werden sollen, falls der Betreffende gefunden wird.

Wird um Fahndung nach einer Person ersucht, die aufgrund Beschlusses festgenommen oder in Verwahrung genommen werden soll, so muss aus dem Ersuchen hervorgehen, was dem Beschluss zugrunde liegt und inwieweit eine Auslieferung des Betreffenden beantragt werden wird, falls man ihn findet. Konnte zur Auslieferungsfrage noch keine Stellungnahme abgegeben werden, so kommt die Fahndung zur Festnahme dennoch in Betracht, wenn ein Auslieferungsersuchen als wahrscheinlich angesehen wird. Dies ist gegebenenfalls in dem Fahndungsantrag anzugeben.

Auch zum Auslieferungsersuchen enthält das Abkommen detaillierte Bestimmungen (Kapitel 6):

[...]

Ein Auslieferungsersuchen ist zu senden: in Dänemark und Norwegen an die Polizei- oder Anklagebehörde des Bezirks, in dem sich der Beschuldigte aufhält; in Finnland an die Polizeiabteilung des Innenministeriums entweder direkt oder über die örtliche Polizeibehörde des Bezirks, in dem sich der Beschuldigte aufhält; in Island an das Justiz- und Kirchenministerium; in Schweden an die Anklagebehörde des Bezirks, in dem sich der Beschuldigte aufhält.

Ist der Aufenthaltsort unbekannt und soll er im Falle einer Fahndung nicht durch das Schengen-Informationssystem (SIS) ermittelt werden, so wird ein Fahndungsersuchen zur Auslieferung durch den eigenen nationalen Kontaktpunkt gestellt. Sobald der Aufenthaltsort geklärt ist, wird das Auslieferungsersuchen an diejenige Behörde übersandt, die nach den vorstehenden Bestimmungen die Sache bearbeiten soll.

2004 wurde das Abkommen dahingehend erweitert, dass die Polizeibehörden der nordischen Länder sich gegenseitig ihre Ausrüstung – mit Ausnahme von Waffen – zur Verfügung stellen können. Zugleich einigte man sich darauf, Rechtsgrundlagen für gemischte Patrouillen zu schaffen, so dass Polizeibeamte eines Landes auf dem Territorium eines anderen Landes tätig werden dürfen.[38] In der Literatur wird der beachtliche Regelungsumfang des Kooperationsabkommens der nordischen Polizeichefs darauf zurückgeführt, dass die geografische, kulturelle und politische Nähe der nordischen Länder eine gute Voraussetzung für ihre Zusammenarbeit in dezentralisierter Form biete,

38. Eine entsprechende Regelung findet sich bereits in den von Dänemark und Schweden im Jahr 2000 erlassenen Gesetzen über die polizeiliche Zusammenarbeit in der Öresundregion. Siehe dazu unten D.9.

ohne dass Souveränitätsprobleme entstehen. Für die polizeiliche Kooperation zwischen Ländern, die einander weniger nahestehen, hält man demgegenüber aus nordischer Sicht einen anderen Grad der rechtlichen Verankerung und der übergeordneten nationalen Kontrolle für notwendig. Wesentliche Voraussetzungen einer guten internationalen polizeilichen Zusammenarbeit seien im Übrigen stets ein generell gutes Kooperationsklima, funktionierende Kommunikation, gegenseitiges Vertrauen und reger Informationsaustausch.[39]

9. Spezielle Bereiche polizeilicher Zusammenarbeit

1984 wurde eine besondere Zusammenarbeit zwischen den nordischen Polizei- und Zollbehörden etabliert: PTN (*Politi-Told-Norden*). Während diese Kooperation ursprünglich auf Drogendelikte beschränkt war, gilt sie heute für alle Formen der schweren, organisierten und grenzüberschreitenden Kriminalität, wie etwa Menschenhandel. Zu den wichtigsten Elementen der PTN-Kooperation gehört der Austausch sowohl allgemeiner Informationen als auch konkreter Hinweisen zur Verwendung im Einzelfall. Deshalb ist besonderer Wert auf die Errichtung einheitlicher Kommunikationssysteme und auf die Vereinbarung gemeinsamer Kriterien für die Registrierung von Meldungen und Angaben gelegt worden. Im Bereich der Drogenkriminalität hat man die Zuständigkeit für die Beobachtung der Entwicklung in Bezug auf bestimmte Drogenarten zwischen den Ländern aufgeteilt (Dänemark: Kokain; Norwegen: Heroin; Schweden: Amphetamin). Es sind auch zahlreiche „Verbindungsoffiziere" in Drittländer ausgesandt worden; dort repräsentiert jeweils ein nordischer Offizier sämtliche nordischen Länder.

Mit Fragen des Straßenverkehrs befasst sich ein anderes Kooperationsorgan, SANT *(SamArbejd Norden Trafik)*. Seit 1997 gab es daneben vorübergehend eine besondere Einsatzgruppe für die sogenannte Rocker-Kriminalität. Ferner finden auf allen Ebenen häufige internordische Treffen zu zahlreichen Themen statt, die bei einem großen Teil der Polizeikräfte zu einem breiten und eingehenden Kenntnisstand über Verhältnisse und Personen in den jeweils anderen Ländern geführt haben.

Eine besonders erwähnenswerte bilaterale Vereinbarung besteht zwischen Dänemark und Schweden, die am 6.10.1999 im Zusammenhang mit der Errichtung einer Brücke über den *Öresund* zwischen Kopenhagen und Malmö einen Staatsvertrag zur polizeilichen Zusammenarbeit im Brückenbereich ge-

39. Vgl. *Auglend u.a.*, S. 1038.

schlossen haben.[40] Auf der Brücke, die am 1.7.2000 für den Verkehr geöffnet wurde, verläuft die Landesgrenze etwa 10,5 km von der dänischen und 5,5 km von der schwedischen Küste entfernt. Polizeibeamte beider Länder können im Brückenbereich unter anderem gemeinsame Patrouillenfahrten durchführen und sind ermächtigt, auf dem jeweils fremden Hoheitsgebiet eine Reihe polizeilicher Maßnahmen zu treffen. So kann beispielsweise die schwedische Polizei einen Autofahrer im dänischen Teil der Brücke anhalten, wenn sie ihn eines Verstoßes gegen die dänische Promillegrenze verdächtigt. Sie kann den Betreffenden bis zur schnellstmöglichen Übergabe an die dänische Polizei festhalten. Bei einem Unfall können schwedische Polizeibeamte auch auf dänischer Seite den Verkehr lenken. Voraussetzung ist in jedem dieser Fälle die Dringlichkeit der Maßnahme. Routinemäßige Verkehrskontrollen dürfen deshalb nur auf dem jeweils eigenen Brückenteil durchgeführt werden. Grenzüberschreitende Observation und Nacheile erfolgen nach den Regeln für die Schengen-Zusammenarbeit. Darüber hinaus dürfen jedoch Polizeibeamte beider Länder nicht nur eine im eigenen Land begonnene Verfolgung jenseits der Grenze fortsetzen, sondern auf dem jeweils fremden Brückenteil auch die Verfolgung einer Person aufnehmen, die dort auf frischer Tat oder auf der Flucht aus einer Haft betroffen wird. Dänemark hat hierbei den Bewegungsradius für schwedische Polizeibeamte über den Brückenbereich hinaus auf 25 km begrenzt, während Schweden umgekehrt auf eine entsprechende Beschränkung verzichtet.

10. Zusammenarbeit im Strafvollzugswesen

Wie bereits oben erwähnt, gibt es spezielle Gesetze, die die Überstellung von verurteilten Personen zum Zwecke der Strafvollstreckung regeln. Auch hier findet eine enge informelle Kooperation in allen Bereichen statt. So treffen sich beispielsweise die jeweiligen Leiter des Gefängniswesens ebenso wie die Sicherheitschefs, die Leiter des Bewährungsvollzugs und die Gefängnisstatistiker in jährlichem Abstand, das leitende Gefängnispersonal jedes zweite Jahr und die (über 100) Rechtspsychiater alle zwei oder drei Jahre.

11. Der Nordische Haftbefehl

Auf manchen Gebieten ist die nordische Zusammenarbeit von der Entwicklung innerhalb der EU überholt worden. Der Europäische Haftbefehl etwa ist in einigen Punkten weiter gehend als die entsprechende Kooperationsverein-

40. Aftale mellem Kongeriget Danmarks regering og Kongeriget Sveriges regering om politimæssigt samarbejde i Øresundsregionen af 6.10.1999. Dänemark: lov nr. 318 af 9.5.2000; Schweden: lag SFS 2000:343.

barung zwischen den nordischen Ländern. Gegenwärtig wird jedoch an der Verwirklichung eines „Nordischen Haftbefehls" gearbeitet, der die innernordische Zusammenarbeit wieder enger als die europäische gestalten wird. Die Grundlage hierfür bildet das „Übereinkommen zur Übergabe zwischen den nordischen Ländern wegen Straftaten (Nordischer Haftbefehl) u.ä." vom 15.12.2005. Teilweise liegen bereits nationale Gesetzentwürfe zu seiner Implementierung vor.[41]

In der Präambel des Übereinkommens heißt es unter anderem:[42]

(3) Aus der erklärten Zielsetzung der nordischen Länder, die Rechtslage auf diesem Gebiet noch geschmeidiger zu gestalten, erwächst der Wunsch nach Abschaffung der bestehenden Auslieferungsvorschriften und Einführung von Regelungen, die auf einem gegenseitig anzuerkennenden Nordischen Haftbefehl beruhen und nach denen die Übergabe stattzufinden hat, sofern nicht einer der in der Konvention genannten Ablehnungsgründe besteht. Ferner wird die Einführung neuer Regelungen für die Übergabe von verurteilten oder verdächtigten Personen zum Zwecke des Strafvollzugs oder der Strafverfolgung es ermöglichen, die mit den gegenwärtigen Auslieferungsprozeduren, unter anderem auch im Rahmen des Europäischen Haftbefehls, verbundene Komplexität abzubauen.

Ein Nordischer Haftbefehl kann ausgestellt werden im Hinblick auf 1) die Strafverfolgung wegen einer Straftat, die nach dem Recht des Landes, in welchem der Haftbefehl ausgestellt worden ist, zu einer Freiheitsstrafe oder einer anderen freiheitsentziehenden Sanktion führen kann, sowie 2) die Vollstreckung eines rechtskräftigen Strafurteils, mit dem eine Freiheitsstrafe oder eine andere freiheitsentziehende Sanktion verhängt worden ist. Dabei wird nicht zwischen eigenen Staatsangehörigen und anderen Personen unterschieden. Ebenso wenig gilt ein Erfordernis der doppelten Strafbarkeit.[43]

Jedes beteiligte Land legt fest, welche lokalen Behörden für die Ausstellung eines Nordischen Haftbefehls beziehungsweise für die Entgegennahme eines solchen und für die Entscheidung über seine Vollstreckung zuständig sind.[44] Zusätzlich kann auch jeweils eine zentrale Behörde bestimmt werden,

41. Dänemark: Gesetzentwurf L 72 2006–07; Norwegen: Forslag til lov om pågripelse og overlevering mellom de nordiske stater på grunn av straffbare forhold (lov om nordisk arrestordre), høringsnotat vom 12.9.2006. In Finnland wird ein entsprechender Gesetzentwurf vorbereitet, siehe dazu http://www.om.fi/32818.htm. Vgl. auch oben D.5.
42. Der Wortlaut des Übereinkommens ist in deutscher Übersetzung im Anhang zu diesem Bericht wiedergegeben.
43. Artikel 2.
44. Artikel 3. Nach den Gesetzentwürfen sollen in Dänemark die örtlichen Polizeidirektoren und in Norwegen die örtlichen Staatsanwälte oder Polizeipräsidenten hierfür zuständig sein; ihre Übergabeentscheidungen sind gerichtlich überprüfbar.

welche die zuständigen lokalen Behörden in ihrer Tätigkeit unterstützt. Die Übersendung des Haftbefehls sowie die weiteren Kontakte erfolgen unmittelbar zwischen der ausstellenden und der vollstreckenden Behörde.[45]

Die Übergabe hat zu erfolgen, sofern nicht ein zwingender oder fakultativer Ablehnungsgrund vorliegt.[46] Gegenüber einem Haftbefehl zum Zwecke der Strafverfolgung ist ein zwingender Ablehnungsgrund beispielsweise dann gegeben, wenn die betreffende Person bereits wegen derselben strafbaren Handlung in einem nordischen Land oder einem EU-Mitgliedsland verurteilt oder freigesprochen worden ist. Ein fakultativer Grund zur Ablehnung der Übergabe besteht unter anderem, wenn das ersuchte Land bereits selbst die betreffende Person wegen derselben Tat strafrechtlich verfolgt oder wenn in diesem oder einem anderen nordischen Land ein begonnenes Ermittlungsverfahren in dieser Sache eingestellt worden ist. Im Gegensatz zum Europäischen Haftbefehl kann jedoch die Übergabe nicht unter Hinweis darauf verweigert werden, dass die Strafverfolgung verjährt ist.

Ein Nordischer Haftbefehl ist stets als Eilsache zu behandeln. Die Entscheidung über die Übergabe muss grundsätzlich innerhalb von drei Tagen nach der Zustimmungserklärung des Betreffenden erfolgen, ohne seine Einwilligung innerhalb von 30 Tagen nach seiner Festnahme.[47] Spätestens fünf Tage nach der Entscheidung über die Vollstreckung des Haftbefehls ist die Übergabe durchzuführen; ausnahmsweise kann die Frist um weitere fünf Tage verlängert werden.[48]

Die verfolgte Person wird bei ihrer Festnahme durch die vollstreckende Behörde über den Nordischen Haftbefehl und dessen Inhalt informiert sowie über die Möglichkeit der Einwilligung in die Übergabe an die ersuchende Behörde belehrt. Der Festgenommene hat Anspruch auf einen Rechtsbeistand und einen Dolmetscher.[49] Eine eventuelle Einwilligungserklärung muss protokolliert werden, und aus dem Protokoll muss hervorgehen, dass der Betreffende die Erklärung freiwillig und in voller Kenntnis der Folgen abgegeben hat. Auch in diesem Zusammenhang hat der Verfolgte ein Recht auf juristischen Beistand.[50] Befindet sich der Betreffende nach Ablauf der im Übereinkommen festgelegten oder einer vereinbarten Übergabefrist noch in Ausliefe-

45. Artikel 8, 13, 14 Abs. 4, 18, 19.
46. Artikel 4 und 5.
47. Artikel 14.
48. Artikel 19 Abs. 1–3.
49. Artikel 9.
50. Artikel 11 Abs. 2–3.

rungshaft, so muss er freigelassen werden.[51] Nach erfolgter Übergabe ist grundsätzlich auch die Weiterübergabe an ein anderes nordisches Land, die Weiterübergabe oder Weiterauslieferung an ein EU-Mitgliedsland sowie die Weiterauslieferung an ein Drittland zulässig.[52]

Der Nordische Haftbefehl geht weiter als der europäische, indem er an kürzere Fristen gebunden ist und weniger Ablehnungsgründe vorgesehen sind. Nach dem nordischen Übereinkommen gilt ferner nicht der Spezialitätsgrundsatz, das heißt, es besteht die Möglichkeit, den Übergebenen im Urteilsland auch wegen anderer als derjenigen Straftaten zu verfolgen, die dem Haftbefehl zugrunde liegen.[53] Ein markannter Unterschied zum EU-Rahmenbeschluss liegt schließlich in dem generellen Verzicht auf das Erfordernis der doppelten Strafbarkeit und auf Anforderungen an einen bestimmten gesetzlichen Strafrahmen (abgesehen davon, dass die Tat mit Freiheitsstrafe in beliebiger Höhe bedroht sein muss). Um die Bedeutung des Verzichts auf doppelte Strafbarkeit zu veranschaulichen, seien folgende Beispiele genannt:

In Finnland und Norwegen liegt die sexuelle Schutzaltersgrenze bei 16 Jahren, in Dänemark und Schweden hingegen bei 15 Jahren und in Island bei 14 Jahren. In einer Strafsache wegen Beischlafs mit einem 14-jährigen Kind können im Rahmen des nordischen Haftbefehlsverfahrens isländische Behörden die Übergabe eines Beschuldigten an die Nachbarländer nicht mit der Begründung ablehnen, dass die Tat nach isländischem Recht nicht strafbar ist. Das gleiche gilt für dänische und schwedische Behörden im Falle eines Nordischen Haftbefehls aus Finnland oder Norwegen wegen sexuellen Umgangs mit einer 15-jährigen Person.

Die Strafbarkeit wegen Trunkenheitsfahrt im Straßenverkehr beginnt in Norwegen und Schweden bei einem Alkoholgehalt von 0,2 ‰ im Blut, in Dänemark und Finnland bei 0,5 ‰. Unter Anwendung des Nordischen Haftbefehls können die norwegischen und schwedischen Behörden die Übergabe eines Verkehrssünders nach Maßgabe ihrer eigenen, strengeren Promillegrenze verlangen.

Nach norwegischem Verkehrsstrafrecht macht sich ein Autofahrer strafbar, der innerhalb von sechs Stunden nach Beendigung einer Fahrt, wegen der er mit einer polizeilichen Verfolgung rechnet oder rechnen muss, Alkohol oder Drogen zu sich nimmt.[54] Die übrigen nordischen Länder können sich gegenüber einem in Norwegen ausgestellten Nordischen Haftbefehl nicht darauf berufen, dass ihre Rechtsordnungen keine entsprechende Regelung kennen.

51. Artikel 19 Abs. 6 i.V.m. Abs. 2–5.
52. Artikel 24. Als Drittland gilt in diesem Zusammenhang ein Land, das weder zu den nordischen Ländern noch zu den Mitgliedstaaten der EU zählt.
53. Artikel 23.
54. § 22 Abs. 2 norw. Verkehrsgesetz *(vegtrafikkloven)*. Eine ähnliche Regelung gilt auf den Färöern: § 16 Abs. 1 løgtingslógarkunngerd nr. 14 af 2.3.1988 úm ferdslu.

In Schweden ist – anders als in den übrigen nordischen Ländern – die Gefangenenflucht für einen Inhaftierten selbst nicht mit Strafe bedroht. Dies können die schwedischen Behörden gegenüber einem Nordischen Haftbefehl nicht als Ablehnungsgrund geltend machen.

Umgekehrt ist in Schweden die Inanspruchnahme sexueller Dienste gegen Entgelt in größerem Umfang strafbar als in den Nachbarländern. Im Falle eines in Schweden ausgestellten Nordischen Haftbefehls kommt es insoweit allein auf das strengere schwedische Strafrecht an.

Die angeführten Beispiele bilden nur eine kleine Auswahl von unterschiedlichen Strafrechtsnormen innerhalb des nordischen Rechtskreises. Die beteiligten Länder, die sich sonst in vielfältiger Weise nahestehen, sind von der jeweils eigenen Regelung überzeugt, und der Versuch, die Abweichungen im Wege einer materiellrechtlichen Harmonisierung einzuebnen, würde in der Politik wie in der Bevölkerung auf starken Widerstand stoßen.[55]

12. Ausblick

In den Bevölkerungen der nordischen Länder besteht ein verbreiteter Wunsch nach mehr Zusammenarbeit zwischen ihren Staaten. Eine in jüngster Zeit durchgeführte Untersuchung hat ergeben, dass 74 % der Dänen eine auf Dauer angelegte nordische Zusammenarbeit wünschen; für eine Kooperation im Rahmen der EU sprachen sich 80 % der Befragten aus. In Schweden und Finnland ist die Identifikation mit dem Norden deutlich stärker als die mit der Europäischen Union.[56]

Entsprechende Einstellungen findet man auch unter den juristischen Fachleuten. So hat der Leiter der schwedischen Obersten Anklagebehörde, Reichsankläger *Fredrik Wersäll*, in einem kürzlich erschienenen Aufsatz[57] dem Wunsch nach fortgesetzter und erweiterter nordischer Zusammenarbeit im Bereich des Strafrechts in markanter Weise Ausdruck verliehen. Er stellt fest, dass in den nordischen Ländern unvergleichlich gute Bedingungen für eine enge rechtliche Zusammenarbeit gegeben sind und dass tatsächlich bereits

55. Bei den parlamentarischen Beratungen des dänischen Gesetzentwurfs zur Implementierung des Nordischen Haftbefehls verweigerten zwei Fraktionen ihre Zustimmung. Die eine (Enhedslisten) wollte an dem Erfordernis der doppelten Strafbarkeit festhalten. Denn es sei völlig unangemessen zu verlangen, „dass jeder einzelne Bürger das Recht aller übrigen nordischen Länder kennt". Die andere Fraktion *(Dansk Folkeparti)* berief sich auf die besonders weitgehende Meinungsäußerungsfreiheit in Dänemark und machte geltend, dass dänische Staatsbürger nicht ausgeliefert werden dürften, weil sie hiervon Gebrauch machten. (Vgl. Retsudvalgets betænkning af 29. marts 2007).
56. Politiken 8.11.2006.
57. Straffrättslig samarbete i ett gränslöst Norden, NTfK 2006, 122 ff.

seit langer Zeit eine sehr effektive und gut funktionierende Kooperation zwischen den nordischen Anklagebehörden und den nordischen Polizeibehörden stattfindet. In den letzten Jahren habe allerdings die entsprechende Zusammenarbeit innerhalb der EU eine derartige Dynamik entwickelt, dass sie den Norden nahezu eingeholt habe. Die in die europäische Entwicklung investierten Kräfte seien zulasten der nordischen Kooperation gegangen. In Bezug auf den Nordischen Haftbefehl beklagt *Wersäll*, dass man bei seiner Konzeption von dem EU-Rahmenbeschluss, und nicht von bestehenden nordischen Regelungen ausgegangen sei.

> Die nordische Zusammengehörigkeit, das Vertrauen in die Rechtsordnungen der jeweiligen nordischen Nachbarländer und vor allem die rechtlichen Übereinstimmungen innerhalb des Nordens sowie die langjährige enge Zusammenarbeit zwischen unseren Strafverfolgungsbehörden bietet die Grundlage für eine bedeutend ehrgeizigere und weitergehende Kooperation als sie jemals innerhalb der EU zustande kommen kann. Dies ist ein Vorteil, den wir nutzen müssen. [...]
>
> Die Gründe, die im vorigen Jahrhundert für eine effektive und weitgehende nordische Zusammenarbeit in Strafsachen sprachen, sind heute noch gewichtiger. [...]
>
> Zu der Vision von einem grenzenlosen Norden gehört eine *vollständige Durchführung des Prinzips der gegenseitigen Anerkennung und Vollstreckung von Beschlüssen, die im Ermittlungsverfahren und im Hauptverfahren getroffen werden.* Ein Beschluss, der in einem nordischen Land getroffen worden ist, sollte ohne irgendeine Prüfung in den übrigen nordischen Ländern anerkannt werden und vollstreckbar sein. Zu einer solchen Vision gehört auch, dass Personen innerhalb des Nordens ebenso einfach über die Landesgrenzen hinweg zwangsweise an einen anderen Ort verbracht werden können, wie dies heute innerhalb ein und desselben Landes im Rahmen eines Ermittlungs- oder Hauptverfahrens möglich ist. [...]
>
> Zur vollständigen Verwirklichung der Vision von einem grenzenlosen Norden auf dem Gebiet des Strafrechts gehört auch, dass jedes nordische Land *auf seinem Territorium hoheitliche Maßnahmen durch Strafverfolgungsbehörden der übrigen nordischen Länder* akzeptiert. [...]
>
> Eine derartige Reform wäre meines Erachtens nicht besonders aufsehenerregend. Ich sehe dies eher als eine ganz natürliche Entwicklung. [...] Bemerkenswert ist es eigentlich vielmehr, dass wir es innerhalb des Nordens nicht gewagt haben, Regelungen zu treffen, die der Wirklichkeit, mit der sich unsere Polizeibeamten und Staatsanwälte seit verschiedenen Jahrzehnten nicht zuletzt in der täglichen Zusammenarbeit an den Landesgrenzen konfrontiert sehen, besser angepasst sind. [...][58]

Die Strafrechtswissenschaft ist weltweit von einer gewissen Trägheit geprägt, und auch die Gesetzgeber nehmen gewöhnlich Rechtsänderungen nur dann vor, wenn vernünftigerweise zu erwarten ist, dass sie zu einer wesentlichen

58. NTfK 2006, 123 ff. (Kursivierungen wie im Originaltext.)

Verbesserung führen. Mit der Politisierung, die in neuerer Zeit im strafrechtlichen Bereich stattfindet, sind jedoch gesetzgeberische Maßnahmen zu einem Wert an sich geworden, zu einem „Signal". Dies gilt sowohl für viele nationale Rechtsordnungen als auch für die EU. Die Entwicklung erweckt den Eindruck, als komme es mehr auf die Harmonisierung als solche an, und weniger darauf, ob ein Änderungsgesetz tatsächlich die Rechtslage verbessert. Es scheint zu genügen, dass kein wesentlicher Rückschritt eintritt.[59]

Entsprechende Tendenzen sind in der nordischen Zusammenarbeit nicht zu beobachten; dies liegt möglicherweise daran, dass dieser Bereich gerade in den letzten Jahren von den Ereignissen und Bemühungen auf europäischem Niveau überlagert war und in den Ausbau der nordischen Kooperation weniger Kraft investiert worden ist.[60] Dem politischen Argument stehen aber auch einige der Gesichtspunkte entgegen, die stets als besonders wertvolle Elemente der nordischen rechtlichen Zusammenarbeit angeführt wurden, etwa dass eine gründliche Gesetzesvorarbeit es erfordert, die Erfahrungen und Vorbehalte aller beteiligten Länder mit einzubeziehen. In diesem Zusammenhang ist es natürlich von entscheidender Bedeutung, das rechtsvergleichende Material zu berücksichtigen, bevor die Überlegungen abgeschlossen sind.[61] Wenn die nordischen Länder sich künftig wieder verstärkt ihrer internen strafrechtlichen Kooperation zuwenden, wofür die Ansätze zur Verwirklichung des Nordischen Haftbefehls ein Indiz sind, wird sich erweisen, inwieweit es ihnen gelingt, den bisherigen Standard zu wahren.

E. Die rechtliche Struktur

Die nordische Zusammenarbeit in Strafsachen basiert, wie oben dargestellt, auf der gegenseitigen Achtung staatlicher Souveränität und verzichtet auf die Einführung überstaatlicher Organe. Sie stützt sich wesentlich auf übereinstimmende Grundauffassungen und harmonisierte Rechtsvorschriften. Die Harmonisierung materiellen Rechts erfolgt dabei zu einem großen Teil ohne Anwendung völkerrechtlicher Instrumente. Vielmehr werden in gemeinsamen Besprechungen und Beratungen unter Fachleuten einheitliche Lösungen für bestimmte Sachverhalte erarbeitet und durch die jeweiligen nationalen Gesetzgebungen verwirklicht. Diese Vorgehensweise wirft weder rechtliche noch politische Probleme auf; sie berührt allein *nationales Recht*.

59. Vgl. *Waaben*, SvJT 1969, 106; *Strömholm*, Festskrift til W.E. von Eyben, S. 188.
60. Siehe dazu die vorstehend zitierten Äußerungen des schwedischen Reichsanklägers *Wersäll*.
61. Vgl. *Strömholm*, S. 179 f.

Eine zweite Form der strafrechtlichen Zusammenarbeit, insbesondere im Hinblick auf die Ausübung grenzüberschreitender Hoheitsgewalt gegenüber Personen, die sich in einem anderen Land befinden, erfolgt auf der klassischen Grundlage völkerrechtlicher Verträge und Abkommen. Auch diese Kooperationsform ist rechtlich und politisch unproblematisch; es handelt sich hier um *internationales Strafrecht* im weiteren Sinne.

Der Wunsch nach fortgesetzter und vertiefter Zusammenarbeit[62] hat zum Ziel, dass sich der europäische Norden in noch stärkerem Maße zu einem Gebiet entwickelt, in dem für innerstaatliche und grenzüberschreitende hoheitliche Maßnahmen die gleichen Regeln gelten. In mancher Hinsicht entspricht bereits jetzt die zwischen den nordischen Staaten geschaffene internationale Rechtslage derjenigen, die innerhalb der einzelnen Länder als nationales Recht für die Zusammenarbeit zwischen verschiedenen Behörden besteht.[63] Dabei ist zu beachten, dass in Dänemark und Finnland besondere Verhältnisse insoweit herrschen, als zu diesen Staaten autonome Landesteile mit eigenen Strafbestimmungen gehören: zu Dänemark die Färöer und Grönland, zu Finnland die Åland-Inseln. Neben den klassischen Kooperationsformen auf nationalrechtlicher und völkerrechtlicher Basis tritt damit im nordischen Rechtskreis ein weiteres Modell hinzu, nämlich das des *interlokalen Strafrechts*.

Das interlokale Strafrecht regelt die innerstaatliche Strafrechtsanwendung für den Fall, dass innerhalb eines Staates ein oder mehrere Teilgebiete mit eigenen, territorial begrenzten Strafrechtsordnungen existieren.[64] Es beantwortet die Frage, welches Recht anzuwenden ist, wenn der Täter innerhalb eines solchen Teilgebiets gehandelt hat, aber außerhalb desselben vor Gericht steht. Somit ist das interlokale Strafrecht einerseits nationales Recht, denn es betrifft ausschließlich innerstaatliche Sachverhalte. Zum anderen handelt es sich – im Unterschied zum internationalen Strafrecht im engeren Sinne[65] – um

62. Siehe näher dazu oben D.12.
63. Zur Zusammenarbeit der Strafverfolgungsbehörden auf nationaler Ebene siehe im Einzelnen die Landesberichte für Dänemark, Finnland, Island, Norwegen und Schweden in diesem Buch.
64. In der dänischen Lehre wird hierfür der Begriff „interprovinzielles Strafrecht" verwendet, während als „interlokales Strafrecht" die Anwendung verschiedener örtlich begrenzter Rechtsvorschriften innerhalb eines einzelnen Teilgebiets bezeichnet wird; vgl. *Greve*, Det strafferetlige ansvar, S. 101; *Ravn*, Juristen 1996, 419 ff.
65. Hierbei handelt es sich um Rechtsanwendungsnormen, mit denen der nationale Gesetzgeber einseitig den Umfang der eigenen Strafgewalt im Verhältnis zu anderen Staaten abgrenzt, nicht aber zwischen verschiedenen berührten Rechtsordnungen eine Wahl trifft.

echte Kollisionsnormen, die beim Zusammentreffen verschiedener Strafrechtsordnungen bestimmen, welche im Einzelfall zur Anwendung kommt.

Weder in Dänemark noch in Finnland ist das interlokale Strafrecht gesetzlich geregelt, sondern es gilt als Gewohnheitsrecht. Übereinstimmend mit dem interlokalen Strafrecht anderer Länder bildet auch hier das Tatortprinzip den maßgeblichen Anknüpfungspunkt. Das heißt, die in einem autonomen Teilgebiet begangene Tat wird stets nach den dort geltenden Strafbestimmungen beurteilt, selbst wenn das Verfahren in einem anderen Teilgebiet desselben Staates stattfindet und am Gerichtsort ein anderes als das Tatortrecht gilt. Der Richter hat in diesem Fall somit „fremdes" Recht anzuwenden. Im Unterschied zu den Regeln des internationalen Strafrechts kennt das interlokale Strafrecht weder das Erfordernis der doppelten Strafbarkeit noch das Prinzip der *lex mitior*. Das Tatortrecht ist also auch dann maßgebend, wenn die Tat nach dem Recht des Gerichtsortes überhaupt nicht oder mit einer milderen Strafe bedroht ist. Freilich bezieht sich das Tatortprinzip nur auf die materiellen Strafbestimmungen; das Verfahren wird nach den Prozessvorschriften des Gerichtsortes durchgeführt.

Im Verhältnis zwischen Finnland und den Åland-Inseln werden die Regeln des interlokalen Strafrechts unter anderem praktisch relevant im Bereich des Straßenverkehrsstrafrechts. Hier bestehen Abweichungen hinsichtlich der angedrohten Strafhöhe für Gefährdungen der Verkehrssicherheit[66] sowie hinsichtlich der Grenze des Alkoholgehalts in der Atemluft bei Trunkenheitsfahrten.[67] Auch zwischen Dänemark und den Färöern kommen Kollisionsfälle bei Straßenverkehrsdelikten vor. Das färöische Verkehrsgesetz enthält eine Bestimmung, nach der sich ein Autofahrer strafbar macht, wenn er innerhalb von sechs Stunden nach Beendigung einer Fahrt, wegen der er mit einer polizeilichen Verfolgung rechnen muss, Alkohol oder Drogen zu sich nimmt.[68] Im dänischen wie auch im grönländischen Recht findet sich keine derartige Vorschrift. Dennoch ist nach den Regeln des interlokalen Strafrechts jeder Richter im Königreich Dänemark verpflichtet, auf einen entsprechenden Sachverhalt, der sich auf den Färöern abgespielt hat, das färöische Tatortrecht anzuwenden.

66. Kap. 23 § 1 finn. Strafgesetz: Geldstrafe oder Gefängnis bis zu sechs Monaten; § 73 Straßenverkehrsgesetz für die Landschaft Åland: Geldstrafe oder Gefängnis bis zu drei Monaten.
67. Kap. 23 §§ 3/4 finn. Strafgesetz: mindestens 0,22/0,53 Milligramm pro Liter; §§ 75/75a Straßenverkehrsgesetz für die Landschaft Åland: mindestens 0,25/0,60 Milligramm pro Liter.
68. § 16 Abs. 1 løgtingslógarkunngerd úm ferdslu.

Eine besondere Entwicklung hat die Praxis zwischen Dänemark und Grönland genommen. Auf Grönland gilt ein eigenständiges Kriminalgesetz[69] mit Jurisdiktionsregeln, die den Anwendungsbereich dieses Gesetzes nach den Prinzipien des *internationalen Strafrechts* festlegen. Darin wird das grönländische Hoheitsgebiet als Inland behandelt; es fehlt jedoch eine Bestimmung, aus der hervorgeht, dass das übrige dänische Königreich nicht Ausland ist. Aus diesem Grund werden heute Strafsachen im dänisch-grönländischen Verhältnis nach den Regeln des internationalen Strafrechts gehandhabt, obwohl es sich zweifellos um innerstaatliche Angelegenheiten handelt, die eigentlich dem interlokalen Strafrecht unterliegen.

Da die Strafdrohungen und das Sanktionensystem des grönländischen Strafrechts erheblich von denen des dänischen abweichen, hat dies praktische Konsequenzen, wie folgendes Beispiel illustriert:

Ein Grönländer begeht während eines Studienaufenthalts in Dänemark eine Vergewaltigung, die erst nach seiner Heimkehr aufgedeckt und in Grönland (entsprechend dem aktiven Personalitätsprinzip) angeklagt wird. Ist der Täter geständig, so kann die Tat nach grönländischem Recht beurteilt und möglicherweise mit einer Geldstrafe geahndet werden. Bestreitet er den Tatvorwurf, so wird die Sache mit Rücksicht auf die erforderliche Beweisaufnahme nach Dänemark verwiesen und dort (entsprechend dem Territorialitätsprinzip) nach dänischem Strafrecht abgeurteilt. Hier muss der Täter mit einer Freiheitsstrafe von mindestens einem Jahr rechnen.

In der Lehre ist diese Praxis wiederholt kritisiert und eine Rückkehr zum interlokalen Strafrecht gefordert worden. Als Einwand hiergegen wird unter anderem geltend gemacht, dass das grönländische Rechtssystem sich auf Laienrichter stütze und diese nicht in der Lage seien, ein ihnen weitgehend unbekanntes Strafrecht (das dänische) anzuwenden. Das geltende grönländische Kriminalgesetz enthält in § 4c folgende Bestimmung:

Hat der Täter seinen Wohnsitz nicht in Grönland oder sind seine Beziehungen zur grönländischen Gesellschaft so lose, dass die Voraussetzungen für eine Anwendung der Maßregeln dieses Gesetzes nicht vorliegen, so kann die Sache in Dänemark anhängig gemacht oder zur Verfolgung dorthin verwiesen werden.

Über die Verweisung entscheidet die Anklagebehörde.[70] In dem gegenwärtig vorliegenden Entwurf eines neuen Kriminalgesetzes für Grönland[71] ist die

69. Kriminallov for Grønland nr. 55 af 5.3.1954 in der Fassung der Bekanntmachung nr. 49 af 13.2.1979 mit späteren Änderungen.
70. Vgl. *Senholt*, Den grønlandske kriminalret, S. 67 f.
71. Betænkning om det grønlandske retsvæsen, nr. 1442.

Beibehaltung der Vorschrift (als § 7) vorgesehen. In dem ansonsten sehr umfassenden Reformgutachten werden diese Bestimmung und die Jurisdiktionsfragen nicht einmal erwähnt. Abgesehen von dem hier geschilderten wenig vorbildlichen Beispiel ist zu erwägen, ob die Entwicklung der EU in Richtung eines einheitliches Rechtsraumes es nahelegt, die Grundsätze des interlokalen Strafrechts für die interne Rechtsanwendung zu übernehmen.[72]

72. Zur Anwendung des Tatortrechts, auch im Hinblick auf bestimmte Fragen der Strafzumessung, siehe *Greve*, Festschrift für Albin Eser, S. 751 ff.

Anhang

Auszüge aus dem Übereinkommen zur Übergabe zwischen den nordischen Ländern wegen Straftaten (Nordischer Haftbefehl)

Kapitel 1: Allgemeine Grundsätze

Artikel 1. Definition und Pflicht zur Vollstreckung des Nordischen Haftbefehls

1. Der Nordische Haftbefehl ist eine justizielle Entscheidung, die ein nordisches Land mit dem Ziel getroffen hat, dass ein anderes nordisches Land eine verfolgte Person zum Zwecke der Strafverfolgung oder der Vollstreckung einer Freiheitsstrafe oder einer anderen freiheitsentziehenden Sanktion festnimmt und übergibt.

2. Ein Europäischer Haftbefehl, der von Dänemark, Finnland oder Schweden nach dem Rahmenbeschluß des Rates der Europäischen Union vom 13. Juni 2003 über den Europäischen Haftbefehl und über das Verfahren der Übergabe zwischen den Mitgliedstaaten ausgefertigt worden ist, wird als ein Nordischer Haftbefehl nach diesem Übereinkommen betrachtet.

3. Die [nordischen] Länder vollstrecken jeden Nordischen Haftbefehl auf der Grundlage des Prinzips gegenseitiger Anerkennung und gemäß den Bestimmungen dieses Übereinkommens.

Artikel 2. Anwendungsbereich für den Nordischen Haftbefehl

1. Ein Nordischer Haftbefehl kann ausgestellt werden wegen eines Sachverhalts, der nach dem Recht des ausstellenden Landes mit Freiheitsstrafe oder einer anderen freiheitsentziehenden Sanktion geahndet werden kann (Strafverfolgung), oder wenn eine Freiheitsstrafe oder eine andere freiheitsentziehende Sanktion verhängt worden ist (Strafvollstreckung).

2. Die Übergabe zur Strafverfolgung oder Strafvollstreckung wegen mehrerer Straftaten kann selbst dann stattfinden, wenn die in Abs. 1 genannten Voraussetzungen nur hinsichtlich einer der Taten erfüllt sind.

3. Straftaten, die nach dem Recht des ausstellenden Landes als solche definiert sind, führen zur Vollstreckung auf der Grundlage eines Nordischen Haftbefehls unter den in diesem Übereinkommen festgelegten Bedingungen und ohne Kontrolle einer doppelten Strafbarkeit.

Artikel 3. Festlegung der zuständigen justiziellen Behörden u.a. sowie Definition des Drittlandes

1. Ausstellende justizielle Behörde ist diejenige justizielle Behörde in dem ausstellenden Land, die nach dem Recht dieses Landes für die Ausstellung eines Nordischen Haftbefehls zuständig ist.

2. Vollstreckende justizielle Behörde ist diejenige justizielle Behörde in dem vollstreckenden Land, die nach dem Recht dieses Landes für die Vollstreckung eines Nordischen Haftbefehls zuständig ist.

3. Jedes Land kann eine Zentralbehörde benennen, welche die zuständigen justiziellen Behörden unterstützt.

4. Jedes Land erklärt bei der Ratifikation dieser Konvention, welche justiziellen Behörden nach seinem nationalen Recht zuständig sind und ob eine Zentralbehörde benannt worden ist.

5. Unter „Drittland" ist in diesem Übereinkommen jedes Land außerhalb des Nordens und der EU zu verstehen.

Artikel 4. Obligatorische Gründe zur Ablehnung der Vollstreckung eines Nordischen Haftbefehls

Die vollstreckende justizielle Behörde lehnt die Vollstreckung eines Nordischen Haftbefehls in folgenden Fällen ab:

1) wenn die Straftat, die dem Nordischen Haftbefehl zugrunde liegt, in dem vollstreckenden Land unter eine Amnestie fällt und dieses Land nach seiner eigenen Rechtsordnung die Strafgewalt über die Tat hat;
2) wenn die verfolgte Person wegen derselben Taten von einem nordischen Land oder einem Mitgliedsland der EU rechtskräftig verurteilt worden ist, vorausgesetzt dass die gegebenenfalls verhängte Sanktion vollstreckt wurde, sich in der Vollstreckung befindet oder nach dem Recht des Urteilslandes nicht mehr vollstreckt werden kann;
3) wenn die Person, auf die sich ein Nordischer Haftbefehl bezieht, nach dem Recht des vollstreckenden Landes aufgrund ihres Alters nicht für die dem Nordischen Haftbefehl zugrunde liegenden Taten strafrechtlich verantwortlich gemacht werden kann.

Artikel 5. Fakultative Gründe zur Ablehnung der Vollstreckung eines Nordischen Haftbefehls

Die vollstreckende justizielle Behörde kann die Vollstreckung eines Nordischen Haftbefehls ablehnen:

1) wenn die Person, auf die sich der Nordische Haftbefehl bezieht, bereits in dem vollstreckenden Land wegen derselben Tat wie derjenigen, die dem Nordischen Haftbefehl zugrunde liegt, strafrechtlich verfolgt wird;
2) wenn die dem Nordischen Haftbefehl zugrunde liegende Tat nach dem Recht des vollstreckenden Landes als ganz oder teilweise im Hoheitsgebiet dieses Landes oder an einem damit gleichgestellten Ort begangen gilt und die Tat nach dem Recht des vollstreckenden Landes keine Straftat darstellt;
3) wenn die verfolgte Person wegen derselben Taten von einem Drittland[73] rechtskräftig verurteilt worden ist, vorausgesetzt dass die gegebenenfalls verhängte Sanktion vollstreckt wurde, sich in der Vollstreckung befindet oder nach dem Recht des Urteilslandes nicht mehr vollstreckt werden kann;
4) wenn die justiziellen Behörden des vollstreckenden Landes beschlossen haben, entweder keine Strafverfolgung wegen der dem Nordischen Haftbefehl zugrunde liegenden Tat einzuleiten oder die Strafverfolgung einzustellen, oder wenn in Bezug auf den Verfolgten in einem anderen nordischen Land wegen derselben Tat eine rechtskräftige Entscheidung getroffen worden ist, die einer weiteren Strafverfolgung entgegensteht;
5) wenn der Nordische Haftbefehl zum Zwecke der Vollstreckung eines Strafurteils oder einer anderen freiheitsentziehenden Sanktion ausgestellt worden ist und der Verfolgte sich in dem vollstreckenden Land aufhält, dessen Staatsangehöriger oder dort ansässig ist und dieses Land sich selbst verpflichtet, die Strafe oder die andere freiheitsentziehende Sanktion gemäß dem nationalen Recht zu vollstrecken.

Artikel 6. Bedingte Übergabe

Wenn ein Nordischer Haftbefehl zum Zwecke der Strafverfolgung ausgestellt wurde und die Person, auf die er sich bezieht, Staatsangehöriger oder Einwohner des vollstreckenden Landes ist, kann die Übergabe unter der Bedingung erfolgen, dass der Betreffende nach seiner Anhörung an das vollstreckende Land überstellt wird, um dort die Freiheitsstrafe oder die sonstige freiheitsentziehende Sanktion zu verbüßen, zu der er in dem ausstellenden Land verurteilt worden ist.

73. Der Begriff des Drittlandes ist in Artikel 3 Nr. 5 definiert als „jedes Land außerhalb des Nordens und der EU".

Artikel 7. Inhalt und Form des Nordischen Haftbefehls

1. Der Nordische Haftbefehl enthält folgende Angaben gemäß dem Formular im Anhang:

a) die Identität und Staatsangehörigkeit des Verfolgten,
b) Name, Anschrift, Telefon- und Faxnummer sowie E-Mail-Adresse der justiziellen Behörde im Ausstellungsland,
c) Angaben darüber, ob ein vollstreckbares Urteil, ein Festnahmebeschluss oder eine andere vollstreckbare Entscheidung mit gleicher Rechtskraft vorliegt, die unter Artikel 1 und 2 fällt,
d) Art und rechtliche Beschreibung der Straftat,
e) eine Beschreibung, unter welchen Umständen die Straftat begangen worden ist, insbesondere Tatzeit, Tatort und in welchem Umfang der Verfolgte sich an ihr beteiligt hat,
f) die verhängte Strafe, sofern es sich um ein rechtskräftiges Urteil handelt, oder der in dem ausstellenden Land gesetzlich festgelegte Strafrahmen für die Straftat des Verfolgten,
g) soweit möglich, andere Rechtsfolgen der Straftat.

2. Ist der Haftbefehl wegen mehrerer Straftaten ausgestellt, so genügt ein Festnahme- oder Verhaftungsbeschluss wegen einer der Straftaten.

Kapitel 2: Übergabeverfahren

Artikel 8. Übersendung eines Nordischen Haftbefehls

1. Ist der Aufenthaltsort des Verfolgten bekannt, so kann die ausstellende justizielle Behörde den Nordischen Haftbefehl direkt an die vollstreckende justizielle Behörde senden.

2. Ist der Aufenthaltsort des Verfolgten nicht bekannt, so kann das ausstellende Land eines oder mehrere der nordischen Länder ersuchen, im Rahmen eines jeweiligen nationalen Ermittlungsverfahrens den Betreffenden zur Fahndung auszuschreiben. Sobald der Aufenthaltsort bekannt ist, wird der Nordische Haftbefehl schnellstmöglich an das betreffende Land gesendet.

3. Die ausstellende justizielle Behörde kann gemäß Art. 95 des Übereinkommens vom 19. Juni 1990 über die Durchführung des Schengener Übereinkommens vom 14. Juni 1985 über die schrittweise Aufhebung der Kontrollen an den gemeinsamen Grenzen beschließen, den Verfolgten an das Schengener Informationssystem zu melden. Eine Meldung an das Schengener Informationssystem entspricht einem mit den in Artikel 7 Abs. 1 genannten Angaben versehenen Nordischen Haftbefehl. Während einer Übergangszeit, d.h. bis das Schengener Informationssystem imstande ist, sämtliche in Artikel 7 genannten Angaben weiterzuleiten, entspricht die Meldung einem Nordi-

schen Haftbefehl, bevor dieser bei der vollstreckenden justiziellen Behörde vorschriftsmäßig eingegangen ist.

4. Ist die Behörde, bei der ein nordischer Haftbefehl eingeht, nicht für seine Bearbeitung zuständig, so sendet sie ihn unverzüglich weiter an die in ihrem Land zuständige Behörde und unterrrichtet die ausstellende justizielle Behörde hiervon.

Artikel 9. Rechte des Verfolgten

1. Wird ein Verfolgter festgenommen, so informiert die vollstreckende justizielle Behörde gemäß ihrem nationalen Recht den Betreffenden über den Nordischen Haftbefehl und dessen Inhalt sowie über die Möglichkeit, einer Übergabe an die ausstellende justizielle Behörde zuzustimmen.

2. Ein Verfolgter, der zum Zwecke der Vollstreckung eines Nordischen Haftbefehls festgenommen wird, hat ein Recht auf Beistand durch einen juristischen Berater und einen Dolmetscher gemäß dem nationalen Recht des vollstreckenden Landes.

Artikel 10. Auslieferungshaft

1. Wird eine Person aufgrund eines Nordischen Haftbefehls festgenommen, so entscheidet die vollstreckende justizielle Behörde, ob der Betreffende gemäß dem nationalen Recht des vollstreckenden Landes in Auslieferungshaft verbleibt. Der Betreffende kann gemäß dem nationalen Recht des vollstreckenden Landes zu jedem beliebigen Zeitpunkt vorläufig freigelassen werden unter der Voraussetzung, dass die zuständige Behörde dieses Landes alle erforderlichen Maßnahmen trifft, um eine Flucht des Betreffenden zu verhindern.

2. Zur Förderung des Ermittlungsverfahrens und zur Sicherung der Übergabe sind die in den einzelnen nationalen Rechtsordnungen vorgesehenen Rechtsmittel anzuwenden.

Artikel 11. Einwilligung in die Übergabe u.a.

1. Erklärt die festgenommene Person ihre Einwilligung in die Übergabe, eventuell auch in die Verfolgung wegen anderer, vor der Anlasstat begangener Straftaten im Sinne von Artikel 23 Abs. 2 b, so wird diese Einwilligungserklärung gegenüber der vollstreckenden justiziellen Behörde gemäß dem nationalen Recht des vollstreckenden Landes abgegeben.

2. Die Länder treffen die erforderlichen Maßnahmen dafür, dass die Einwilligung nach Abs. 1 in einer Weise eingeholt wird, aus der hervorgeht, dass der Betreffende die Erklärung freiwillig und in Kenntnis der damit verbunde-

nen Folgen abgegeben hat. Im Hinblick hierauf hat der Festgenommene ein Recht auf juristischen Beistand.

3. Die Einwilligungserklärung wird gemäß dem nationalen Recht des vollstreckenden Landes zu Protokoll genommen.

4. Die Einwilligungserklärung kann unter Bezugnahme auf das nationale Recht des vollstreckenden Landes zurückgenommen werden.

Artikel 12. Vernehmung der verfolgten Person

Willigt der Festgenommene nicht gemäß Artikel 11 in die Übergabe ein, so hat er einen Anspruch darauf, von der vollstreckenden justiziellen Behörde gemäß dem nationalen Recht des vollstreckenden Landes vernommen zu werden.

Artikel 13. Entscheidung über die Übergabe

1. Die vollstreckende justizielle Behörde trifft die Entscheidung über die Übergabe des Betreffenden innerhalb der Fristen und zu den Bedingungen, wie sie in diesem Übereinkommen festgelegt sind.

2. Ist die vollstreckende justizielle Behörde der Ansicht, dass die von dem ausstellenden Land übersandten Angaben nicht ausreichend sind, um eine Übergabeentscheidung zu treffen, so fordert sie unverzüglich die notwendigen ergänzenden Angaben an, und mit Rücksicht auf die nach Artikel 14 einzuhaltenden Fristen kann sie eine Frist für die Zusendung dieser Angaben setzen.

3. Die ausstellende justizielle Behörde kann jederzeit der vollstreckenden justiziellen Behörde ergänzende sachdienliche Angaben zuleiten.

Artikel 14. Fristen und Verfahren in Verbindung mit der Entscheidung über die Vollstreckung eines Nordischen Haftbefehls

1. Ein Nordischer Haftbefehl ist als Eilsache zu behandeln und zu vollstrecken.

2. In den Fällen, in denen der Verfolgte seine Zustimmung zur Übergabe erteilt, muss spätestens 3 Tage nach der Zustimmung eine abschließende Entscheidung über die Vollstreckung des Nordischen Haftbefehls getroffen werden.

3. In anderen Fällen muss spätestens 30 Tage nach der Festnahme des Verfolgten eine abschließende Entscheidung über die Vollstreckung des Nordischen Haftbefehls getroffen werden.

4. In Einzelfällen, in denen keine abschließende Entscheidung innerhalb der in Abs. 2 und 3 festgelegten Fristen getroffen wird, unterrichtet die vollstreckende justizielle Behörde alsbald die ausstellende justizielle Behörde

hierüber sowie über die Gründe dafür. In einem solchen Fall wird die Entscheidung schnellstmöglich getroffen.

5. Solange die vollstreckende justizielle Behörde noch keine abschließende Entscheidung über die Vollstreckung des Nordischen Haftbefehls getroffen hat, hat sie sich zu vergewissern, dass die materiellen Bedingungen für eine Übergabe weiterhin erfüllt sind.

6. Jede Ablehnung der Vollstreckung eines Nordischen Haftbefehls ist zu begründen.

Artikel 15. Entscheidung in Fällen konkurrierender Ersuchen

1. Haben mehrere nordische Länder einen Haftbefehl für dieselbe Person ausgestellt, so entscheidet die vollstreckende justizielle Behörde darüber, welcher Haftbefehl vollstreckt werden soll, und zwar unter gehöriger Berücksichtigung aller Umstände, insbesondere der relativen Schwere der Tat und des Begehungsortes, der jeweiligen Ausstellungsdaten der Nordischen Haftbefehle sowie der Frage, ob die Haftbefehle zum Zwecke der Strafverfolgung oder zum Zwecke der Vollstreckung einer Freiheitsstrafe oder einer anderen freiheitsentziehenden Sanktion ausgestellt worden sind.

2. Entsteht ein Konflikt zwischen einem Nordischen Haftbefehl und einem Europäischen Haftbefehl oder einem Auslieferungsersuchen eines Drittlandes oder eines EU-Mitgliedslandes, so entscheidet die zuständige Behörde in dem vollstreckenden Land darüber, ob der Nordische Haftbefehl, der Europäische Haftbefehl oder das Auslieferungsersuchen Vorrang haben soll, und zwar unter gehöriger Berücksichtigung aller Umstände, insbesondere der in Abs. 1 genannten sowie derjenigen, die in dem anzuwendenden Übereinkommen oder Vertrag angeführt sind.

3. Dieser Artikel berührt nicht die Verpflichtungen der nordischen Länder gemäß dem Statut für den Internationalen Strafgerichtshof oder im Verhältnis zu den internationalen Tribunalen für Verbrechen gegen humanitäres Völkerrecht.

Artikel 16. Vorrechte und Immunitäten

1. Genießt die verfolgte Person in dem vollstreckenden Land ein Vorrecht oder Immunität gegenüber Strafvollstreckung oder Strafverfolgung, so laufen die in Artikel 14 genannten Fristen erst ab dem Zeitpunkt, zu dem das Vorrecht oder die Immunität aufgehoben und die justizielle Behörde des vollstreckenden Landes hiervon unterrichtet worden ist. Das vollstreckende Land stellt sicher, dass die materiellen Voraussetzungen der Übergabe erfüllt sind, wenn der Verfolgte ein solches Vorrecht oder eine solche Immunität nicht länger genießt.

2. Obliegt die Aufhebung des Vorrechts oder der Immunität einer Behörde in dem vollstreckenden Land, so richtet die vollstreckende justizielle Behörde unverzüglich ein entsprechendes Ersuchen an die betreffende Behörde. Obliegt die Aufhebung des Vorrechts oder der Immunität einer Behörde eines anderen Landes oder einer internationalen Organisation, so ist die ausstellende justizielle Behörde für das Ersuchen zuständig.

Artikel 17. Konkurrierende internationale Verpflichtungen

Dieses Übereinkommen beeinträchtigt nicht die Verpflichtungen des vollstreckenden Landes, wenn der Verfolgte an dieses Land von einem EU-Mitgliedsland oder einem Drittland übergeben oder ausgeliefert worden ist und der Betreffende gemäß den Regeln, nach denen die Auslieferung stattgefunden hat, gegen eine Weiterübergabe geschützt ist. Das vollstreckende Land trifft alle notwendigen Maßnahmen, um das EU-Mitgliedsland oder das Drittland, welches den Verfolgten übergeben oder ausgeliefert hat, alsbald um Zustimmung zu ersuchen, dass der Betreffende an das ausstellende Land übergeben werden kann. Die in Artikel 14 genannten Fristen laufen erst von dem Tag, an dem diese Spezialitätsregeln entfallen.

Artikel 18. Unterrichtung über die Entscheidung

Die vollstreckende justizielle Behörde unterrichtet unverzüglich die ausstellende Behörde darüber, inwieweit der Nordische Haftbefehl vollstreckt werden wird.

Artikel 19. Frist für die Übergabe des Verfolgten

1. Der Verfolgte wird schnellstmöglich zu einem zwischen den beteiligten Behörden vereinbarten Termin übergeben.

2. Der Betreffende wird spätestens 5 Tage nach der abschließenden Entscheidung über die Vollstreckung des Nordischen Haftbefehls übergeben.

3. Wenn es sich aufgrund besonderer Umstände als unmöglich erweist, den Verfolgten innerhalb der in Abs. 2 festgesetzten Frist zu übergeben, nehmen die vollstreckende justizielle Behörde und die ausstellende justizielle Behörde unverzüglich Kontakt miteinander auf und vereinbaren einen neuen Termin für die Übergabe. Die Übergabe hat innerhalb von 5 Tagen nach Ablauf der Frist des Abs. 2 zu erfolgen.

4. Wenn es sich aufgrund von Umständen, die keinem der Länder zuzurechnen sind, als unmöglich erweist, den Verfolgten innerhalb der in Abs. 3 festgesetzten Frist zu übergeben, nehmen die vollstreckende justizielle Behörde und die ausstellende justizielle Behörde Kontakt miteinander auf und vereinbaren einen neuen Termin für die Übergabe.

5. Eine Übergabe kann aus schwerwiegenden humanitären Gründen ausnahmsweise vorläufig ausgesetzt werden, beispielsweise wenn gewichtige Gründe für die Annahme bestehen, dass die Übergabe Leib oder Leben des Verfolgten eindeutig in Gefahr bringen würde. Der Nordische Haftbefehl ist zu vollstrecken, sobald diese Gründe nicht länger bestehen. Die vollstreckende justizielle Behörde unterrrichtet unverzüglich die ausstellende Behörde hiervon, und sie vereinbaren einen neuen Termin für die Übergabe.

6. Befindet sich der Betreffende nach Ablauf der in Abs. 2–5 genannten Fristen noch in Auslieferungshaft, so wird er freigelassen.

Artikel 20. Aussetzung der Übergabe oder vorläufige Übergabe

1. Die vollstreckende justizielle Behörde kann, nachdem sie die Vollstreckung eines Nordischen Haftbefehls beschlossen hat, die Übergabe des Verfolgten aussetzen, damit der Betreffende in dem vollstreckenden Land strafrechtlich verfolgt werden kann oder, falls er bereits verurteilt worden ist, damit er eine wegen einer anderen als der Anlasstat gegen ihn verhängte Strafe innerhalb dieses Landes verbüßen kann.

2. Anstatt die Übergabe auszusetzen, kann die vollstreckende justizielle Behörde unter Bedingungen, die zwischen den vollstreckenden und den ausstellenden justiziellen Behörden vereinbart werden, den Verfolgten vorläufig an das ausstellende Land übergeben. Die Vereinbarung erfolgt schriftlich, und die Bedingungen sind für alle Behörden des ausstellenden Landes bindend.

Artikel 21. Transit

Personen, die von einem nordischen Land an ein anderes nordisches Land übergeben werden sollen, können ohne besondere Erlaubnis über oder durch eines oder mehrere der übrigen nordischen Länder geführt werden.

Kapitel 3: Wirkungen der Übergabe

Artikel 22. Anrechnung von Zeiten der Auslieferungshaft im vollstreckenden Land

1. Das ausstellende Land rechnet jeden Zeitraum, in dem der Verfolgte im Zusammenhang mit der Vollstreckung eines Nordischen Haftbefehls in Auslieferungshaft war, auf die Gesamtdauer der von ihm in dem ausstellenden Land zu verbüßenden Freiheitsstrafe oder anderen freiheitsentziehenden Sanktion an.

2. In diesem Zusammenhang übersendet die vollstreckende justizielle Behörde gleichzeitig mit der Übergabe alle Angaben über Auslieferungshaftzei-

ten des Verfolgten aufgrund des Nordischen Haftbefehls an die ausstellende justizielle Behörde.

Artikel 23. Eventuelle Strafverfolgung wegen anderer Straftaten

1. Eine Person, die aufgrund eines Nordischen Haftbefehls zur Strafverfolgung oder Vollstreckung eines Strafurteils oder einer anderen freiheitsentziehenden Sanktion übergeben worden ist, kann wegen anderer vor der Übergabe begangener Straftaten als derjenigen, wegen der die Übergabe erfolgt ist, zur Verantwortung gezogen werden, es sei denn

a) eine Übergabe wegen der betreffenden Straftaten wäre gemäß Artikel 4 ausgeschlossen,

b) eine Übergabe wäre gemäß Artikel 27 nach nationalem Recht abgelehnt worden,[74]

c) eine Übergabe wegen der betreffenden Straftat hätte nach Artikel 5 Abs. 2 oder 4 abgelehnt werden können und das vollstreckende Land verweigert die Zustimmung.

2. Ungeachtet der Bestimmung in Abs. 1 kann eine Person, die aufgrund eines Nordischen Haftbefehls zur Strafverfolgung oder Vollstreckung eines Strafurteils oder einer anderen freiheitsentziehenden Sanktion übergeben worden ist, wegen anderer vor der Übergabe begangener Straftaten als derjenigen, wegen der die Übergabe erfolgt, zur Verantwortung gezogen werden, wenn

a) der Betreffende, nachdem er die Möglichkeit hatte, das nordische Land, an welches er übergeben worden ist, zu verlassen, hiervon 45 Tage nach seiner endgültigen Freilassung keinen Gebrauch gemacht hat oder in dieses Land, nachdem er es verlassen hatte, zurückgekehrt ist,

b) der Betreffende sich vor oder nach der Übergabe mit einer Strafverfolgung wegen anderer Straftaten einverstanden erklärt hat.

Artikel 24. Weiterübergabe oder Weiterauslieferung

1. Eine Person, die an ein anderes nordisches Land zur Strafverfolgung oder Vollstreckung eines Strafurteils oder einer anderen freiheitsentziehenden Sanktion übergeben worden ist, kann an ein anderes nordisches als das vollstreckende Land weiter übergeben werden aufgrund eines Nordischen Haftbefehls, der wegen einer vor der Übergabe begangenen Straftat ausgestellt ist, sofern nicht die Übergabe durch das ursprünglich ausstellende Land an das

74. Artikel 26 und 27 enthalten Sonderregelungen für die Übergabe von/nach Island.

nunmehr ausstellende Land gemäß Artikel 26 oder 27 nach nationalem Recht abgelehnt worden wäre.

2. Eine Person, die an ein anderes nordisches Land aufgrund eines Nordischen Haftbefehls übergeben worden ist, kann gemäß den rechtlichen Bestimmungen des ausstellenden Landes wegen einer vor der Übergabe begangenen Straftat an ein EU-Land weiter übergeben oder weiter ausgeliefert oder an ein Drittland weiter ausgeliefert werden, wenn

a) der Betreffende selbst sich hiermit einverstanden erklärt,
b) der Betreffende, obwohl er 45 Tage ungehindert das Land, an welches er übergeben worden war, hätte verlassen können, hiervon keinen Gebrauch gemacht hat oder, nachdem er das Land verlassen hatte, freiwillig zurückgekehrt ist, oder
c) das vollstreckende Land seine Zustimmung erteilt. Die Zustimmung kann nur erteilt werden, wenn die Übergabe wegen der betreffenden Straftat nach den rechtlichen Bestimmungen des vollstreckenden Landes hätte erfolgen können.

Artikel 25. Übergabe von Gegenständen

1. Die vollstreckende justizielle Behörde hat gemäß dem nationalen Recht des vollstreckenden Landes und auf Ersuchen der ausstellenden justiziellen Behörde oder auf eigene Initiative Gegenstände zu beschlagnahmen und zu übergeben,

a) die als Beweismaterial benötigt werden, oder
b) die der Verfolgte durch die Straftat erlangt hat.

2. Die in Abs. 1 genannten Gegenstände sind zu übergeben, selbst wenn der Nordische Haftbefehl nicht vollstreckt werden kann, weil der Verfolgte verstorben oder entwichen ist.

3. Werden die in Abs. 1 genannten Gegenstände innerhalb des vollstreckenden Landes beschlagnahmt oder konfisziert, so kann dieses Land sie im Zusammenhang mit einer laufenden Strafverfolgung vorläufig zurückbehalten oder sie dem ausstellenden Land unter der Bedingung übergeben, dass sie später zurückgegeben werden.

4. Jegliche Rechte des vollstreckenden Landes oder eines Dritten an den in Abs. 1 genannten Gegenständen bleiben bestehen. Wenn solche Rechte bestehen, hat das ausstellende Land unverzüglich nach Abschluss der Strafverfolgung die Gegenstände unentgeltlich an das vollstreckende Land zurückzugeben.

Kapitel 4: [Besondere Regelungen zur Übergabe an/von Island]

Kapitel 5: Allgemeine und abschließende Bestimmungen

Artikel 28. Verhältnis zu anderen rechtlichen Instrumenten

1. Dieses Übereinkommen findet Anwendung zwischen Dänemark, Finnland, Island, Norwegen und Schweden.

2. Die Bestimmungen des Übereinkommens berühren nicht die Verpflichtungen der nordischen Länder aufgrund des Rahmenbeschlusses über den Europäischen Haftbefehl oder anderer Auslieferungsvereinbarungen mit Drittländern.

3. Die nordischen Länder können nach Inkraftteten des Übereinkommens bilaterale oder multilaterale Verträge oder Vereinbarungen mit EU-Mitgliedsländern oder Drittländern schließen. Solche Verträge und Vereinbarungen müssen die Beziehungen zu den nicht an ihnen beteiligten nordischen Ländern unberührt lassen.

Artikel 29. [Inkrafttreten]

Zitierte und ergänzende Literatur

Abrahamsson, Olle, Det nordiska lagstiftningssamarbetets framtid i ett EU-perspektiv. Svensk Juristtidning 2001, 1–11.

Asp, Petter, Nordic Judicial Co-operation in Criminal Matters. Uppsala 1998.

Auglend, Ragnar L./Mæland, Henry John/Røsandhaug, Knut, Politirett. 2. Aufl. Oslo 2004.

Bernitz, Ulf, Nordic legislative cooperation in the new Europe. A challenge for the Nordic countries in the EU perspective. Scandinavian Studies in Law 2000, Volume 39, 29–58.

Bernitz, Ulf/Wiklund, Ola (Hrsg.), Nordiskt lagstiftningssamarbete i det nya Europa. Stockholm 1996.

Betænkning om det grønlandske retsvæsen, nr. 1442. Kopenhagen 2004.

Carsten, Gebhard, Nordischer Juristentag. Rabels Zeitschrift für ausländisches und internationales Privatrecht 1973, 37. Jahrgang, 80–100.

Clausen, Julius, Skandinavismen, Historisk fremstillet. Kopenhagen 1900.

Cornils, Karin/Verch, Ulrike, Landesbericht Dänemark. In: Sabine Gleß/-Rainer Grote/Günter Heine (Hrsg.), Justitielle Einbindung und Kontrolle von Europol. Bd. 1: Nationale und europäische Strafverfolgung. Freiburg 2001, S. 9–74.

Dahlberg, Matts/Drangel, Bo/Kring, Claes, Utlämning för brott från Sverige till Danmark, Finland, Island och Norge. Svensk Juristtidning 1984, 597–619. Den nordiske politisamarbejdsaftale, www.politi.no/publikasjoner/-nordisk.doc

Den nordiske strafferetskomités betænkning om forældelse i nordisk strafferet. In: Straffelovrådets betænkning nr. 433/1966 om strafferetlig forældelse m.v., S. 42–50.

Den nordiske strafferetskomités betænkning om konfiskation. In: Straffelovrådets betænkning nr. 355/1964 om konfiskation, S. 91–103.

Den nordiske strafferetskomités betænkning om prøveløsladelse. Nordisk Tidsskrift for Kriminalvidenskab 1970, 61–80.

Ekeberg, Birger, Nordisk rättsgemenskap. In: O.A. Borum/Knud Illum (Hrsg.), Festskrift til Henry Ussing. Kopenhagen 1951, S. 110–125.

v. Eyben, W.E., Krise i nordisk lovsamarbejde? Tidsskrift for Rettsvitenskap 1960, 298–322.

Femti år, Nordisk Råd 1952–2002. Til nordisk nytte? Kopenhagen 2002.

Frände, Dan, Något om rättsskyddet vid utlämning från Finland. In: Risto Koulu et al. (Hrsg.), Velka, vakuus ja prosessi. Helsinki 2001, S. 15–29.

Garde, Peter, Dansk Kriminalistforening 1899–1999. Nordisk Tidsskrift for Kriminalvidenskab 1999, Sondernummer.

Greve, Vagn, Færdselsstrafferet. 3. Aufl. Kopenhagen 2001.

Greve, Vagn, Det strafferetlige ansvar. 2. Aufl. Kopenhagen 2004.

Greve, Vagn, Strafzumessung im internationalen Strafrecht. In: Jörg Arnold et al. (Hrsg.), Menschengerechtes Strafrecht. Festschrift für Albin Eser. München 2005, S. 751–763.

Harck, Sten, Landesbericht Dänemark. In: Sabine Gleß/Rainer Grote/Günter Heine (Hrsg.), Justitielle Einbindung und Kontrolle von Europol. Bd. 2: Grundlagen und Grenzen präventiv-polizeilicher Ermittlungstätigkeit in den Rechtsordnungen ausgewählter Mitgliedstaaten. Freiburg 2001, S. 165–212.

Hellner, Jan, Unification of Law in Scandinavia. American Journal of Comparative Law 1968, 88–126.

Hellner, Jan, Rechtsvereinheitlichung im skandinavischen Rechtskreis. In: Helmut Coing u.a. (Hrsg.), Methoden der Rechtsvereinheitlichung. Frankfurt 1974, S. 27–34.

Henricson, Ib, Politiret. 3. Aufl. Kopenhagen 2004.

Herlitz, Nils, Nordiskt samarbete inom offentlig rätt? In: Festskrift tillägnad Birger Ekeberg. Stockholm 1950, S. 267–279.

Høigård, Cecilie, Tretti års virke. Oslo 1992.

Horned, Owe, Aktuella praktiska och rättsliga problem vid överförande av straffverkställighet. Nordisk Tidsskrift for Kriminalvidenskab 1994, 183–196.

Hurwitz, Stephan, Nordisk kriminalretligt samarbejde. Nordisk Tidsskrift for Kriminalvidenskab 1949, 74–75.

Jareborg, Nils/Asp, Petter (Hrsg.), Svensk internationell straffprocessrätt. Uppsala 1995.

Jensen, Asbjørn, EF's betydning for det nordiske lovsamarbejde. Tidsskrift for Rettsvitenskap 1988, 524–540.

Lidbom, Carl, Den nordiska rättsenhetens problem i dag. Svensk Juristtidning 1973, 273–278.

Nordiska rådet. Stockholm 1994.

Magnuson, Lars, Inbördes rättshjälp. Svensk Juristtidning 1991, 497–527.

Modeen, Tore, Rechtsvereinheitlichungsbestrebungen in den nordischen Staaten. Zeitschrift für vergleichende Rechtswissenschaft 1970, 156–172.

NORD 1987:36, Nordiska samarbetsorgan. Pohjoismaisia yhteistyöelimiä. Stockholm 1987.

NORD 1992:17, Straffrättslig jurisdiktion i Norden. Stockholm 1992.

NORD 1994:11, Karlsson, Svenolof (Hrsg.), Norden är död – Länge leve Norden! Stockholm 1994.

Nordström, Marianne, Internationellt polissamarbete. In: Nils Jareborg/Petter Asp (Hrsg.), Svensk internationell straffprocessrätt. Uppsala 1995, S. 283–329.

NU 15/1967, Om forældelse i nordisk strafferet. Betænkning afgivet af Den nordiske Strafferetskomité. Stockholm 1967.

NU 3/70, Prøveløsladelse. Ehdonalaiseen vapauteen päästäminen. Betænkning afgivet af Den nordiske strafferetskomité. Stockholm 1970; auch abgedruckt in: Nordisk Tidsskrift for Kriminalvidenskab 1970, 61–80.

NU 1971:9, Avräkning av häktningstid m.m. Stockholm 1971.

NU 1975:5, Bötesstraffet. Sakko rangaistus. Betänkande avgivet av Nordiska straffrättskommittén. Stockholm 1975.

NU 1976:8, Cooperation agreements between the Nordic countries. A compilation of some of the basic cooperation agreements between Denmark, Finland, Iceland, Norway and Sweden. Stockholm 1976.

NU 1976:32, Oversikt over det nordiske lovsamarbeides utvikling og resultater. Stockholm 1977.

NU B 1977:25, Straffsystemer i Norden. Stockholm 1977.

NU A 1978:4, Cooperation agreements between the Nordic countries. Stockholm 1978.

NU 1979:3, Nordic Council, Instruments and Achievements. Stockholm 1979.

NU 1980:13, Alternativer til frihedsstraf. Vapaus rangaistuksen vaihtoehdot. Delbetænkning afgivet af Nordisk Strafferetskomité. Stockholm 1981.

NU 1982:3, Nordiska samarbetsorgan. Stockholm 1982.

NU 1984:2, Straffutmåling. Rangaistuksen mitoittaminen. Betenkning avgitt av Nordisk Strafferettskomité. Stockholm 1984.

NU 1986:2, Företagsböter. Yhteisösakko. Betänkande avgivit av Nordiska straffrättskommittén. Stockholm 1986.

Opsahl, Torkel, Gjennomføring av fellesskapslovgivning, særlig direktiver, i Skandinavia. Lov og Rett 1971, 97–116.

Påle, Karin, Villkor för utlämning. Uppsala 2003.

Program og principper for det nordiske justitssamarbejde [2005], www.norden.org/samarbejdsområder/lovgivning/strategi/samarbejdsprogram.

Ravn, Lene, Interprovinsiel strafferet og frakendelse af førerret. Juristen 1996, 414–435.

Romander, Holger, Om överföring av åtal inom Norden. In: Hans M. Michelsen u.a. (Hrsg.), Rett og rettssal. Festskrift til Rolv Ryssdal. Oslo 1984, S. 371–377.

Senholt, Leif, Den grønlandske kriminalret – kommentarer til kriminallov for Grønland, m.v. Kopenhagen 1984.

Sinding, Gerd/Lerche, Michael, Offererstatningsloven med kommentarer. Kopenhagen 2005.

Stigel, Ole/Jensen, Nils Erik, Politiets og anklagemyndighedens samarbejde med udenlandske myndigheder. Anklagemyndighedens Årsberetning 1976, S. 25–52.

Strömholm, Stig, Nordiskt samarbete, utvecklingslinjer och argument. In: Mogens Koktvedgaard (Hrsg.), Festskrift til Professor, dr.jur. W.E. von Eyben. Kopenhagen 1982, S. 173–189.

TemaNord 2000:614, Utvecklingen av det nordiska lagstiftningssamarbetet under inverkan av EU och EES. Kopenhagen 2000.

Turner, Barry, The other European community: the Nordic Council. London 1981.

Ulrich, Stein, Internationalt politisamarbeid. Nordisk Tidsskrift for Kriminalvidenskab 1994, 161–182.

Vento, Harri (Hrsg.), Pohjoinen raja – avoin raja. Nordisk gräns – öppen gräns. Rovaniemi 1986.

Waaben, Knud, Retssammenligning og retsfællesskab i nordisk strafferet. Svensk Juristtidning 1969, 102–112.

Wallmén, Olof, Nordiska rådet och nordiskt samarbete. Stockholm 1966.

Wendt, Frantz Wilhelm, Nordisk Råd 1952–1978, struktur, arbejde, resultater. Stockholm 1979.

Wendt, Frantz Wilhelm, Cooperation in the Nordic Countries: Achievements and Obstacles. Stockholm 1981.

Wersäll, Fredrik, Straffrättsligt samarbete i ett gränslöst Norden. Nordisk Tidsskrift for Kriminalvidenskab 2006, 122–126.

Abkürzungsverzeichnis

Abs.	Absatz
Art.	Artikel
DNA	Desoxyribonukleinsäure
EU	Europäische Union
EES; EWR; EØS	Europeiska ekonomiska samarbetsområdet; Europäischer Wirtschaftsraum; Det europæiske økonomiske samarbejdsområde
ff.	fortfolgende
Hrsg.	Herausgeber
i.V.m.	in Verbindung mit
Kap.; kap.	Kapitel
L	Lovforslag (dänischer Gesetzentwurf)
lag, lov, lög	Gesetz
m.m.; m.v.	med mera, med videre (und ähnliche(s), und dergleichen)
NORD	Nordisk betænkning (Publikationsreihe des Nordischen Rates und des Nordischen Ministerrates)
Nr.; nr.	Nummer
NTfK	Nordisk Tidsskrift for Kriminalvidenskab (gesamtnordische Zeitschrift für Strafrecht und Kriminologie)
NTfS	Nordisk Tidsskrift for Strafferet (gesamtnordische Zeitschrift für Strafrecht)
NU	Nordisk utredningsserie (Publikationsreihe des Nordischen Rates und des Nordischen Ministerrates)
norw.	norwegisch
PTN	Politi-Told-Norden (Zusammenarbeit zwischen nordischen Polizei- und Zollbehörden)
S.	Seite
SANT	SamArbejd Norden Trafik (Zusammenarbeit zwischen nordischen Straßenverkehrsbehörden)
SFS	Svensk författningssamling (schwedisches Gesetzblatt)

SIS	Schengen-Informationssystem
SvJT	Svensk Juristtidning (schwedische Juristenzeitung)
TfR	Tidsskrift for Rettsvitenskap (norwegische Zeitschrift für Rechtswissenschaft)
u.a.	und andere
u.ä.	und ähnliche(s)
Vgl.	vergleiche

Freiheitsentziehende Maßnahmen gegen gefährliche, strafrechtlich verantwortliche (Rückfall-)Täter in Dänemark

A. Einführung

1. Überblick über das Sachproblem

Bei Rückfalltätern kommt in erster Linie eine nach den allgemeinen Strafzumessungsregeln verschärfte Gefängnisstrafe in Betracht. Zugleich kann ein erhebliches Rückfallrisiko der vorzeitig bedingten Entlassung aus dem Strafvollzug entgegenstehen. Für gleichartigen Rückfall sehen bestimmte Deliktstatbestände im Besonderen Teil des Strafgesetzes sowie auch im Nebenstrafrecht einen erhöhten Strafrahmen vor.[1]

Als eine spezielle Rechtsfolge für besonders gefährliche Straftäter steht nach dänischem Recht die Verwahrung *(forvaring)* zur Verfügung.[2] Es handelt sich um eine zeitunbestimmte freiheitsentziehende Sanktion, die durch den Tatrichter anstelle einer Gefängnisstrafe verhängt und überwiegend in der mit psychiatrisch und psychologisch speziell geschultem Personal ausgestatteten Vollzugsanstalt Herstedvester vollstreckt wird.

2. Rechtlicher Rahmen im Überblick

a) Strafe

Die allgemeinen Bestimmungen zur Strafschärfung wegen Rückfalls finden sich in §§ 81 Nr. 1, 84 des dänischen Strafgesetzes (*straffelov*, strl.).[3] Sie sind 2004 im Zusammenhang mit einer umfassenden Revision des Strafzumessungsrechts und der Strafrahmen des Besonderen Teils neu eingeführt bzw.

1. Dazu im Einzelnen unten B.
2. Siehe dazu unten C.
3. Siehe den Gesetzeswortlaut im Anhang.

geändert worden.[4] Fast ein halbes Jahrhundert zuvor (1961) hatte der Gesetzgeber die allgemeine Strafschärfungsregel (§ 82 strl. a.F.) abgeschafft, nach der die Strafe bis zur doppelten Höhe des gesetzlichen Strafrahmens, maximal jedoch bis auf 20 Jahre Gefängnis, angehoben werden konnte, wenn der Täter gewerbs- oder gewohnheitsmäßig gehandelt hatte. Die ehemalige Vorschrift (§ 80 strl. a.F.), dass bei der Strafzumessung der frühere Lebenswandel – das heißt vor allem frühere Kriminalität – des Angeklagten besonders zu berücksichtigen war, wurde 1973 aufgehoben.[5] Anstelle der allgemeinen Rückfallschärfung wurden bei bestimmten einzelnen Straftatbeständen erhöhte Strafdrohungen für den Fall gleichartiger Rückfälligkeit eingeführt. Diese gesetzgeberische Technik einer deliktsspezifischen Strafrahmenerweiterung ist auch nach der Reform von 2004 erhalten geblieben. Dabei wurde ihr zuvor auf erwachsene Straftäter begrenzter Anwendungsbereich auf Minderjährige ausgedehnt und der Zeitraum für die Rückfallwirkung einer Vortat von fünf auf zehn Jahre verlängert (§ 84 strl.). Zusätzlich gilt nunmehr eine allgemeine Strafzumessungsregel, nach welcher es innerhalb des gesetzlichen Strafrahmens als verschärfend anzusehen ist, wenn der Angeklagte wegen einer für die aktuelle Strafsache relevanten Tat vorbestraft ist (§ 81 Nr. 1 strl.).

b) Spezielle freiheitsentziehende Sicherungsmaßnahmen

Die Verwahrung ist heute in §§ 70 ff. strl. geregelt.[6] Bei der Einführung des geltenden Strafgesetzes von 1930 gab es zwei Arten der zeitunbestimmten Verwahrung, die sich von der heutigen deutlich unterschieden: Die damalige „Sicherungsverwahrung“ (*sikkerhedsforvaring*, § 65 strl. a.F.) konnte gegen gefährliche Rückfalltäter verhängt werden. Sie war u.a. für sogenannte Gewohnheitsverbrecher im Bereich der Eigentums- und Vermögenskriminalität gedacht, erlangte in der Praxis aber keine nennenswerte Bedeutung. Die zweite Verwahrungssanktion, die „Psychopathenverwahrung“ (*psykopatforvaring*, § 70 strl. a.F.) war eine besondere Reaktionsform für psychisch entwicklungsgehemmte, geschwächte oder gestörte – darunter auch sexuell abnorme – Straftäter. Ihre ursprüngliche Bezeichnung wurde später in „Verwahrung“ geändert. Diese Sanktion spielte in der Praxis eine erhebliche Rolle. Sie wurde sowohl gegen vielfach rückfällige Vermögens- und Eigentumsdelinquenten als auch gegen Sittlichkeits- und Gewaltverbrecher angewendet. Im Zuge des wachsenden Behandlungspessimismus, der ab den 1960er Jahren die nordische Kriminalpolitik prägte, wurden die Sicherungsverwahrung und

4. Durch Gesetz Nr. 218 vom 31.3.2004.
5. Durch Gesetz Nr. 319 vom 13.6.1973.
6. Siehe den Gesetzeswortlaut im Anhang.

die (Psychopathen-)Verwahrung wegen ihrer unbestimmten Dauer als unverhältnismäßig und ungerecht kritisiert und schließlich 1973 abgeschafft. Der mit den damaligen Reformvorarbeiten befasste Strafgesetzrat *(Straffelovrådet)* hielt es jedoch für geboten, die Möglichkeit einer zeitunbestimmten Freiheitsentziehung für besonders gefährliche Rückfalltäter nicht gänzlich aufzugeben, sondern in gewissem Umfang beizubehalten, und zwar nunmehr begrenzt auf Gewaltdelikte.[7] Entsprechend dieser Empfehlung wurde 1973 die Verwahrung in ihrer heutigen Form eingeführt.[8] Ausschlaggebend war der Gesichtspunkt der Gefährlichkeit: Bei einigen (wenigen) Gewaltverbrechern sei damit zu rechnen, dass die Verhängung und Vollstreckung einer zeitbestimmten Freiheitsstrafe keine hinreichend individualpräventive Reaktion darstelle. Einem naheliegenden Risiko schwerer oder unberechenbarer Aggressionshandlungen dürfe die Gesellschaft nicht ausgesetzt werden.[9]

3. Generelle Zwecke und Anwendungsmaßstäbe

a) Strafe

Nachdem in der ersten Hälfte des 20. Jahrhunderts individualpräventive Ziele und der Behandlungsgedanke stark im Vordergrund gestanden hatten, wird heute der Strafzweck betont nüchtern formuliert: Die Androhung, Verhängung und Vollstreckung von Strafe soll dazu beitragen, die Kriminalität zu begrenzen. Auf der Ebene der kriminalisierenden Gesetzgebung liegt der Schwerpunkt auf der positiven, normbestätigenden und moralbildenden Generalprävention. Die Strafdrohung soll dazu dienen, Menschen von bestimmten unerwünschten Verhaltensweisen abzuhalten. Eine gerichtlich verhängte Strafe soll proportional zur Schwere der begangenen Tat sowie zur Schuld des Täters bemessen werden und dessen persönliche Verhältnisse berücksichtigen. Im Vollzug der (Freiheits-)Strafe wird zum einen das Ziel verfolgt, den Verurteilten zu einem kriminalitätsfreien Leben zu motivieren und zu befähigen, und zum anderen die nötige Kontrolle über ihn auszuüben, um die Vollstreckung der Sanktion zu gewährleisten und die Allgemeinheit vor eventueller Gefahr durch weitere Straftaten zu schützen.[10]

7. Betænkning om de strafferetlige særforanstaltninger, Nr. 667, Kopenhagen 1972, S. 73 ff., 145 f.
8. Durch Änderungsgesetz Nr. 320 vom 13.6.1973.
9. Betænkning Nr. 667/1972, S. 76 f.
10. Vgl. *Vagn Greve*, Straffene. 2. Aufl. Kopenhagen 2002, S. 36–47; *Hans Jørgen Engbo*, Straffuldbyrdelsesret. 2. Aufl. Kopenhagen 2005, S. 24–29.

b) Spezielle freiheitsentziehende Sicherungsmaßnahmen

Dem zuletzt genannten Sicherungszweck kommt bei der Verhängung und Vollstreckung der Verwahrung besonderes Gewicht zu.[11] Ihre Anwendungsvoraussetzungen stellen auf die Gefährlichkeit des Angeklagten und auf die Notwendigkeit dieser Maßnahme ab, um einer erheblichen bzw. naheliegenden Gefahr für Leib, Leben oder Freiheit anderer vorzubeugen. Sicherheitsvorkehrungen zum Schutz der Allgemeinheit spielen auch im Verwahrungsvollzug eine entscheidende Rolle.

B. Schutz im Rahmen allgemeiner strafrechtlicher Regelungen (insbesondere zur Strafzumessung)

1. Neben oder anstelle spezieller Regelungen?

Das dänische Sanktionensystem kennt als allgemeine freiheitsentziehende Strafe heute nur die Gefängnisstrafe (§§ 31 ff. strl.).[12] Eine allgemeine freiheitsbeschränkende Sanktionsart ist die bedingte Verurteilung (§§ 56 ff. strl.), die mit der Auflage gemeinnütziger Arbeit verbunden und/oder mit einer unbedingten Gefängnisstrafe von höchstens sechs Monaten kombiniert werden kann.

Als spezielle Rechtsfolgen für bestimmte Tätergruppen sind die Jugendsanktion für schwer belastete junge Rechtsbrecher (§ 74 a), die Verwahrung (§§ 70 ff.) für rückfallgefährdete Gewaltverbrecher und Sexualstraftäter sowie besondere Reaktionen gegenüber geisteskranken, psychisch gestörten oder entwicklungsgehemmten Tätern (§§ 68 ff.) vorgesehen.[13] Die Verhängung dieser speziellen Rechtsfolgen kommt jeweils anstelle der allgemeinen Sanktionen in Betracht.

Bei der Strafzumessung sind bestimmte Umstände, die im Zusammenhang mit einer besonderen Gefährlichkeit des Angeklagten stehen, als strafschärfend innerhalb des gesetzlichen Strafrahmens zu berücksichtigen. Ein erhebliches Risiko des Rückfalls in nicht nur bagatellartige Kriminalität stellt zudem einen Hinderungsgrund für die bedingt vorzeitige Entlassung aus dem Anstaltsvollzug dar.[14]

11. *Hans Jørgen Engbo*, Straffuldbyrdelsesret, S. 243 f.; *Vagn Greve*, Straffene, S. 192–199.
12. Die früher daneben bestehende Strafform der Haft (§§ 44–49 strl. a.F.) wurde überwiegend im Nebenstrafrecht, vor allem bei Trunkenheit im Straßenverkehr, angewandt und 2001 abgeschafft.
13. Im Einzelnen hierzu unten C und D.
14. Siehe dazu unten 2.c).

2. *Einzelne freiheitsentziehende Instrumente im Kontext von Strafzumessung und -vollstreckung*

a) Gefängnisstrafe

Gefängnis (*fængsel*, §§ 33 ff.) wird für eine Dauer von mindestens sieben Tagen und höchstens 16 Jahren oder auf Lebenszeit verhängt. In Fällen einer zulässigen Überschreitung des gesetzlichen Strafrahmens kann auf Gefängnis bis zu 20 Jahren erkannt werden. Dies gilt insbesondere im Hinblick auf die Bildung einer Gesamtstrafe für mehrere Straftaten, die bei besonders erschwerenden Umständen eine der angedrohten Höchststrafen bis um die Hälfte übersteigen darf (§ 88 Abs. 1 Satz 2 strl.). Von der Möglichkeit, den erweiterten Strafraum bis zu 20 Jahren Gefängnis zu nutzen, wird in der Praxis kein Gebrauch gemacht.

Eine fakultative Strafrahmenerweiterung wegen gleichartigen Rückfalls ist bei einzelnen Straftatbeständen des Besonderen Teils vorgesehen. So können die für vorsätzliche Körperverletzung, schwere Körperverletzung und besonders schwere Körperverletzung angedrohten Höchststrafen bis um die Hälfte erhöht werden, wenn der Täter wegen einer mit vorsätzlicher Gewalt verbundenen Tat vorbestraft ist (§ 247 Abs. 1 strl.). Die Höchststrafe für Sachbeschädigung kann von 18 Monaten auf sechs Jahre angehoben werden, wenn die Tat in systematischer oder organisierter Weise begangen wurde oder der Täter wegen vorsätzlicher Sachbeschädigung, schwerer Brandstiftung, Brandstiftung, Herbeiführens einer Explosion, Störung der Verkehrssicherheit, Störung von Kommunikations- und Versorgungsanlagen und Denkmalsbeschädigung vorbestraft ist (§ 291 Abs. 2 strl.).

Gefängnis auf Lebenszeit ist als Höchststrafe bei vorsätzlicher Tötung, schwerer Brandstiftung, Angriff auf den Luft- oder Seeverkehr, Terrorismus sowie einigen Staatsschutzdelikten vorgesehen. In der Praxis beschränkt sich der Anwendungsbereich auf Fälle der vorsätzlichen Tötung. Die lebenslange Gefängnisstrafe fungiert als zeitunbestimmter Freiheitsentzug und ist wegen dieser Unbestimmtheit stark kritisiert worden.[15] Ihre Beibehaltung wurde damit begründet, dass die Gefährlichkeit des Verurteilten und damit der zeitliche Bedarf seiner Einsperrung zum Urteilszeitpunkt nur schwer einzuschätzen sei und sich oft erst nach einiger Dauer des Freiheitsentzugs feststellen

15. *Vagn Greve*, Fængsel på livstid – eller fængsel i 21 år? Lov & Ret 1993, Nr. 11, S. 25 ff.; *Per Ole Träskman*, Utestängning genom tidsobestämd inspärring – det problematiska livtidsstraffet. In: Vagn Greve u.a. (Hrsg.), Nytter det? Kopenhagen 2001, S. 151–169.

lasse.[16] Nachdem der Vollzug einer lebenslangen Gefängnisstrafe früher nur im Gnadenwege vorzeitig beendet werden konnte, besteht nunmehr die Möglichkeit einer bedingten Strafrestaussetzung, und zwar durch Anordnung des Justizministers nach einer Verbüßungszeit von mindestens 12 Jahren (§ 41).[17] Die durchschnittliche Verbüßungsdauer liegt etwa bei 17 Jahren.[18]

b) Strafzumessungskriterien

Nach der allgemeinen Regel für die Festsetzung der Strafe (§ 80 strl.) sind bei der Strafzumessung die Schwere der Straftat und Feststellungen über den Täter zu gewichten, wobei der Gesichtspunkt einer einheitlichen Rechtsanwendung zu beachten ist. Bei der Beurteilung der Schwere der Straftat ist zu berücksichtigen, welcher Schaden, welche Gefahr und welche Verletzung mit ihr verbunden waren und inwieweit der Täter diese Umstände erkannte oder hätte erkennen müssen. Relevante Feststellungen über den Täter sind solche, die sich auf dessen allgemeine persönliche und soziale Verhältnisse, sein Verhalten vor und nach der Tat sowie seine Beweggründe für die Tatbegehung beziehen. Mit dem Kriterium des Täterverhaltens vor der Tat finden Vorstrafen, insbesondere wegen gleichartiger Kriminalität, bereits hier Eingang in die Strafzumessungserwägungen.[19]

Darüber hinaus enthält § 81 strl. eine (nicht abschließende) Aufzählung von Strafschärfungsgründen, darunter die folgenden:

1) dass gegen den Täter bereits früher eine für die vorliegende Strafsache bedeutsame Verurteilung ergangen ist,
3) dass die Tat besonders geplant war oder im Rahmen umfassender Kriminalität begangen worden ist,
4) dass der Täter wesentlich ernstere als die tatsächlich eingetretenen Folgen beabsichtigt hatte,
5) dass der Täter besondere Rücksichtslosigkeit gezeigt hat,
11) dass die Tat von einer Person begangen worden ist, die eine Strafe oder eine andere strafrechtliche Rechtsfolge freiheitsentziehender Art verbüßt,

16. Straffelovrådets betænkning om straffastsættelse og strafferammer I. Almindelig del. Bet. Nr. 1424, Kopenhagen 2002, S. 245–248 (mit abweichender Stellungnahme von *Vagn Greve*, S. 248 f.).
17. Siehe auch unten B.2.c).
18. *Gorm Toftegaard Nielsen*, Strafferet 2. Sanktionerne. 2. Aufl. Kopenhagen 2005, S. 16 f., 27.
19. Vgl. *Asbjørn Jensen* in Kommenteret straffelov. Almindelig del. 8. Aufl. Kopenhagen 2005, S. 407.

12) die Tat von einem ehemaligen Insassen gegen die betreffende Institution oder eine dort angestellte Person begangen worden ist.

Im Zusammenhang mit dem Kriterium früherer Verurteilungen (Nr. 1) wird darauf abgestellt, ob sie für die aktuelle Strafsache relevant sind. Dies trifft in erster Linie bei gleichartiger Rückfälligkeit zu, kann aber auch in anderen Fällen gegeben sein. Entscheidend ist eine konkrete Würdigung der früheren und aktuellen Kriminalität. Eine zeitliche Grenze für die Berücksichtigung von Vorstrafen sieht das Gesetz nicht vor.

In Bezug auf diejenigen Straftatbestände des Besonderen Teils, die eine Strafrahmenanhebung für Wiederholungstaten vorsehen,[20] legt § 84 Abs. 3 strl. fest, dass die Rückfallwirkung erlischt, wenn seit der Verbüßung[21] der früheren Strafe zehn Jahre vergangen sind. Diese Frist, die bei Freiheitsstrafen mit der bedingten oder unbedingten Entlassung aus dem Strafvollzug beginnt, ist 2004 von fünf auf zehn Jahre verlängert worden. Es ist aber keine Voraussetzung, dass in der Verurteilung wegen der früheren Tat überhaupt eine konkrete Strafe verhängt worden ist[22] oder gar deren Vollstreckung begonnen hat.

c) Vermeidung strafvollzugsreduzierend wirkender Vergünstigungen

Über eine bedingt vorzeitige Entlassung aus dem Strafvollzug wird in der Regel nach Verbüßung von zwei Dritteln der Strafzeit, ausnahmsweise nach der Hälfte, entschieden (§§ 38 Abs. 1–2, 40 a strl.). Die Aussetzung der Reststrafe zur Bewährung setzt jedoch u.a. voraus, dass die bedingte Freilassung des Verurteilten nicht „unangebracht erscheint“ (§ 38 Abs. 5 strl.). Als unangebracht wird sie nach regelmäßiger Praxis dann angesehen, wenn ein erhebliches Risiko des Rückfalls in nicht nur bagatellartige Kriminalität besteht und dieses Risiko durch Nachsorgemaßnahmen der Bewährungshilfe voraussichtlich nicht begrenzt werden kann.[23] Die Entlassungsentscheidung wird während des Strafvollzugs vom Leiter der Vollzugsanstalt bzw. von der zentralen Vollzugsverwaltung getroffen.[24] Nach Zwei-Drittel-Verbüßung stellt

20. Siehe dazu oben B.2.a).
21. Der Verbüßung wird insoweit ein rechtskräftiger Erlass oder Wegfall der Strafe gleichgesetzt.
22. Zur bedingten Verurteilung ohne Strafausspruch siehe unten B.3.
23. Ziff. 6–12 Vejledning om løsladelse af dømte, der udstår fængselsstraf. VEJ Nr. 29 vom 19.4.2006. Vgl. *Hans Jørgen Engbo*, Straffuldbyrdelsesret, S. 346–348.
24. Für Verurteilte mit einer Strafe ab acht Jahren oder im Fall einer bedingten Entlassung vor Ablauf von zwei Dritteln der Strafzeit entscheidet die zentrale Vollzugsbehörde im

die bedingte Aussetzung des Strafrestes einen gewöhnlichen Schritt im Vollzugsablauf dar, sodass eine Ablehnung begründet werden muss und gerichtlich überprüfbar ist.

Die Probezeit, die mit Bewährungsaufsicht und Weisungen verbunden werden kann, darf drei Jahre nicht überschreiten. Wenn der Strafrest mehr als drei Jahre beträgt, kann jedoch eine Probezeit bis zu fünf Jahren festgesetzt werden (§ 39 strl.). Begeht der vorzeitig Entlassene eine neue Straftat während der Probezeit, so kann die Verbüßung der Reststrafe angeordnet werden (§ 40 strl.).

Seit 2001 ist eine bedingte Strafrestaussetzung auch im Fall einer auf Lebenszeit verhängten Gefängnisstrafe vorgesehen (§ 41 strl.).[25] Der Justizminister entscheidet über die vorzeitige Entlassung auf Probe nach Ablauf von 12 Vollzugsjahren.[26] Nach einer Verbüßungszeit von 14 Jahren kann der Verurteilte einen ablehnenden Beschluss gerichtlich überprüfen lassen (§ 112 Nr. 6 Strafvollstreckungsgesetz, *straffuldbyrdelseslov*, sfbl.). Auch hier ist die Bewährungsentlassung unzulässig, wenn sie mit Rücksicht auf die Gefährlichkeit des Verurteilten unangebracht erscheint, das heißt wenn ein erhebliches Risiko erneuter schwerer Straftaten besteht.[27]

3. *Freiheitsbeschränkende Maßnahmen als mildere Mittel*

Eine eigene Sanktionsform mit Strafcharakter stellt die bedingte Verurteilung dar (§§ 56 ff. strl). Sie erfolgt entweder in Form eines reinen Schuldspruchs, bei dem die Straffestsetzung für die Dauer einer Bewährungszeit ausgesetzt wird, oder in der Weise, dass das Gericht bereits eine konkrete Strafe festlegt und deren Vollstreckung ganz oder teilweise zur Bewährung aussetzt. Eine bedingte Verurteilung erfolgt in aller Regel anstelle der Verhängung einer (unbedingten) Gefängnisstrafe. Die Länge der alternativ infrage kommenden Freiheitsstrafe ist dabei nicht begrenzt; sie liegt in der Praxis jedoch nur sehr selten über zwei Jahren. Der Hauptanwendungsbereich für bedingte Verurteilungen ist die Vermögenskriminalität (mit Ausnahme von Raub). Ersttäter werden häufiger bedingt verurteilt als Wiederholungstäter, sozial Angepasste

Justizministerium; §§ 25 ff. Bekendtgørelse om løsladelse af dømte, der udstår fængselsstraf. BEK Nr. 318 vom 19.4.2006. Vgl. *Gorm Toftegaard Nielsen*, Strafferet 2, Sanktionerne, S. 28.

25. Früher war eine vorzeitige Entlassung aus dem Vollzug der lebenslangen Freiheitsstrafe nur durch Begnadigung möglich.
26. Eine Begnadigung ist weiterhin auch vor diesem Zeitpunkt möglich.
27. Betænkning om en lov om fuldbyrdelse af straf m.v. Bet. Nr. 1355, Kopenhagen 1998, S. 38.

häufiger als Arbeitslose, Alkohol- oder Drogenabhängige; gegenüber jungen und alten Straftätern wird die bedingte Verurteilung häufiger angewandt als gegenüber Angeklagten im Alter zwischen 21 und 40 Jahren.[28]

Die bedingte Verurteilung kann mit Bewährungsaufsicht und verschiedenen Weisungen verbunden werden (§ 57 strl.), darunter Aufenthaltsverbote an bestimmten Plätzen und Kontaktverbote mit bestimmten Personen. Falls dies nicht als ausreichend erscheint, kann (zusätzlich) die Auflage gemeinnütziger Arbeit für eine Dauer von mindestens 30 und höchstens 240 Stunden erteilt werden (§§ 62 ff. strl.). Sofern eine weitere Verschärfung der bedingten Verurteilung erforderlich ist, etwa gegenüber einem Wiederholungs- oder Mehrfachtäter, kann das Gericht sie mit einem kurzen unbedingten Freiheitsentzug verbinden (sogenanntes Kombinationsurteil *[kombinationsdom]*). Es bestimmt in diesem Fall, dass ein Teil der festgesetzten Strafe, jedoch höchstens sechs Monate, zu vollstrecken ist, während die Verurteilung im Übrigen für bedingt erklärt wird (§ 58 Abs. 1 strl.).

Die Verbüßung einer unbedingten Freiheitsstrafe außerhalb der Vollzugsanstalt mit elektronischer Fußfessel ist 2005 eingeführt worden, und zwar für Personen, die wegen eines Straßenverkehrsdelikts zu einer Gefängnisstrafe bis zu drei Monaten verurteilt worden sind. Für gefährliche Rückfalltäter kommt diese Vollzugsvariante nicht in Betracht.

4. Fragen der Rückwirkung (zuungunsten Betroffener)

a) Änderungen der Rechtslage zwischen Tatbegehung und Aburteilung

Bei Änderungen der Rechtslage zwischen Begehung und Aburteilung einer Tat bestimmen sich deren Strafbarkeit und die Strafe grundsätzlich nach dem späteren Gesetz, jedoch mit der Maßgabe, dass die Entscheidung dadurch nicht strenger als nach dem früheren Gesetz ausfallen darf (§ 3 Abs. 1 strl.). Ergibt ein Vergleich, dass die neue Rechtslage im Ergebnis für den Angeklagten ungünstiger ist, so muss das frühere Gesetz angewendet werden. Das Rückwirkungsverbot bezieht sich nur auf die zwischenzeitliche Änderung von Gesetzen und auf deren Grundlage erlassenen Verwaltungsvorschriften, nicht auf eine geänderte Rechtsauffassung oder Strafzumessungspraxis der Gerichte.

b) Änderungen der Rechtslage während der Strafverbüßung

Das Rückwirkungsverbot in § 3 strl. gilt nur für Gesetzesänderungen, die sich auf die Strafbarkeit einer Tat oder die für sie vorgesehene Strafdrohung be-

28. *Vagn Greve*, Straffene, S. 127.

ziehen. Es gilt hingegen nicht für geänderte Bestimmungen zur Strafvollstreckung, einschließlich Vorschriften zur bedingten Aussetzung des Strafrestes.

C. Schutz durch Verhängung einer speziellen freiheitsentziehenden Sicherungsmaßnahme

1. Neben oder anstelle von Strafe?

Anstelle einer Gefängnisstrafe kommt als alternative freiheitsentziehende Sanktion die Verwahrung gemäß § 70 ff. strl. in Betracht.

2. Generelle täterseitige Voraussetzungen

Die Verwahrung ist eine besondere Rechtsfolge für gefährliche strafrechtlich verantwortliche Personen, sie kann aber auch gegenüber einer Person angewendet werden, die zur Tatzeit geisteskrank, entwicklungsgehemmt oder in ihren psychischen Funktionen gestört und deshalb zurechnungsunfähig oder vermindert zurechnungsfähig war, sofern im Übrigen die Voraussetzungen des § 70 strl. erfüllt sind.[29] Eine besondere untere oder obere Altersgrenze besteht nicht.

3. Voraussetzungen bezüglich Vortat(en)

Eine gesetzliche Vorgabe hinsichtlich Art, Anzahl oder Bestrafung eventueller Vortaten gibt es nicht. Es wird nicht einmal zwingend vorausgesetzt, dass der Angeklagte überhaupt vorbestraft ist. Entscheidend ist seine aktuelle Gefährlichkeit. Deren Beurteilung wird auf die Art und Schwere der Anlasstat sowie auf Angaben über die Persönlichkeit des Angeklagten gestützt. In diesem Zusammenhang ist auch seine eventuelle frühere Kriminalität zu berücksichtigen. Die Gewichtung eventueller Vortaten ist dabei wiederum abhängig von der Art der Anlasstat: Bei Gewaltverbrechern wird der Rückfälligkeit grundsätzlich eine größere Bedeutung beigemessen als bei Sexualstraftätern.[30]

4. Voraussetzungen bezüglich Anlasstaten

Der Angeklagte muss sich eines der in § 70 Abs. 1 Nr. 1 strl. abschließend aufgezählten schweren Gewaltverbrechen – vorsätzliche Tötung, Raub, Freiheitsberaubung, schwere Körperverletzung, Bedrohung, Brandstiftung – oder des Versuchs einer dieser Straftaten bzw. der Vergewaltigung oder einer anderen schweren Sexualstraftat oder des Versuchs hierzu (§ 70 Abs. 2 Nr. 1

29. Siehe dazu unten D.a).
30. Näher dazu unten 4 und 5.

strl.) schuldig gemacht haben. Eigentums- oder Vermögensdelikte sind nur dann erfasst, wenn sie mit der Anwendung oder Androhung von Gewalt verbunden sind. Die Ausgliederung der Sexualstraftaten aus dem ursprünglichen Deliktskatalog und ihre gesonderte Regelung erfolgte erst durch eine Gesetzesänderung im Jahr 1997.[31]

5. Voraussetzungen bezüglich (fortbestehender) Gefährlichkeit des Täters

a) Sachliche Kriterien

Ferner muss der Angeklagte eine Gefahr für Leben, Leib, Gesundheit oder Freiheit anderer darstellen. Ist die Anlasstat ein schweres Gewaltverbrechen, so muss die Gefahr „naheliegend“ sein (Abs. 1), bei einem Sexualstraftäter wird nur eine „erhebliche“ Gefahr verlangt (Abs. 2). Mit dieser 1997 eingeführten Unterscheidung sollte nach den Gesetzesmotiven die Anwendung der Verwahrung gegenüber schweren Sexualstraftätern erleichtert werden.[32] In jedem Fall ist die Beurteilung der Gefährlichkeit auf die aktuell begangene Tat sowie auf die Persönlichkeit des Angeklagten zu stützen, wobei eventuelle frühere Straftaten „insbesondere“ (Abs. 1) bzw. „unter anderem“ (Abs. 2) zu berücksichtigen sind. Bei Gewaltverbrechern wird demnach der Rückfälligkeit grundsätzlich eine größere Bedeutung beigemessen als bei Sexualstraftätern. Auch diese Unterscheidung sollte dazu dienen, die Anwendungsvoraussetzungen für die Verwahrung gegenüber Sexualstraftätern zu lockern. Während zuvor in der Praxis erst beim zweiten Rückfall eine Verwahrung in Betracht gezogen worden war, sollte dies nun bereits nach einmaligem Rückfall und bei Vorliegen eines erheblichen Wiederholungsrisikos sogar für Ersttäter möglich sein.[33]

b) Besondere Verfahrensregeln zur Beurteilung des konkreten Einzelfalles

Im Hinblick auf die Einschätzung der Gefahr wird in der Praxis regelmäßig ein rechtspsychiatrisches Gutachten eingeholt, selbst wenn keine Anzeichen für eine gesundheitliche Störung vorliegen. Die sogenannte Mentaluntersuchung wird von der Rechtspsychiatrischen Klinik in Kopenhagen, von einem Facharzt für Psychiatrie oder von einem Amtsarzt durchgeführt. Sie kann ambulant oder stationär erfolgen. In der Regel wird das Untersuchungsergebnis dem Gerichtsmedizinischen Rat *(Retslægerådet)* als sachverständigem Organ vorgelegt. Dieser Rat äußert sich betont zurückhaltend über die Fähig-

31. Änderungsgesetz Nr. 274 vom 15.4.1997.
32. Folketingstidende 1996/97, Tillæg A, S. 101, 111.
33. Folketingstidende 1996/97, Tillæg A, S. 111.

keit von Psychiatern, ein Rückfallrisiko einzuschätzen.[34] Auch in der Wissenschaft wird die Prognose skeptisch betrachtet.[35]

6. Weitere sachliche Voraussetzungen

Die Verwahrung muss anstelle einer Gefängnisstrafe notwendig sein, um der bestehenden Gefahr vorzubeugen. Dies bedeutet beispielsweise, dass die Verwahrung nicht indiziert ist, wenn als Alternative die Verhängung einer lebenslangen Gefängnisstrafe in Betracht kommt. Auch eine sehr lange zeitbestimmte Gefängnisstrafe kann im Einzelfall ausreichend sein, um dem Sicherheitsbedürfnis der Allgemeinheit Rechnung zu tragen.[36]

7. Rechtsfolgen

a) Art

Die Verwahrung wird nach den allgemeinen Strafvollzugsregeln vollstreckt (§§ 1, 105 sfbl.), jedoch vorzugsweise in der Vollzugsanstalt Herstedvester, die mit psychiatrisch und psychologisch speziell geschultem Personal sowie besonderen Sicherheitsvorkehrungen ausgestattet ist.[37]

b) Dauer

Die Verwahrung ist eine zeitunbestimmte Sanktion, die aufrecht zu erhalten ist, solange die Gefährlichkeit des Verurteilten fortdauert (§ 72 Abs. 1 strl.). Es besteht die Möglichkeit einer probeweisen Entlassung (§ 72 Abs. 2 strl.) mit der Maßgabe, dass der Betreffende bei mangelnder Bewährung unmittelbar in den Vollzug zurückgeführt und dies nachträglich gerichtlich überprüft wird.

34. Siehe etwa Jahresberichte des Gerichtsmedizinischen Rates RÅ 1988, S. 137, 1995 S. 79, 99.
35. *Vagn Greve*, Straffene, S. 192–195; *Gorm Toftegaard Nielsen*, Strafferet 2, S. 31 f..
36. Beispiele aus der höchstrichterlichen Rechtsprechung: keine Notwendigkeit der Verwahrung gegenüber 14 Jahren Gefängnis (U 1986.898 H) bzw. neun Jahren Gefängnis (U 1992.849 H); in einem anderen Fall (U 1998.1377 H) wurde die alternative Verurteilung zu zehn Jahren Gefängnis nicht als ausreichend angesehen.
37. Die übrigen Insassen dieser Anstalt sind Strafgefangene und Untersuchungshäftlinge, bei denen ein besonderer Bedarf an psychiatrischer Betreuung besteht.

8. Prozedurale Fragen

a) Zuständigkeit für Entscheidungen über Verhängung, Aufhebung bzw. Lockerung

Zuständig für die Verhängung und die Aufhebung der Verwahrung ist allein das Tatgericht. Das Gericht (nicht die Vollzugsverwaltung) entscheidet auch über eine probeweise Entlassung, und zwar auf Antrag der Anklagebehörde.

b) Mögliche Zeitpunkte der Anordnung

Das Gericht ordnet die Verwahrung im Taturteil an. Eine nachträgliche Anordnung der Verwahrung ist ausschließlich in der Weise möglich, dass eine Zwangsmaßnahme nach §§ 68 oder 69 strl. gegen eine geisteskranke, entwicklungsgehemmte oder in ihren psychischen Funktionen gestörte Person durch gerichtlichen Beschluss in Verwahrung umgewandelt wird (§ 72 Abs. 2 strl.).

c) Mögliche Anlässe und Zeitpunkte der Überprüfung betr. Fortdauer/Lockerung/Aussetzung/Aufhebung

Wenn anzunehmen ist, dass die Voraussetzungen für eine probeweise Entlassung erfüllt sind, ersucht die Vollzugsanstalt die Anklagebehörde, die Sache dem Gericht vorzulegen. Nach Ablauf von drei Jahren der Verwahrung ist jährlich die Frage zu prüfen, ob ein entsprechendes Ersuchen an die Anklagebehörde gestellt werden soll. Die Anstaltsleitung erörtert diese Frage anlässlich einer ihrer Besprechungen mit dem Justizministerium bzw. dem Zentralen Vollzugsamt. Das Ersuchen an die Anklagebehörde ergeht grundsätzlich im Zusammenhang mit dem Jahrestreffen zwischen dem Reichsankläger und dem Justizministerium bzw. dem Zentralen Vollzugsamt.[38] Auch der Verurteilte selbst und sein Rechtsbeistand sind berechtigt, ein entsprechendes Ersuchen an die Anklagebehörde zu richten. Wird ihrem Antrag nicht stattgegeben, so kann ein erneutes Ersuchen nicht vor Ablauf eines halben Jahres nach der Ablehnungsentscheidung gestellt werden (§ 72 Abs. 2 Satz 3 strl.).

d) Regelungen zur Einbeziehung von Sachverständigen in die Entscheidungsfindung

Für ihre Entscheidung, ob ein Ersuchen an die Anklagebehörde gestellt werden soll, holt die Anstaltsleitung die Stellungnahme eines Facharztes für Psychiatrie ein.[39] Falls das Ersuchen von dem Verurteilten selbst oder seinem

38. §§ 1–3 Bekendtgørelse om behandlingen af sager om prøveudskrivning af forvaringsdømte. BEK Nr. 393 vom 17.5.2001.
39. § 4 BEK Nr. 393 vom 17.5.2001.

Rechtsbeistand an die Anklagebehörde gerichtet wird, holt diese ein entsprechendes fachärztliches Gutachten ein.

9. Fragen der Rückwirkung (zuungunsten Betroffener)

a) Anwendung auf Taten, die vor der Rechtsänderung begangen wurden und nach dieser abgeurteilt werden

Im Fall einer Gesetzesänderung während des Zeitraums zwischen der Begehung und der Aburteilung einer Tat ist nach § 3 Abs. 1 strl. grundsätzlich das zum Urteilszeitpunkt geltende Recht anzuwenden, es sei denn, das frühere Recht war milder.[40] Eine besondere Regelung enthält § 4 strl. für die Verhängung anderer Sanktionen als Gefängnis oder Geldstrafe. Für bestimmte in § 4 Abs. 1 strl. aufgezählte Rechtsfolgen – darunter auch die Verwahrung – kommt es stets allein auf das zur Urteilszeit geltende Recht an; für andere muss gemäß § 4 Abs. 2 strl. die Rechtsgrundlage auch zur Tatzeit bestanden haben.[41]

Mit Rücksicht auf den strafähnlichen Charakter der Verwahrung, der insbesondere auch im Zusammenhang mit Art. 7 EMRK anerkannt ist, wird von dänischen Strafrechtswissenschaftlern allerdings geltend gemacht, dass die Verwahrung entgegen dem Wortlaut des § 4 Abs. 1 strl. nicht verhängt werden dürfte, wenn dies zum Zeitpunkt der Tatbegehung nicht gesetzlich vorgesehen war.[42]

b) Anwendung auf Personen, die im Zeitpunkt der Gesetzesänderung rechtskräftig abgeurteilt waren

Tritt die Gesetzesänderung erst nach der Verurteilung in Kraft und entfällt damit die Strafbarkeit der Tat, so entfällt auch eine für die Tat verhängte, aber noch nicht vollstreckte Strafe (§ 3 Abs. 2, § 4 Abs. 3 strl.). Von den genannten Bestimmungen nicht erfasst ist der Fall, dass die Strafbarkeit der Tat bestehen bleibt und allein die Sanktionsnorm nachträglich geändert wird. Die dabei entstehende Rechtslage für bereits verurteilte Personen wird üblicherweise durch Übergangsvorschriften in dem jeweiligen Änderungsgesetz geregelt.

Bei der Reform von 1973 überließ es der Gesetzgeber ausdrücklich den Gerichten zu entscheiden, wie mit den bei Inkrafttreten des neuen Gesetzes in

40. Vgl. oben B.4.a).
41. Siehe den Gesetzeswortlaut von §§ 3 und 4 strl. im Anhang.
42. *Knud Waaben*, Strafferettens almindelige del I. Ansvarslæren. 4. Aufl. Kopenhagen 1997, S. 96; *Gorm Toftegaard Nielsen*, Strafferet I. Ansvaret. 3. Aufl. Kopenhagen 2008, S. 299 f.

Sicherungsverwahrung bzw. (Psychopathen-)Verwahrung einsitzenden Personen zu verfahren war (§ 6 des Änderungsgesetzes).[43] Eine allgemeine Übergangsregelung hielt man angesichts der Verschiedenartigkeit der betroffenen Personen für unmöglich. Die Gerichte hatten in jedem Einzelfall durch Urteil festzulegen, welche Sanktion an die Stelle der verhängten Sicherungsverwahrung oder (Psychopathen-)Verwahrung treten sollte: eine Gefängnisstrafe (sofern die neuen gesetzlichen Voraussetzungen für die Verwahrung nicht erfüllt waren), psychiatrische Zwangspflege (sofern dies nach den neuen Bestimmungen geboten war) oder Verwahrung nach den neuen Vorschriften. Da auch die früheren Verwahrungsformen bereits zeitunbestimmt gewesen waren, ergab sich insofern keine rückwirkende Benachteiligung für die Betroffenen.

Personen, die bei Inkrafttreten des Änderungsgesetzes aus der Sicherungsverwahrung bzw. (Psychopathen-)Verwahrung bedingt entlassen waren und sich in der Bewährungszeit befanden, wurden behandelt wie bedingt vorzeitig Entlassene aus dem Gefängnisstrafvollzug mit einer ausgesetzten Reststrafe von sechs Monaten und einer Bewährungszeit von zwei Jahren.

D. Anwendung anderer Regeln über Freiheitsentziehung bzw. Freiheitsbeschränkung

1. Unterbringung psychisch Kranker

Personen, die zur Tatzeit aufgrund von Geisteskrankheit oder eines damit gleichzustellenden Zustands zurechnungsunfähig waren, sowie in höherem Grad geistig Behinderte werden nicht bestraft (§ 16 Abs. 1 strl.). Dies gilt auch für die in leichterem Grad geistig Behinderten und solche Personen, die sich zur Tatzeit in einem mit geistiger Behinderung gleichzustellenden Zustand befanden, sofern nicht besondere Umstände für die Verhängung einer Strafe sprechen (§ 16 Abs. 2 strl.).

Gegenüber einer Person, die nach § 16 strl. freigesprochen wird, kann das Gericht jedoch eine spezielle Rechtsfolge nach § 68 strl. anordnen. Sofern weniger eingreifende Maßnahmen wie Bewährungsaufsicht, Anordnungen bezüglich Aufenthaltsort oder Arbeit, Entziehungskur, psychiatrischer Behandlung u.Ä. nicht ausreichend sind, kann angeordnet werden, dass der Betreffende in einem psychiatrischen Krankenhaus oder einer Einrichtung für Personen mit weitgehender psychischer Behinderung untergebracht oder unter Aufsicht mit der Möglichkeit einer verwaltungsrechtlichen Unterbringung gestellt oder in ein geeignetes Heim oder eine Anstalt zur besonderen Pflege

43. Näher dazu Betænkning Nr. 667/1972, S. 149 f.

oder Fürsorge eingewiesen wird. Sind die Voraussetzungen des § 70 strl. erfüllt, so kann auch eine Unterbringung in Verwahrung erfolgen.

Befand sich der Täter bei der Tatbegehung in einem Zustand, der durch mangelhafte Entwicklung, Schwächung oder Störung der psychischen Funktionen bedingt, aber nicht von der in § 16 strl. genannten Art war, so kann das Gericht, sofern es dies für zweckdienlich befindet, anstatt eine Strafe zu verhängen, auch hier Maßnahmen im Sinne von § 68 Satz 2 strl. anordnen (§ 69 strl.).

Die speziell für geisteskranke und psychisch gestörte Straftäter vorgesehenen Rechtsfolgen gemäß §§ 68 und 69 strl. werden unter dem Gesichtspunkt der Behandlung und des Schutzes, nicht aber nach allgemeinen Strafzumessungserwägungen festgesetzt. Für die Dauer einer Krankenhauseinweisung oder einer Heimunterbringung ist weniger die Art und Schwere der begangenen Straftat als vielmehr die Rückfallgefahr maßgebend. Um die zeitliche Unbestimmtheit dieser Maßregeln im Interesse einer größeren Rechtssicherheit einzuschränken, ist im Jahr 2000 eine grundsätzliche Höchstdauer von fünf Jahren eingeführt worden (§§ 68 a, 69 a strl.). Ausgenommen von dieser Regelung sind Strafsachen wegen schwerer Gewalt- und Sexualverbrechen sowie Brandstiftung.

2. "Präventiver Polizeigewahrsam" (Polizeirecht statt Strafrecht)

Gemäß § 5 Polizeigesetz (*lov om politiets virksomhed, politiloven*, pl.) ist die Polizei verpflichtet, Gefahren einer Störung der öffentlichen Ordnung sowie Gefahren für die Sicherheit einzelner Personen oder der Allgemeinheit abzuwehren. Sofern weniger eingreifende Mittel zur Gefahrenabwehr nicht ausreichend sind, kann die Polizei denjenigen, von dem die Gefahr ausgeht, unter Anwendung von Zwang in Gewahrsam nehmen (§ 5 Abs. 3, § 15 Nr. 1 pl.). Die Freiheitsentziehung muss so kurzzeitig und schonend wie möglich erfolgen und soll nach Möglichkeit nicht länger als sechs Stunden andauern.

Gegenüber gefährlichen Geisteskranken besteht die Möglichkeit einer zwangsweisen Unterbringung und Behandlung in einer psychiatrischen Einrichtung, selbst wenn sie keine Straftat begangen haben.[44] Dies gilt im Hinblick auf Selbstgefährdung ebenso wie auf Fremdgefährdung.

44. § 6 Bekendtgørelse af lov om frihedsberøvelse og tvang i psykiatrien, Nr. 111 vom 1.11.2006.

3. *Anwendung freiheitsbeschränkender Maßnahmen auf polizeirechtlicher Grundlage*

Im Rahmen ihrer Aufgabe der Gefahrenabwehr ist die Polizei auch befugt, Verbote und Gebote auszusprechen, die etwa den Aufenthalt an bestimmten Plätzen und den Kontakt mit bestimmten Personen betreffen.

E. Aktuelle Reformbestrebungen

Es bestehen derzeit keine Reformbestrebungen auf dem Gebiet freiheitsentziehender Maßnahmen gegen gefährliche, strafrechtlich verantwortliche (Rückfall-)Täter.

Wie bereits oben (C.9.a) erwähnt, wird in der dänischen Strafrechtswissenschaft vereinzelt die Ansicht vertreten, dass die in § 4 Abs. 1 strl. ausdrücklich vorgesehene Rückwirkung von gesetzlichen Bestimmungen zur Verwahrung aufgrund des strafähnlichen Charakters dieser Sanktion unzulässig sei. Der Gesetzeswortlaut steht dem jedoch entgegen.

Eine in der öffentlichen Diskussion häufig geäußerte Kritik richtet sich gegen die verbreitete Praxis der chemischen Kastration im Verwahrungsvollzug für Sexualverbrecher. Formell handelt es sich um eine freiwillige Behandlung. Jedoch beeinflusst eine Weigerung des Verwahrten die Entscheidung der Anstaltsleitung über seine Entlassung. In diesem Zusammenhang wird geltend gemacht, dass über eventuelle Langzeitwirkungen der verwendeten Medikamente bisher noch keine Erkenntnisse vorliegen.

Weder diese Beanstandungen noch die seit Langem bestehende Skepsis gegenüber der Zuverlässigkeit von Rückfallprognosen haben zu konkreten Änderungsvorhaben geführt.

F. Rechtstatsächliches Material

1. *Beispielsfälle aus der Praxis*

Beispiele aus der höchstrichterlichen Rechtsprechung:[45]

U 1996.103 H; U 1999.965 H: Der zur Tatzeit 22-jährige Angeklagte war viermal vorbestraft wegen schwerer Gewalttaten (darunter schwerer Raub). Obwohl im rechtspsychiatrischen Gutachten eine naheliegende Gefahr i.S. von § 70 Abs. 1 Nr. 2 strl. festgestellt worden war, hob der Oberste Gerichtshof das erstinstanzliche Verwahrungsurteil auf und verhängte für die aktuelle Tat (Raub) eine Gefängnisstrafe von zwei Jahren und sechs Monaten. Das Gericht begründete dies mit der Jugend und Unreife des Angeklagten sowie

45. Entscheidungen des Obersten Gerichtshofs (*Højesteret*, H), veröffentlicht in *Ugeskrift for Retsvæsen* (U). Weitere Beispiele in Fußnote 36.

mit der allgemein gebotenen Zurückhaltung in der Anwendung der Verwahrung. Als derselbe Angeklagte sich kurz nach seiner Entlassung aus dem Anstaltsvollzug erneut mehrerer schwerer Gewalttaten (darunter schwerer Raub und Nötigung) schuldig gemacht hatte, wurde er zu Verwahrung verurteilt und diese Entscheidung vom Obersten Gerichtshof bestätigt.

U 1998.906 H: Der wegen besonders gefährlicher Körperverletzung Angeklagte war zuvor mehrfach wegen einschlägiger Taten verurteilt worden, zuletzt sechs Jahre vor der aktuellen Tat. Auf der Grundlage des rechtspsychiatrischen Gutachtens erkannte das Landgericht auf Verwahrung. Der Oberste Gerichtshof hingegen verneinte eine naheliegende Gefahr i.S. von § 70 Abs. 1 Nr. 2 strl. und verurteilte den Angeklagten zu sechs Jahren Gefängnis.

U 2003.818 H: Der Angeklagte, mehrfach vorbestraft (u.a. wegen vorsätzlicher Tötung und schwerer Gewaltanwendung), hatte sich einer schweren Bedrohung und eines Tötungsversuchs schuldig gemacht. Entgegen dem rechtspsychiatrischen Gutachten und der Schwurgerichtsentscheidung fand der Oberste Gerichtshof es bedenklich, eine naheliegende Gefährlichkeit anzunehmen, und erkannte auf drei Jahre Gefängnis.

U 2006.970 und 2406 H: Der zur Tatzeit 17-jährige, nicht vorbestrafte Angeklagte wurde schuldig befunden, eine 18-jährige Frau unmotiviert und in besonders brutaler Weise (mehr als 27 Messerstiche in Hals, Brust und Bauch, Würgegriff und Faustschlägen ins Gesicht) getötet zu haben. In dem psychiatrischen Gutachten wurde die Verwahrung befürwortet, der Rechtsmedizinische Rat fand dagegen die Indikation einer Verwahrung nicht hinreichend sicher belegt. Das Untergericht erkannte auf acht Jahre Gefängnis (die Höchststrafe für minderjährige Straftäter), das Obergericht ordnete Verwahrung an, der Oberste Gerichtshof bestätigte das erstinstanzliche Urteil.

U 2007.2399 H: Das Verwahrungsurteil des Schwurgerichts gegen einen zwölfmal einschlägig vorbestraften Mann, der nach Entweichen aus dem Anstaltsvollzug seine frühere Geliebte mehrfach auf besonders brutale und gefährliche Weise misshandelt hatte, wurde vom Obersten Gerichtshof bestätigt.

U 2008.649 H: In dieser Strafsache wegen Raubes und wiederholter besonders gefährlicher Körperverletzung, begangen während eines Ausgangs aus dem Anstaltsvollzug, wurde der Angeklagte mit Rücksicht darauf, dass er sechsmal einschlägig vorbestraft war, zu Verwahrung verurteilt.

U 2008.905 H: Das Schwurgericht hatte mit 16 zu 8 Stimmen den Angeklagten wegen besonders gefährlicher Körperverletzung zu einem Jahr und sechs Monaten Gefängnis verurteilt; das Minderheitsvotum lautete auf Verwahrung. Der Angeklagte war mehrfach vorbestraft, u.a. war er 1994 wegen vorsätzlicher Tötung zu 15 Jahren Gefängnis verurteilt worden und hatte die aktuelle Tat während der Bewährungszeit begangen. Der Oberste Gerichtshof sah trotz des langen Zeitabstands zu dem Tötungsdelikt eine naheliegende Gefahr i.S. von § 70 Abs. 1 Nr. 2 strl. für gegeben an und erkannte auf Verwahrung.

2. Statistische Angaben

Im Durchschnitt ergehen drei bis vier Verwahrungsurteile pro Jahr (1998: 7; 1999: 3; 2000: 3; 2001: 4; 2002: 4; 2003: 1; 2004: 5; 2005: 4; 2006: 0; 2007: 3).[46]

2007 befanden sich durchschnittlich 30,6 Verurteilte in Verwahrung. Diese Zahl ist in den letzten zehn Jahren kontinuierlich gestiegen. 1998 lag sie noch bei 19,9 Personen.[47]

Die durchschnittliche Vollstreckungsdauer nimmt ebenfalls zu und liegt heute bei etwa zehn Jahren.

G. Schlussbemerkung

Aufgrund von Art und Schwere der Anlasstaten sowie auch angesichts der Vorverurteilungen wäre für den Beschwerdeführer M. (BS) nach dänischem Recht die Anordnung der Verwahrung anstelle einer Gefängnisstrafe in Betracht gekommen.

Dies hätte vorausgesetzt, dass im Strafverfahren wegen der Anlasstat eine Mentaluntersuchung durchgeführt worden wäre mit der Feststellung einer von dem Angeklagten ausgehenden naheliegenden Gefahr für Leib, Leben oder Freiheit anderer, dass der Gerichtsmedizinische Rat die Gefährlichkeit des Angeklagten bestätigt und das Gericht sich dieser Einschätzung angeschlossen hätte. Die Verwahrung hätte im Strafurteil wegen der Anlasstat verhängt werden müssen und nicht nachträglich angeordnet werden können. Die Fortdauer der zeitlich unbestimmten Verwahrung wäre spätestens nach Ablauf von drei Vollzugsjahren jährlich zu überprüfen.

Vor dem Hintergrund der Rechtspraxis während der letzten zehn Jahre spricht eine gewisse Wahrscheinlichkeit dafür, dass in einem Fall wie dem des BS die Verwahrung angeordnet worden wäre, jedoch kann nicht mit Sicherheit davon ausgegangen werden.

46. http://www.statistikbanken.dk/statbank5a/default.asp?w=1024; Danmarks Statistik (Hrsg.), Kriminalitet 2007, S. 73.
47. http://kriminalforsorgen.dk

Anhang

Auszüge aus dem dänischen Strafgesetz (*straffelov*, strl.) vom 15.4.1930 in der Fassung der Bekanntmachung Nr. 1260 vom 23.10.2007

§ 3

Stk. 1. Er den ved en handlings påkendelse gældende straffelovgivning forskellig fra den, der gjaldt ved handlingens foretagelse, afgøres spørgsmålet om strafbarhed og straf efter den senere lov, dog at afgørelsen ikke derved må blive strengere end efter den ældre lov. Beror ophøret af lovens gyldighed på ydre, strafskylden uvedkommende forhold, bliver handlingen at bedømme efter den ældre lov.
Stk. 2. Bortfalder uden for sidstnævnte tilfælde ved lov en handlings strafbarhed, bortfalder også den for sådan handling idømte, men ikke fuldbyrdede straf. Den dømte kan forlange, at spørgsmålet om straffens bortfald ved påtalemyndighedens foranstaltning indbringes for den ret, der har påkendt sagen i første instans. Afgørelsen træffes ved kendelse.

§ 4

Stk. 1. Hvorvidt den strafbare handling skal medføre retsfølger af sådan art som i §§ 56–61, 62–70, 73 og 79 nævnt, afgøres efter den ved handlingens påkendelse gældende lovgivning.
Stk. 2. Andre retsfølger af handlingen indtræder, for så vidt intet modsat er bestemt, kun, når dette var hjemlet også ved den ved handlingens foretagelse gældende lovgivning.
Stk. 3. Bestemmelsen i § 3, stk. 2, finder tilsvarende anvendelse på andre retsfølger af handlingen end straf, hvis deres indtræden var betinget af handlingens strafbarhed.

§ 68

Hvis en tiltalt frifindes for straf i medfør af § 16, kan retten træffe bestemmelse om anvendelse af andre foranstaltninger, der findes formålstjenlige for at forebygge yderligere lovovertrædelser. Såfremt mindre indgribende foranstaltninger som tilsyn, bestemmelser vedrørende opholdssted eller arbejde, afvænningsbehandling, psykiatrisk behandling m.v. ikke findes tilstrækkelige, kan det bestemmes, at den pågældende skal anbringes i hospital for sindslidende, i institution for personer med vidtgående psykiske handicap eller under tilsyn med mulighed for administrativ anbringelse eller i egnet hjem eller institution til særlig pleje eller forsorg. Anbringelse i forvaring kan ske under de betingelser, der er nævnt i § 70.

§ 68 a

Stk. 1. Medfører en foranstaltning efter § 68 eller § 72, jf. § 68, at den dømte skal anbringes i institution, eller giver foranstaltningen mulighed herfor, fastsættes en længstetid på 5 år for denne foranstaltning. Længstetiden omfatter også foranstaltninger, som senere fastsættes efter § 72, jf. § 68, og som medfører en lempelse af den hidtidige foranstaltning. Under særlige omstændigheder kan retten efter anmodning fra anklagemyndigheden ved kendelse fastsætte en ny længstetid på 2 år.
Stk. 2. I de tilfælde, der er omhandlet i stk. 1, fastsættes dog i almindelighed ingen længstetid, hvis den dømte findes skyldig i drab, røveri, frihedsberøvelse, alvorlig voldsforbrydelse, trusler af den i § 266 nævnte art, brandstiftelse, voldtægt eller anden alvorlig sædelighedsforbrydelse eller i forsøg på en af de nævnte forbrydelser. Er der ikke fastsat en længstetid, indbringer anklagemyndigheden spørgsmålet om ændring eller endelig ophævelse af foranstaltningen for retten 5 år efter afgørelsen, medmindre spørgsmålet har været forelagt for retten inden for de sidste to år. Derefter forelægges spørgsmålet for retten mindst hvert andet år.
Stk. 3. Ved andre foranstaltninger end de i stk. 1 nævnte fastsættes en længstetid for foranstaltningen, der ikke kan overstige 3 år. Under særlige omstændigheder kan retten efter anmodning fra anklagemyndigheden ved kendelse forlænge længstetiden. Den samlede tid for foranstaltningen kan ikke overstige 5 år.

§ 69

Befandt gerningsmanden sig ved den strafbare handlings foretagelse i en tilstand, der var betinget af mangelfuld udvikling, svækkelse eller forstyrrelse af de psykiske funktioner, og som ikke er af den i § 16 nævnte beskaffenhed, kan retten, såfremt det findes formålstjenligt, i stedet for at idømme straf træffe bestemmelse om foranstaltninger som nævnt i § 68, 2. pkt.

§ 69 a

Stk. 1. Medfører en foranstaltning efter § 69, at den dømte skal anbringes i institution, eller giver foranstaltningen mulighed herfor, fastsættes en længstetid på 5 år for denne foranstaltning og en længstetid for opholdet, der i almindelighed ikke kan overstige 1 år. Længstetiden på 5 år omfatter også foranstaltninger, som senere fastsættes efter § 72, jf. § 69 og § 68, 2. pkt., og som medfører en lempelse af den hidtidige foranstaltning. Under særlige omstændigheder kan retten efter anmodning fra anklagemyndigheden ved kendelse fastsætte en ny længstetid på 2 år for foranstaltningen eller en ny længstetid for opholdet.
Stk. 2. I de tilfælde, der er omhandlet i stk. 1, fastsættes dog i almindelighed ingen længstetid for foranstaltningen, hvis den dømte findes skyldig i drab, røveri, frihedsberøvelse, alvorlig voldsforbrydelse, trusler af den i § 266 nævnte art, brandstiftelse, voldtægt eller anden alvorlig sædelighedsforbrydelse eller i forsøg på en af de nævnte forbrydelser. § 68 a, stk. 2, 2. og 3. pkt., finder tilsvarende anvendelse.
Stk. 3. Ved andre foranstaltninger end de i stk. 1 nævnte fastsættes en længstetid for foranstaltningen, der ikke kan overstige 3 år. Under særlige omstændigheder kan retten efter anmodning fra anklagemyndigheden ved kendelse forlænge længstetiden. Den samlede tid for foranstaltningen kan ikke overstige 5 år.

§ 70

Stk. 1. En person kan dømmes til forvaring, hvis

1) han findes skyldig i drab, røveri, frihedsberøvelse, alvorlig voldsforbrydelse, trusler af den i § 266 nævnte art eller brandstiftelse eller i forsøg på en af de nævnte forbrydelser, og
2) det efter karakteren af det begåede forhold og oplysningerne om hans person, herunder navnlig om tidligere kriminalitet, må antages, at han frembyder nærliggende fare for andres liv, legeme, helbred eller frihed, og
3) anvendelse af forvaring i stedet for fængsel findes påkrævet for at forebygge denne fare.

Stk. 2. En person kan endvidere dømmes til forvaring, hvis

1) han findes skyldig i voldtægt eller anden alvorlig sædelighedsforbrydelse eller i forsøg herpå, og
2) det efter karakteren af det begåede forhold og oplysningerne om hans person, herunder om tidligere kriminalitet, må antages, at han frembyder væsentlig fare for andres liv, legeme, helbred eller frihed, og
3) anvendelse af forvaring i stedet for fængsel findes påkrævet for at forebygge denne fare.

§ 72

Stk. 1. Det påhviler anklagemyndigheden at påse, at en foranstaltning efter §§ 68, 69 eller 70 ikke opretholdes i længere tid og videre omfang end nødvendigt.

Stk. 2. Bestemmelse om ændring eller endelig ophævelse af en foranstaltning efter §§ 68, 69 eller 70 træffes ved kendelse efter anmodning fra den dømte, bistandsværgen, anklagemyndigheden, institutionens ledelse eller kriminalforsorgen. Anmodning fra den dømte, bistandsværgen, institutionens ledelse eller kriminalforsorgen fremsættes over for anklagemyndigheden, der snarest muligt indbringer spørgsmålet for retten. Tages en anmodning fra den dømte eller bistandsværgen ikke til følge, kan ny anmodning ikke fremsættes, før der er forløbet et halvt år fra kendelsens afsigelse.

Stk. 3. Bestemmelsen i § 59, stk. 2, finder tilsvarende anvendelse på afgørelser efter stk. 2. Er der spørgsmål om ændring af foranstaltningen på grund af ny lovovertrædelse, afgøres spørgsmålet dog af den ret, der behandler sagen vedrørende overtrædelsen.

§ 81

Det skal ved straffens fastsættelse i almindelighed indgå som skærpende omstændighed,

1) at gerningsmanden tidligere er straffet af betydning for sagen,

   [...]

§ 84

Stk. 1. Det er en betingelse for anvendelse af bestemmelser om forhøjet straf eller andre retsfølger i gentagelsestilfælde, at gerningsmanden, inden den pågældende på ny forbrød sig, i den danske stat er fundet skyldig i en begået strafbar handling, som loven tillægger gentagelsesvirkning på den nu begåede, eller forsøg på eller medvirken til en sådan.

Stk. 2. Retten kan tillægge straffedomme afsagt uden for den danske stat samme gentagelsesvirkning som de her i landet afsagte.

Stk. 3. Gentagelsesvirkningen ophører, når der, førend den nye strafbare handling blev begået, er forløbet 10 år, efter at den tidligere straf er udstået, endelig eftergivet eller bortfaldet. Er den tidligere straf en bødestraf, regnes den nævnte frist fra datoen for den endelige dom eller bødens vedtagelse. Med hensyn til betingede domme regnes fristen fra den endelige dom.

Deutsche übersetzung*

§ 3*

(1) Ist das zur Zeit der Aburteilung einer Tat geltende Strafrecht verschieden von dem, das zur Zeit der Tatbegehung galt, so bestimmen sich Strafbarkeit und Strafe nach dem späteren Gesetz, jedoch mit der Maßgabe, dass die Entscheidung dadurch nicht strenger als nach dem früheren Gesetz ausfallen darf. Beruht das Außerkrafttreten des Gesetzes auf äußeren, die Strafwürdigkeit nicht berührenden Umständen, so ist die Tat nach dem früheren Gesetz zu beurteilen.
(2) Entfällt abgesehen von dem letzteren Fall die Strafbarkeit einer Tat durch Gesetz, so entfällt auch die für eine solche Tat verhängte, aber noch nicht vollstreckte Strafe. Der Verurteilte kann verlangen, dass die Anklagebehörde die Frage des Wegfalls der Strafe dem Gericht vorlegt, das die Sache erstinstanzlich abgeurteilt hat. Die Entscheidung ergeht durch Beschluss.

§ 4

(1) Inwiefern die Tat Rechtsfolgen der in §§ 56-61, 62-70, 73 und 79 genannten Art nach sich zieht, bestimmt sich nach den zur Zeit ihrer Aburteilung geltenden Gesetzen.
(2) Andere Rechtsfolgen der Tat treten, soweit nichts Gegenteiliges bestimmt ist, nur ein, wenn dies auch nach den zur Zeit der Tatbegehung geltenden Gesetzen vorgesehen war.
(3) Die Vorschrift des § 3 Abs. 2 findet entsprechende Anwendung auf andere Rechtsfolgen der Tat als Strafe, wenn deren Eintritt von der Strafbarkeit der Tat abhängig war.

§ 68

Wird ein Angeklagter gemäß § 16 nicht bestraft, so kann das Gericht andere Maßregeln anordnen, die es für zweckdienlich befindet, um weiteren Straftaten vorzubeugen. Sofern weniger eingreifende Maßnahmen wie Bewährungsaufsicht, Anordnungen bezüglich Aufenthaltsort oder Arbeit, Entziehungskur, psychiatrischer Behandlung u.ä. nicht ausreichend sind, kann angeordnet werden, dass der Betreffende in einem psychiatrischen Krankenhaus oder einer Einrichtung für Personen mit weitgehender psychischer Behinderung untergebracht oder unter Aufsicht mit der Möglichkeit einer verwaltungsrechtlichen Unterbringung gestellt oder in ein geeignetes Heim oder eine Anstalt zur besonderen Pflege oder Fürsorge eingewiesen wird. Eine Unterbringung in Sicherungsverwahrung kann unter den in § 70 genannten Voraussetzungen erfolgen.

* Deutsche Übersetzung *Karin Cornils/Vagn Greve*.

§ 68 a

(1) Hat eine Maßregel nach § 68 oder § 72 i.V.m. § 68 zur Folge oder eröffnet sie die Möglichkeit, dass der Verurteilte in einer Anstalt untergebracht wird, so ist für diese Maßregel eine Höchstdauer von 5 Jahren festzusetzen. Die Höchstdauer umfasst auch Maßnahmen, die später gemäß § 72 i.V.m. § 68 angeordnet werden und die zu einer Erleichterung der bisherigen Maßregel führen. Unter besonderen Umständen kann das Gericht auf Antrag der Anklagebehörde durch Beschluss eine neue Höchstdauer von 2 Jahren festsetzen.
(2) In den Fällen des Abs. 1 wird jedoch in der Regel keine Höchstdauer festgesetzt, wenn der Verurteilte der Tötung, des Raubes, der Freiheitsberaubung, eines schweren Gewaltverbrechens, der Bedrohung im Sinne von § 266, der Brandstiftung, der Vergewaltigung oder eines anderen schweren Sittlichkeitsverbrechens oder des Versuchs eines der genannten Verbrechen schuldig befunden wird. Ist keine Höchstdauer festgesetzt worden, so legt die Anklagebehörde 5 Jahre nach der Entscheidung dem Gericht die Frage einer Änderung oder endgültigen Aufhebung der Maßregel vor, sofern nicht diese Frage innerhalb der letzten 2 Jahre dem Gericht vorgelegt worden ist. Danach ist die Frage dem Gericht mindestens jedes zweite Jahr vorzulegen.
(3) Für andere als die in Abs. 1 genannten Maßregeln wird eine Höchstdauer festgesetzt, die 3 Jahre nicht überschreiten darf. Unter besonderen Umständen kann das Gericht auf Antrag der Anklagebehörde durch Beschluss die Höchstdauer verlängern. Die Gesamtdauer der Maßregel darf 5 Jahre nicht überschreiten.

§ 69

Befand sich der Täter bei Begehung der strafbaren Handlung in einem Zustand, der durch mangelhafte Entwicklung, Schwächung oder Störung der psychischen Funktionen bedingt und nicht von der in § 16 genannten Art war, so kann das Gericht, sofern es dies für zweckdienlich befindet, anstatt eine Strafe zu verhängen, Maßnahmen im Sinne von § 68 Satz 2 anordnen.

§ 69 a

(1) Hat eine Maßregel nach § 69 zur Folge oder eröffnet sie die Möglichkeit, dass der Verurteilte in einer Anstalt untergebracht wird, so ist eine Höchstdauer von 5 Jahren für diese Maßregel festzusetzen und eine Höchstdauer für die Unterbringung, die in der Regel 1 Jahr nicht überschreiten darf. Die Höchstdauer von 5 Jahren umfasst auch Maßnahmen, die später nach § 72 i.V.m. § 69 und § 68 Satz 2 angeordnet werden und zu einer Erleichterung der bisherigen Maßregel führen. Unter besonderen Umständen kann das Gericht auf Antrag der Anklagebehörde durch Beschluss eine neue Höchstdauer von 2 Jahren für die Maßregel oder eine neue Höchstdauer für die Unterbringung festsetzen.
(2) In den Fällen des Abs. 1 wird jedoch in der Regel keine Höchstdauer für die Maßregel festgesetzt, wenn der Verurteilte der Tötung, des Raubes, der Freiheitsberaubung, eines schweren Gewaltverbrechens, der Bedrohung im Sinne von § 266, der Brandstiftung, der Vergewaltigung oder eines anderen schweren Sittlichkeitsverbrechens oder des Versuchs eines der genannten Verbrechen schuldig befunden wird. § 68 a Abs. 2 Satz 2 und 3 finden entsprechende Anwendung.
(3) Für andere als die in Abs. 1 genannten Maßregeln wird eine Höchstdauer festgesetzt, die 3 Jahre nicht überschreiten darf. Unter besonderen Umständen kann das Gericht auf

Antrag der Anklagebehörde durch Beschluss die Höchstdauer verlängern. Die Gesamtdauer der Maßregel darf 5 Jahre nicht überschreiten.

§ 70

(1) Jemand kann zu Verwahrung verurteilt werden, wenn
1. er der Tötung, des Raubes, der Freiheitsberaubung, eines anderen schweren Gewaltverbrechens, der Bedrohung im Sinne von § 266 oder der Brandstiftung oder des Versuchs eines der genannten Verbrechen schuldig befunden wird und
2. aufgrund der Art der begangenen Tat und der Feststellungen über seine Person, insbesondere über frühere Kriminalität, anzunehmen ist, dass er eine naheliegende Gefahr für Leben, Leib, Gesundheit oder Freiheit anderer darstellt, und
3. die Verwahrung anstelle einer Gefängnisstrafe notwendig ist, um dieser Gefahr vorzubeugen.

(2) Jemand kann ferner zu Verwahrung verurteilt werden, wenn
1. er der Vergewaltigung oder eines anderen schweren Sittlichkeitsverbrechens oder des Versuchs einer solchen Straftat für schuldig befunden wird und
2. aufgrund der Art der begangenen Tat und der Feststellungen über seine Person, unter anderem über frühere Kriminalität, anzunehmen ist, dass er eine erhebliche Gefahr für Leben, Leib, Gesundheit oder Freiheit anderer darstellt, und
3. die Verwahrung anstelle einer Gefängnisstrafe notwendig ist, um dieser Gefahr vorzubeugen.

§ 72

(1) Es obliegt der Anklagebehörde, dafür Sorge zu tragen, dass eine Maßnahme nach §§ 68, 69 oder 70 nicht für längere Zeit und in weiterem Umfang als notwendig aufrechterhalten wird.

(2) Eine Entscheidung über die Änderung oder endgültige Aufhebung einer Maßnahme nach §§ 68, 69 oder 70 ergeht durch Beschluss auf Antrag des Verurteilten, des Beistands, der Anklagebehörde, der Anstaltsleitung oder des Strafvollzugsamtes. Ein Antrag des Verurteilten, des Beistands, der Anstaltsleitung oder des Strafvollzugsamtes ist an die Anklagebehörde zu richten, die die Frage so bald als möglich dem Gericht vorlegt. Wird einem Antrag des Verurteilten oder des Beistands nicht stattgegeben, so kann ein neuer Antrag frühestens nach Ablauf eines halben Jahres seit dem Erlass des Beschlusses gestellt werden.

(3) [Grundsätzliche Zuständigkeit des erstinstanzlichen Gerichts]

§ 81

Bei der Festsetzung der Strafe ist es im Allgemeinen als erschwerender Umstand zu werten, wenn
1. gegen den Täter bereits früher eine für die vorliegende Strafsache bedeutsame Verurteilung ergangen ist,

   […]

§ 84

(1) Die Anwendung der Vorschriften über eine erhöhte Strafe oder andere Rechtsfolgen bei Rückfall setzt voraus, dass der Täter, bevor er erneut straffällig geworden ist, im dänischen Staat einer begangenen strafbaren Handlung, der das Gesetz im Verhältnis zu der später begangenen Tat Rückfallwirkung beimisst, oder des Versuchs oder der Beteiligung an einer solchen strafbaren Handlung schuldig befunden worden ist.

(2) Das Gericht kann einem im Ausland ergangenen Strafurteil die gleiche Rückfallwirkung beimessen wie den im Inland ergangenen.

(3) Die Rückfallwirkung entfällt, wenn vor der Begehung der neuen strafbaren Handlung 10 Jahre vergangen waren, seitdem die frühere Strafe verbüßt, rechtskräftig erlassen oder erloschen war. War die frühere Strafe eine Geldstrafe, so beginnt die genannte Frist mit dem Datum des rechtskräftigen Urteils oder der Annahme der Geldstrafe. Bei bedingten Urteilen beginnt die Frist mit dem rechtskräftigen Urteil.

Abkürzungsverzeichnis

Abs.	Absatz
a.F.	alte Fassung
Aufl.	Auflage
BEK	bekendtgørelse – Bekanntmachung, Anordnung
Bet.	betænkning – (Reform-)Gutachten
bzw.	beziehungsweise
EMRK	Europäische Konvention zum Schutze der Menschenrechte und Grundfreiheiten
ff.	fortfolgende
H	Højesteret – Oberster Gerichtshof
Hrsg.	Herausgeber
i.S.	im Sinne
m.v.	med videre – und Weiteres
pl.	lov om politiets virksomhed, politiloven – Polizeigesetz
Nr.	Nummer
S.	Seite
sfbl.	straffuldbyrdelseslov – Strafvollstreckungsgesetz
strl.	straffelov – Strafgesetz
U	Ugeskrift for Retsvæsen – juristische Fachzeitschrift
u.a.	und andere, unter anderem
u.Ä.	und Ähnliches
VEJ	vejledning – Richtlinie
vgl.	vergleiche

Participation in Crime: Criminal Liability of Leaders of Criminal Groups and Networks in Denmark[1]

I. General description of the legal system's approach to forms of participation

A. Introduction

1. Terminology

The Danish Criminal Code contains only one common concept for offenses of participation. Section 23 of the Criminal Code, which is the general rule, uses the Danish word *medvirken*, which linguistically can be translated to *participation*. The word assumes that there is more than one (potentially) liable party. The code further uses the Danish word *gerningsmand*, i.e., "the man who commits the act", here translated to "offender". It is utilized as a term both for one person, who single-handedly is (potentially) liable for an offense, as well as for one or more (potential) participators; about co-perpetrators see especially the rules for determining the penalty in Sections 80–84 of the Criminal Code (which are recited below in section D.2). In the legal literature the term *gerningsmand* is sometimes substituted with the gender-neutral synonym *gerningsperson*, i.e., "the person who commits the act".

1. Prof. *Vagn Greve* is professor of criminal law at the University of Copenhagen. The report is translated by *Malene Frese Jensen*. Quotations are translated from Danish unless indicated otherwise.

2. The Danish kingdom

The Kingdom of Denmark consists of three regions: Denmark, the Faroe Islands and Greenland. The three regions have different legislation, including different criminal codes, the latter of which in many areas are quite dissimilar as the Greenlandic criminal code to a great extent reflects an ideology fundamentally different from the Danish and the Faroese. These two are essentially identical. Only Danish criminal law is described in the following; the substance of the report will in essence convey the Faroese law but not necessarily the Greenlandic.

3. Categorization of crimes

The Danish criminal law does not make a differentiation between a category of serious offenses and another concerning less serious offenses. Further – as for the matters discussed in this report – exactly the same general rules apply to offenses that fall under the Special Part of the Criminal Code, as to offenses that are criminalized pursuant to special areas of legislation. The Criminal Code used to be called the Civil Criminal Code to set it apart from the Military Criminal Code. A Military Criminal Code is still in effect,[2] but even so, its rules of participation are generally the same as those that apply in the civil criminal law.[3]

In this unitary system of Denmark it is thus permissible, as a rule, to assume that theoretical analyses and case law from one area of criminal law also can be taken as an indication of what applies in other areas of criminal law. Yet, this should not be construed as complete homogeneity. There are special provisions and there are special kinds of offenses for which the general rules do not apply or do not apply fully; such special rules can result in both an extension as well as a restriction of the criminal liability.

4. History and ideology

Danish criminal law was in the eighteen hundreds strongly influenced by the German participation theories of the time. However, around the turn of the century the differentiations between categories of participators and offenders were strongly criticized in Danish-Norwegian legal literature. The 1930 Danish Criminal Code consequently departed from these principles and stipulated that there is an independent basis of liability for the participants. It further established that the blame and thus the sentencing decision could not be tied to

2. Law No. 530 of 24 June 2005.
3. Compare Report No. 1435, p. 371.

the differentiation participator-offender; rather the actual circumstances of each individual person should be the basis for determining the sentence. Consequently – depending on the given circumstances – the fact that several individuals are involved can be both an aggravating as well as a mitigating factor compared to those situations, where one individual single-handedly commits an equivalent offense.

Words like "participate" are sometimes used in indictments and judgments. It is important to note that the use of such words, or the omission of their use, has no significance for the finding of guilt. It is not a category different from the one that concerns individuals, who have carried out everything single-handedly.

The 1930 Criminal Code is still in effect. No real changes have been made since 1930 as for the rules about criminal liability for participation. The provisions governing the sentencing decision have, on the other hand, been radically restructured and specified in 2004,[4] but this restructuring, specification and rewording have not changed the fundamental principles. We thus consistently apply an *Einheitstäterbegriff*. In the Danish legal literature the participation system is characterized as being "negative", because it declines to differentiate between the different groups of criminally liable parties.[5] Neither in the legal literature nor politically has this *Einheitstäter*-system been criticized.

In modern times the criminal liability of corporations has steadily been extended, resulting in legal persons now almost always being liable on equal terms with physical persons.[6]

In the Special Part of the Criminal Code offenses are typically worded "Any person who does such and such ..."; in the special areas of legislation other models are used. Common is that "any" as a rule includes single-handedly liable individuals as well as participants, and physical as well as legal persons.

4. Law No. 219 of 31 March 2004 about changes of the Criminal Code and the Administration of Justice Act (changes of sentencing ranges and provisions about sentencing, etc.).
5. See *Hurwitz*, Almindelig del (General Part), pp. 493 ff., and *Greve*, Det strafferetlige ansvar (The Criminal Liability), pp. 161 ff.
6. This is the case both as for the Criminal Code, pursuant to its Section 306, as well as for the Military Criminal Code, pursuant to its Section 8(2), and also the great majority of special areas of legislation.

B. Basic structure and consequences of the legal system's approach to forms of participation[7]

1. How and where the legal system deals with forms of participation

The general rules about participation can be found in the Criminal Code's fourth chapter about "Attempt and Complicity". In the legal literature it is pointed out how similar the function of the attempt rules and the participation rules is in reality. A narrow word interpretation of the different offense descriptions will, in the typical cases, lead to the conclusion that criminal liability presupposes presence of all elements of the offense and that the criminally liable person actually must have fulfilled all the requirements of the provision. Pursuant to the principle *nulla poena sine lege*, which in Danish law is expressed in Section 1 of the Criminal Code, it would consequently be impossible to hold criminally liable a person, who only had committed part of the elements of a crime or only had aided another person to commit the criminal act. The rules of Chapter 4 thus extend the criminalized area to also include attempt and participation. In parts of the legal literature the rules of participation are consequently regarded as rules that in reality are part of the statutory elements that constitute an offense.[8] In another part of the legal literature the issue of participation is considered a means for defining the circle of individuals that can be held liable.[9] The approach has significance for the systematic and didactical presentation, but the different views of the system has not resulted in conflicting views of the extent of the criminal liability.

The rules of participation in Chapter 4 of the Criminal Code read like this:

§ 23.

(1) The penalty in respect of an offense shall apply to any person who has contributed to the execution of the wrongful act by instigation, advice or action. The punishment may be reduced for any person who has only intended to give assistance of minor importance, or to strengthen an intention already existing and if the offense has not been completed or an intended assistance has failed.

(2) The punishment may similarly be reduced for a person who has contributed to the breach of a duty in a special relationship in which he himself had no part.

(3) Unless otherwise provided, the penalty for participation in offenses that are not punishable more severely than with imprisonment for 4 months may be remitted where the accomplice only intended to give assistance of minor importance or to strengthen an intention already existing, or where his complicity is due to negligence.

7. See further Komm. strl. (Annotated Criminal Code) I, pp. 202 ff. and 218 ff.; *Greve*, Det strafferetlige ansvar (The Criminal Liability), pp. 161 ff.; *Toftegaard Nielsen*, Ansvaret (The Liability), pp. 195 ff.
8. *Toftegaard Nielsen*, Ansvaret (The Liability), pp. 195 ff.
9. *Greve*, Det strafferetlige ansvar (The Criminal Liability), pp. 161 ff.

§ 24.
The accomplice shall not be punished if, under the conditions laid down in Section 22 of this Act [i.e., the rules about withdrawal from attempt to commit an offense single-handedly], he prevents the completion of the offense or takes steps which would have prevented its completion had it not, without his knowledge, already been unsuccessful or averted in some other way.

As it appears, the range of the criminal liability is defined by Section 23(1) 1st period. These rules defining the liable subject are supplemented by the rules in the Chapter 5 of the Criminal Code about legal persons' liability and by various special rules in other areas of the system. When Section 23 mentions "instigation, advice or action", it does not imply that there are special rules for certain forms of participation or that a systematism based on these three forms shall be applied. It has no legal significance whether one characterizes a given conduct in one way or the other, for which reason only the main term of "participation" is used in Danish law.

The other parts of Section 23 concern matters of sentencing and can result in reduced punishment compared to what would have been indicated for a single-handedly committed act. These rules governing the determination of the punishment are supplemented by several provisions in Chapter 10 of the Criminal Code about determining the penalty and by various special rules in other areas of the system; depending on the circumstances the other rules can result in both increased as well as reduced punishment.

Pursuant to Section 2 of the Criminal Code, the general rules, described supra, apply to acts that are criminalized in the Special Part of the Criminal Code as well as in the special areas of legislation. The special areas of legislation include, as mentioned, also the Military Criminal Code.[10]

The Danish Criminal Code does not contain a common provision about the liability for omissions. A doctrine has developed in case law concerning this liability, which quite often is of importance especially for superiors' and other leaders' criminal liability. In keeping with the project description these questions are for the most part disregarded in the following.

2. Overview of forms of participation

Since Danish law, as mentioned above, does not ascribe special significance to the different forms of participation, these questions will only be addressed below in section C.

10. Compare Report No. 1435, p. 371.

3. Consequences of differentiating between forms of participation

As for culpability, the general rules do not distinguish between the individual who personally carry out all the necessary elements, and the individual who participates in carrying them out; see further below in section C. As for determining the punishment, more possibilities emerge – both in aggravating as well as in mitigating respects – when more individuals are involved in the crime; see further below in section D.

C. Description of forms of participation

1. The statutory basis and the range of the liability for participation[11]

In cases where several individuals cooperate in committing an offense the *general* rule in Danish law is Section 23(1) 1st period of the Criminal Code:

> The penalty in respect of an offense shall apply to any person who has contributed to the execution of the wrongful act by instigation, advice or action.

Section 23 of the Criminal Code extends the elements of all crimes unless the provision in question in itself contains a limitation to certain areas of criminal complicity. That is very seldom the case; compare below under section E. Hence, the general rule is that everyone, who cooperates in committing an offense, incurs the same criminal liability as it is stipulated in the statutory basis for the offense. Pursuant to Section 23 each person must be considered individually. The "participator" can thus without any conflict be punished, even if the "main perpetrator" is not punished, for example due to the latter's lack of sufficient *mens rea.*

The liability does not even presuppose that there is an individual, who is considered the "main perpetrator". A group of people, who each individually carry out a minor significant act, can together commit a violation of the law. This is, for example, often the case in the workplace and environment areas.

The participation provisions in Section 23 (and Section 24) of the Criminal Code can be applied to *all types of crimes* – the serious as well as the trivial, the intentional as well as the negligent. According to Section 2 of the Criminal Code the provisions also apply to other laws besides the Criminal Code, including military criminal law. Section 23 encompasses participation to consummated crimes as well as participation in attempted crimes. It is further possible, pursuant to Section 21, to punish for attempted participation.

11. See further Komm. strl. (Annotated Criminal Code) I, pp. 202 ff. and 218 ff.; *Greve*, Det strafferetlige ansvar (The Criminal Liability), pp. 161 ff.; *Toftegaard Nielsen*, Ansvaret (The Liability), pp. 195 ff.

As it follows from the earlier partial quote of Section 23 – "instigation, advice or action" – it is illegal both to influence the will and to influence the ability to violate the law. In Danish law a distinction is often made between "psychological" and "physical" participation. The psychological participation ("instigation") concerns another person's will; such acts of participation include incitements, solicitations, temptations and threats. If the purpose is to overcome another person's opposition it is called "incitement". Physical participation ("action") is all contributing deeds, including information about how the crime can be realized. Generally, it is only of importance whether the person cooperates with one or more other people to carry out actions intended to result in, or which actually do result in, a crime. Examples of participation include standing guard, lending of tools, and financing of illicit enterprises and contracts. "Advice" can, depending on the circumstances, take the form of psychological or physical participation. The influencing does not have to take place through words, but can take place through signs or other means.

A keeper of a gaol was convicted for assault. By twice lifting his fist up and down he had indicated that a guard should hit an inmate. (U.f.R. 1979.858 H)

The contribution, such as advice or an agreement, must be *concrete*, both as for a sufficient identification of victim and time of the crime, as well as for the elements of the crime. In this relation it becomes of some significance that Danish law has a very wide attempt concept; the victim is, for example, sufficiently identified, if the act is aimed at some house in a city or some person in a group. This subject has especially been analyzed within the teachings of attempt; however, when there is liability for attempt there will also be liability for a consummated crime. Inversely, there will be liability for attempt – at least for an attempt in its advanced form – if there would be liability for a consummated crime.

The collaboration can be concrete for a single crime or it can be a longer existing collaboration, where crimes are committed continually. It has no significance for the area of criminal liability as for the objective elements, but it may be of significance as for the subjective elements. If an individual knows that his collaborators several times have committed a crime under certain circumstances, he may be liable if he creates or participates in creating a new, similar situation. If his collaborators previously have committed rape against his female guests, he cannot avoid liability for participation if he once more invites a female friend and does not ensure that the others are not present.

During a ride a taxi driver became aware that the passenger's sack contained smuggled goods. An hour later he agreed to be hired by the same person, who also this time brought along a sack. Acquitted for the first transport, but convicted for participating to smuggling as for the other. (U.f.R. 1961.933 V)

Causation is usually *not* required in the restricted sense. Clumsy aid is still aid; bad advice is still advice. It is punishable as participation if B helps A carry away stolen goods, even if B is so clumsy that it makes the theft considerably more difficult for A. It is punishable for B to stand guard, even if A would have committed exactly the same crime without B's assistance. One has no impunity in regards to one's acts of violence, even if the precise same acts otherwise would have been committed by one's collaborators.

If B stands guard without A knowing so, B is in a situation of participation while A is not. It does not affect their liability, but it means that the special rules for determining the punishment for participation cannot be applied to A, but only to B.

It is difficult to define the objective area of participation exactly. There is, for example, a gradual transition from an *(incidental) cooperation*, which is not included under Section 23, to a negligent participation, which is included by Section 23. It is, however, obvious that not all acts, that are part of a crime's elements, have such a character that it is reasonable to describe the actor as "having contributed to the execution of the wrongful act". For example, several farmers' pollution of a stream following spring farm-work will often lack the joint character, which can prompt the application of Section 23. If it is not a case of cooperation but rather two or more independent occurrences, the applicable rule is not Section 23 but instead the principles of coexisting competing causes.

Gradual transitions also exist between the lawful *attendance of a crime* and the punishable participation through accompaniment of the person or persons, who carry out the actual acts.[12]

Communication over the *internet* involves several technical installations that are placed at the users' disposal. It can, for example, involve electronic message boards. Such interactions will fall within the Criminal Code's concept of participation so that the person, who posts an illegal text on the internet, and the person, who owns the technical installations, objectively are in a participation situation. In most cases the person who is responsible for the technical side is ignorant about the unlawful messages (e.g., racist smear campaigns, invasions of privacy and child pornography), and the necessary *mens rea* will consequently not be present as for that person. If the individual

12. See further *Toftegaard Nielsen*, Ansvaret (The Liability), pp. 209 ff. and below under 3.

has or ought to have the necessary knowledge but does nothing, then criminal liability can incur as for the continued communication on the message board.

Another area of gradual transition is from lawful notification of an illegal state of affairs to a punishable participation by offering *advice* as for a company's future dispositions, e.g., in the tax area. On one hand, the lawyer or accountant shall notify the client about all existing ways of reducing taxes. On the other hand, he must not propose unlawful dispositions.

Some recent judgments illustrate this:

An inn owner was convicted for participation to unlawful business conduct. He had leased the inn to some individuals who did not have trade and alcohol licenses. (U.f.R. 1983.1094 V)

An accountant had "single-handedly ... out of helpfulness toward an – by a co-defendant employed – office assistant in draft form ... drawn up a small part of the accounts, which formed the basis for ... the mentioned amount". He was convicted for participation in regard to violation of the Law of Value-Added Tax by the lower court and the High Court, but was acquitted by the Supreme Court due to expiration of the period of limitation. (U.f.R. 1988.640 H)

A and B attempted to enter a restaurant after midnight. The door keepers refused B entry. A told the door keepers that they would fetch a weapon and shoot them. B was standing next to A, when the statement was made. They left together, then drove together in A's car and got a sawn-off rifle. A carried the rifle when they returned to the restaurant and he fired it at the front hitting a window above the door. As the shot was fired A and B were standing close together. B was convicted for participation in violating the Criminal Code Section 252 about any person, who in a "reckless manner, exposes the life or physical ability of others to impending danger". (FM 1998.139 Ø)

T had participated in serving food and drinks for guests in a room used for gambling. This was not sufficient to convict T for participation in violating the Criminal Code's rule on gambling. (U.f.R. 1991.216 Ø)

T had served food and drinks in a room in which games of cards and dice were being played. The High Court made a reference to the fact that T exchanged money for the gambling machines and convicted him for violating the Criminal Code's rules on gambling. (DIK 1993-95.169 Ø)

2. Participants "behind the scenes"

In cases with a participant acting "behind the scenes", such individual can be punished even if he or she has left the concretization of the actual victims to others in the group. If a drug dealer sends people out in the street with drugs, it has no importance who they sell to. If a gang member supplies fellow members with weapons to assault a rival gang, he can be convicted of consummated assault, regardless of who from the rival gang was attacked. If the weapons were to be used against a certain person but actually were used against another, the person acting "behind the scenes" can only be punished for attempt (as for the intended victim), unless there was a sufficiently concrete awareness that others could be targeted. (In theory, but hardly in practice, a case could be made for liability based on negligence). The individuals, who commit the actual assault in the last example, can be punished for attempted assault on the intended victim and also for the consummated crime against the actual victims. The participant "behind the scenes" needs only to fulfill the very limited objective conditions laid down for an act of participation; such individual can hence be punished for (attempted) participation in arson even if the only objective fact is that he has handed one or more people a box of matches, knowing that it would be used in connection with a planned arson.

3. *Mens rea*[13]

If a person is to be convicted there must have been *mens rea* (intent or negligence). The rules of participation encompass both intentional and negligent conduct, provided that the relevant statutory offense makes liability for negligence possible. It is the common rules of *mens rea* that apply, including the common rules about the significance of mistake of fact and ignorance of the law.

The *mens rea* must include the pertinent elements. If A believes that he is standing guard while B commits a burglary, then he can only be convicted for this, even if B in reality is committing a robbery inside the house. If the guard A believes that B is committing a robbery, while B in reality is committing a burglary, then B shall be punished for burglary and A for attempted robbery.

An explicit *agreement* is not required to incur liability in a participation situation. To some extent it may be *implied* what is to happen. Punishment for participation can only be handed down in cases where another person, in actuality, carries out the criminalized act, if this person's act falls within the agreed upon or anticipated area. As mentioned, each person is considered individually; this can result in one person in a group being convicted for one crime, while others are acquitted or convicted pursuant to another provision. If there is a sufficiently concretized agreement, possibly a presumed agreement, it has no significance for the criminal liability which party to the agreement actually carries out the physical acts.

13. See further Komm. strl. (Annotated Criminal Code) I, pp. 178 ff. and 416 ff.; *Greve*, Det strafferetlige ansvar (The Criminal Liability), pp. 189 ff. and 226 ff.; *Toftegaard Nielsen*, Ansvaret (The Liability), pp. 63 ff.

Three individuals ran after a boy and beat him so that he suffered severe bodily injuries. All three were found liable for the violence as a whole, as it did not exceed what had been foreseeable from the beginning. (U.f.R. 1993.945 V)

It was not considered proven that there was an agreement to use fire weapons against some unarmed attackers. Consequently, only the person who had fired was convicted for this. (U.f.R. 1994.359 V)

Around midnight some young people forced entry into a house that was inhabited by foreigners and assaulted the occupants. Some from the group remained standing outside the house. The court stated: "Since the action was carried out around midnight by a group strong in numbers, the court must consider the violation of the domestic peace to have been an implied agreement or a presumption for the action's purpose so that all the defendants, who did not personally commit the violation of the domestic peace, must be considered as participating to this unlawful act." (U.f.R. 1970.253 Ø)

T had taken part in fetching O in order to harass him. T was present for several hours without intervening to stop the others' maltreatment of O. T was convicted for participation to maltreatment. (DIK 1993-95.15 V)

If the individual had the intention that *the course of events should be interrupted before the consummation of the crime*, e.g., by allowing the other person to be arrested for attempt to commit the crime, there is no basis for convicting for participation to an (attempted) intentional offense. This is true even if participation in attempt is punishable; liability for participation in attempt presupposes that there is intent to consummate the crime. If, for example, a plain-clothed police officer (a decoy) walks slowly down the street in the hopes that a drug dealer will attempt to sell him his goods, it is not a case of participation to drug dealing. If, on the other hand, the individual, in order to infiltrate an organization, assists in selling drugs for a period of time by referring takers (perhaps other police officers), it falls under the rules of participation in drug dealing *(agent provocateur)*. That the motive is to apprehend the persons "behind the scenes" does not affect the criminal liability (but perhaps the sentence). Based on the circumstances it can, however, also be regarded as a case of "material atypicality". Even if the participation rules are considered inapplicable, the result is not necessarily impunity. There can be criminal liability pursuant to the rules of dereliction in public service, and this will often be the most obvious outcome if the rules of police agents have been violated.

The act of participation must be aimed at a *concretized crime*. If a person instigates other to commit crimes in general, there is no basis for punishment. (See, however, below under E.4 about certain special crimes). Section 23 is obviously not an independent statutory basis for punishment. It simply extends other provisions' elements of crimes, and the instigation must be aimed towards one of those. If some people unlawfully possess weapons for the purposes of possible, but uncertain, later use, there is no basis for punishment for attempted murder or bodily harm, but only for unlawful possession of a weapon.

Some defendants had pistols, etc. in their car. Charged for attempted assault of a particularly dangerous character. Acquitted, as it was not proven that they had possessed the weapons with the intent to commit such violence. (U.f.R. 1996.1265 Ø)

4. The liability of legal persons, etc.[14]

a) The statutory basis for criminal liability

By the end of the nineteenth century there was a consensus that legal persons could not be punished. Yet, a number of rules bringing about criminal liability for legal persons were implemented in special areas of legislation during the nineteenth hundreds. The rules of legal persons' criminal liability were changed in 1996.[15] The most important change was the implementation of a new Chapter 5, consisting of the Sections 25–27, in the Criminal Code's General Part. The change did not, however, introduce criminal liability in general for legal persons in all (penal) legislation. Danish law still stipulates that a specific authorization of criminal liability for legal persons shall be incorporated in each law. At present the following wording is used in legislation:

Companies, etc. (legal persons) can be held criminally liable pursuant to the rules of the Criminal Code Chapter 5.

When a particular criminal provision provides the authority for legal persons' liability, the general rule is that Chapter 5 of the Criminal Code's applies. To start with this provides a definition of the different kinds of legal persons; see the listing in Section 26(1) of joint-stock companies, co-operative societies etc, municipalities and state authorities. Compared to previous law a very significant extension of the possible liable subjects is found in Section 26(2), which equals certain big one-person owned businesses with legal persons.

Section 27(1) of the Criminal Code states that: "Criminal liability of a legal person is conditional upon a transgression having been committed within the establishment of this person by one or more persons connected to this legal person or by the legal person himself." Danish law is rather extensive in

14. See further Komm. strl. (Annotated Criminal Code) I, pp. 239 ff.; *Greve*, Det strafferetlige ansvar (The Criminal Liability), pp. 172 ff.; *Toftegaard Nielsen*, Ansvaret (The Liability), pp. 251 ff.; *Greve*, Criminal Responsibility.
15. Law No. 474 of 12 June 1996 amending the Criminal Code (Criminal liability for legal persons).

this area; it is not required that the person acting has a superior position in the company, i.e., that he or she has the authority to enter binding contracts on behalf of the company. Even quite inferior persons can under the circumstances trigger liability for the collective unit. One of the primary reasons for introducing criminal liability for collective units was that the punishment should be in proportion to the company's finances, not to the finances of the low-wage employee, who actually carried out the criminalized act. The criminal liability for companies thus resembles the vicarious tort liability. There is, however, no possibility for recourse against the employee for paid fines.[16] It is not necessary to prove which employee, who has acted in the unlawful manner; proof that it has been done by some employee will suffice. A main reason for making it possible for legal persons to incur criminal liability was exactly to be able to sanction the so-called anonymous faults.

It is in this relation without significance whether the individual has exceeded his or her authority or has acted contrary to instructions, as long as the committed act can be considered a part of the legal person's activities. An employee's act does not eliminate the company's liability solely based on the fact, that the individual has disobeyed the management's instructions.

During sewerage work there was no protection against landslides. The company and the foreman were indicted pursuant to the Law of Work Environment. The foreman was acquitted since he had instructed the workers not to work in the dig. The company was convicted since "the work, which was done … cannot be considered unusual components of the indicted company's activities on the construction site … ". (U.f.R. 1996.615 Ø)

A carpenter, A, helped an electrician on a construction site to mount a wire. Meanwhile, he was standing on the fork of a forklift at a height of 3.25 meter. An indictment was filed against the carpenter company for violating the Law of Work Environment. The company was acquitted by the lower court and the High Court. The latter stated: "Considering that there was a basket that could be attached to … the forklift …, and that one of the defendant's employees at the work site was trained in safety precautions, A's unusual utilization of the forklift is found … to be of such a nature, that the defendant based on the presented information did not have any real possibility for preventing the law violation." But the Supreme Court convicted: "The act is not found to be such an unusual component of the indicted company's activities on the construction site, that the company can be exempted from a fine … ". (U.f.R. 1994.158 H)

An act can be so abnormal that a company cannot be held responsible for it.

Neither will a company be liable, if the act is carried out solely in the own interest of the employee. In such situations the necessary functional correlation to the company is lacking. So is the case, for instance, if a driver, without

16. Pursuant to Section 50(3) of the Criminal Code.

a truck owner's knowledge, transports his own moving load and in the process exceeds the truck's maximum weight.

b) The mens rea

The criminal liability for legal persons is not (necessarily) based purely on objective elements, cf. Section 27 Subsection 1 1st period of the Criminal Code:

> Criminal liability of a legal person is conditional upon a transgression having been committed within the establishment of this person at the fault of one or more persons connected to this legal person or at the fault of the legal person as such.

The *mens rea* condition can be met by an employee acting with the necessary subjective guilt (intent or negligence). If a relevant employee within the legal person has acted with such knowledge or resolve that it would constitute intent, if indictment were to be brought against the individual himself, it is reasonable to say that the legal person has acted with intent. Likewise if the employee has acted with (gross) negligence.

It can happen that the fault of the individual employees is so minor that they judged independently would not be liable, but that the sum (the cumulated fault) becomes of such magnitude that the legal person as such should be held liable.

The *mens rea* can also be connected to "the legal person as such" (last part of Section 27(1) 1st period of the Criminal Code). This will, for example, be the case if the conditions of the company's buildings, manufactory processes, etc. are such that unacceptable risks of violations are created, even if the individual employees cannot be blamed for their separate actions. The company is also liable for the selection, training and supervision of its employees.

c) The liability for physical persons

The fact that a legal person incurs or can incur liability does not preclude that physical persons (also) can incur liability pursuant to the general rules for the same incident. The Ministry of Justice has a commission of experts to give advice about criminal legal issues, the Criminal Law Commission; it is comprised of, among others, the chief justice of the Supreme Court, the Attorney General and a professor of criminal law. This commission has expressed a wish for a development toward making the liability of the company be the primary. This is especially called for when the violation is motivated by a desire to make a gain for the company, when the exercised negligence is not very severe, and when the act is committed by a subordinate employee. Different customs exist in practice in different areas of the law as for who is held liable, i.e., as for indictment and conviction of employees in place of or in addition to indictment and conviction of the company, as well as in relation to how employees are singled out.

There is obviously liability for the management if it is informed about an imminent or occurring criminal act and it, in spite of the fact that it could have prevented the violation, does not interfere.

Within a company, management and an employee may enter into what are generically referred to as *delegation agreements*, whereby it is determined that the employee should be responsible for criminal acts performed. Such agreements are usually considered invalid. A transfer of criminal liability can, however, legally take place by transferring the general authority and responsibility of an area.

Another type of dispositions concerns the use of a *front man*. It happens, for instance, that a bankrupt lets the spouse run a new company in name only. If criminal acts are committed in the company, e.g., in the tax area, there is a question of who is criminally liable. If it is obvious who the actual person in charge is, the criminal liability will usually be placed with this person.

The front man is not necessarily exonerated. He knew, of course, that the enterprise could not be undertaken or actually was not undertaken by him.

5. *The liability of the superior and the subordinate*[17]

a) The superior

A superior, who orders a subordinate to commit a criminal act, is usually held criminally liable for participation. This is the general rule. For public servants it is stipulated explicitly in Section 151 of the Criminal Code like this:

> Any person who aids or abets a subordinate in a public office or function to commit a punishable act in this service is punished, regardless of whether the subordinate is subject to punishment or owing to ignorance or for any other reason is exonerated, pursuant to the provision that concerns the offense.

As it appears, the provision does not just concern issuance of orders. It has further, in itself, implications compared to the general rules of participation in

17. See further Komm. strl. (Annotated Criminal Code) I, pp. 251 ff.; *Greve*, Det strafferetlige ansvar (The Criminal Liability), pp. 179 ff. and 139 ff.; *Toftegaard Nielsen*, Ansvaret (The Liability), pp. 268 ff. and 156 ff.

Section 23 of the Criminal Code, as Section 23's rules of punishment reductions are not replicated.[18]

b) The subordinate

Sweden has a general rule about the significance of a subordinate being ordered to commit the criminal act in Chapter 24 Section 8 of the Swedish Criminal Code:

> An act committed by a person on the order of someone to whom he owes obedience shall not result in his being liable to punishment, if in view of the nature of the obedience due, the nature of the act and the circumstances in general, it was his duty to obey the order.[19]

Danish law does not have a comparable provision, but the state of the law in practice can probably be described in a similar way. The problem is, however, that the provision is circular; it says that an act is not punishable if there is a duty to obey the order. Therefore, it does not give any real guidance. And the principle can neither be taken to mean that the criminal law simply refers to whether there is or is not a civil or administrative legal obligation, e.g., in the way that the employment can be terminated if the order is disobeyed. The rule is that an order to commit a crime shall not be obeyed. The more compelling the interest is in having strong discipline in an area, the easier it is, however, to penetrate the assumption.

As for situations concerning relations between *superiors and subordinates in the private sector*, the outcome is rarely doubtful. The subordinate must refuse to carry out the ordered or accept that unlawful actions bring criminal liability upon him. An order can hence not, in itself, exculpate. This is true no matter whether the two individuals are part of a formal hierarchy, e.g., in a company, or in an informal, yet real, hierarchy, such as within a family or other group.

> A truck owner gave his driver assignments that could not be completed without violating the speed limits. Both were convicted for the speeding violations. (U.f.R. 1935.653 Ø)

Under the circumstances the degree of dependence may, however, be considered in relation to the indictment and the determination of punishment, cf. below about sentencing. The general rules of criminal participation do not apply if the persons role has been quite insignificant, e.g., a junior office girl who

18. See further Komm. strl. (Annotated Criminal Code) II, pp. 115 ff.
19. Translation by the Swedish Ministry of Justice.

merely as part of the regular fulfillment of her duties delivers a letter from one person to another.

If a situation concerning the relations between superiors and subordinates arise within the *public* sector, the problem is not quite so simple. Today the rule is that it is the general law, and not the concrete order, which must be obeyed.

As for *war criminals* it must be assumed that the Danish courts in some form will apply the principles, which have been expressed in Articles 8 and 33 of the Rome Statute of the International Criminal Court.

The law about war criminals from 1946[20] included the following provision as Section 4:

> That the criminal act is carried out according to an order or under the influence of a state of dependence does not exonerate from liability but can be considered a mitigating circumstance, and under particularly mitigating circumstances the punishment may be remitted completely.

The Supreme Court applied the provision and thus dismissed that an extended area of impunity prevails.[21] In actuality the order was given considerable weight in relation to the determination of the punishment.[22]

Section 1(2) of the Treachery Law[23] included a curtailment, which opened up for a possible wider area of impunity:

> The acts comprised by this law, when carried out before August 29, 1943 [when the policy of cooperation buckled, the Danish government resigned, etc.], are not punished if the offender acted pursuant to law, order or instruction given by a lawful Danish authority within

20. Law No. 395 of 12 July 1946 about punishment for war crimes committed during the Second World War.
21. U.f.R. 1950.453 H, also analyzed by *Tamm*, Retsopgøret (The After-War Trials of Collaborators and War Criminals), pp. 631–639. This case concerned the highest-ranking Germans in occupied Denmark, the German Reich's plenipotentiary Best, higher SS and Lieutenant-General of the Police Pancke, as well as the chief of the Gestapo Bovensiepen. By the courts' emphasis on the fact that the defendants had acted under severe pressure, yet never under an imminent and inevitable concrete threat, it is left open by the court what would have applied in such a situation.
22. An example is a case where a Gestapo officer, who at the Lower Court was given the death penalty, but at the High Court was given an eight years prison sentence, because the High Court placed more emphasis on the situation of compulsion, in which the defendant was subject to act under, when carrying out a given order, cf. *Tamm*, Retsopgøret (The After-War Trials of Collaborators and War Criminals), p. 641.
23. Law No. 259 of 1 June 1945 augmenting the Criminal Code concerning treachery and other detrimental acts against the country.

its area of authority. If the act is carried out on or after the mentioned date, charges may, provided the mentioned condition, be dismissed or the punishment may be reduced or under particularly mitigating circumstances be remitted.

In the explanatory notes to the law it was explicitly mentioned that an order to kill always falls outside a Danish official's area of authority.[24]

Section 9 of the present Danish *Military* Criminal Code states:

The fact that a criminal offense is committed pursuant to an order by a superior does not exonerate the person, who has committed the act, from liability, unless the individual was obligated to obeying orders from the superior and was unaware that the order was unlawful, and the order was not obviously unlawful.

This rule is a continuation of the previous military criminal code's equivalent provision.[25] In the notes to the bill behind the existing law, which was implemented in 2005, it is presumed that the provision has the same area of application as ICC Article 33.[26]

In the annotation to the previous military criminal code it is stated: "If the subordinate is in doubt, the order should be obeyed, since it is then not immediately obvious that the order is unlawful. … No investigative obligation is evidently imposed the subordinate, as this would contravene the necessary requirement of the military command to swift compliance of issued orders, without giving the subordinate time for further consideration …".[27] In the Proclamation for the Defense B 3–4, § 4, Subsection 2, it is stipulated that the subordinate, who receives an order that contravenes with a higher superior's order or with regulations, must obey the order if it is upheld after the contravention has been brought to the attention of the order's issuer. This can, however, only apply if the order is lawful. In the annotation to the provision in one of the most highly regarded law collections, Karnov's Law Collection, it is pointed out that the duty to obey the order especially applies in critical situations, where the situation of necessity in itself can cause an otherwise unlawful act to be lawful, and where possibly only the superior fully understands the seriousness of the situation.

24. Cf. *Lundgren*, Tillæg (Augment), p. 6, note 6.
25. Report No. 1435, p. 373.
26. Report No. 1435, pp. 263 ff. and the Parliament's Defense Commission's attachment No. 16 to Bill 54/2004-05.
27. *Biering-Sørensen/Gyde*, Militær straffe- og retsplejelovgivning (Military Criminal Law and Administration of Justice), p. 72.

The provision applies whether the superior knows, or does not know, that the order involves committing a criminal act.

Similar principles apply presumably in other areas, in which there is a special need for swift action in critical situations, e.g., within *police and fire-fighting.*

Problems related to unlawful orders can also occur within the *civil administration.* The question has in recent years been thoroughly discussed in relation to an incident in which the Minister of Justice had instructed the officials at the Ministry of Justice to administrate the area of foreign nationals contrary to the law. In the administrative law literature the state of the law has been summarized this way: "If the unlawfulness, of what the order entails, is obvious, the public official acts in an unlawful manner by obeying and can, in return, not be subject to punishment by refusing to obey. If the unlawfulness is not obvious and the public official – after having expressed his doubt of the unlawfulness – obeys, he cannot be subject to punishment."[28] There is hence a certain presumption that orders are legal. Then again, the legitimization of the quoted perception of the state of the law has been the subject of discussion.[29]

In some areas the citizen has an obligation of obedience toward the police, which is similar to that of public employees, and orders can then, depending on the circumstances, give cause for impunity. Again, it must be presumed that the unlawfulness is not evident.

Subordinates can thus be held criminally liable for participation, even if there is an order from superiors or other forms of guilt on their part. If the subordinate has acted with intent or under other particularly serious circumstances, the subordinate will often be brought into the criminal case. Criminal liability presumes, of course, that the general conditions for punishment are fulfilled. The situation might very well be that the subordinates do not have, and also should not have had, the necessary knowledge of the circumstances, so that they do not fulfill the subjective elements (intent or negligence).

Even if there may be a basis for (a participation) liability, the prosecuting authority often only bring charges against the company, against the person in charge (the owner, the director or board members) and/or against any individual, who has achieved a personal gain from the offense. Such limited prosecution is legal and reasonable. This follows directly from the fact that Denmark adheres to the "*opportunitetsprincip*", i.e., a principle under which

28. *Christensen*, Lydighedspligt (Obligation to Obedience).
29. *Revsbech*, Nyere tendenser (Recent Tendencies), pp. 41 ff.

prosecutors have the discretionary power to wave prosecution on the grounds of public interest, as stipulated in Section 722 of the Administration of Justice Act. Drawing authority from this provision Order No. 621 of 25 June 2001 has been issued, allowing the Chief Constable of Police to waive prosecution, e.g.,

> **§ 1.** …
> 4) In cases against individuals, who have committed an offense within the activities of a legal person, if it is deemed adequate to pursue the criminal case against the legal person, provided it is not an offense,
> a) for which the law imposes an independent and individual liability for single persons for the adherence to the rules, or
> b) for which it follows from administrative guidelines that criminal charges also should be pursued against individuals.

6. Organizations, crowds, etc.

Danish law does not, per se, criminalize participation in a criminal organization. See further below under E.3.

If crimes are committed by large gatherings of people, participation in the gathering can possibly be punished pursuant to provisions about crowds. If a congregation as such commits an offense, e.g., false imprisonment, the individual participants can only be punished if the conditions of Section 23 of the Criminal Code are fulfilled.

D. Effect of form of participation on sentencing

1. Effect of form of participation/contribution to offense on sentencing range

Since Danish law does not differentiate between people “behind the scenes” and participants, or between different forms of participation, all are judged based on the common sentencing ranges of the offenses in question. Yet, there are a few rules, according to which the plurality of liable persons results in or can result in a sentencing range different from that of single-handed activities. See, for example, Section 286 of the Criminal Code about theft, etc. that are committed by “several persons in association”.

2. *Effect of form of participation/contribution to offense on actual sentence imposed*[30]

Since Danish law does not differentiate between different forms of offenders/participants, the general wide rules about choice of sanction and determination of punishment apply, no matter the individual person's contribution.

As the boundaries of the liability for participation are so wide, individuals can easily be held accountable based on contributions that in themselves are quite minor or barely worthy of punishment. The sentence, on the other hand and for this reason, does involve a consideration of the individual's contribution. This takes place as part of an overall consideration of each person's contribution and without the use of concepts such as person "behind the scenes" and (merely a) participator.

Section 23 of the Criminal Code authorizes the consideration of the individual's less significant part in determining the sentence:

(1) … The punishment may be reduced for any person who has only intended to give assistance of minor importance, or to strengthen an intention already existing and if the offense has not been completed or an intended assistance has failed.
(2) The punishment may similarly be reduced for a person who has contributed to the breach of a duty in a special relationship in which he himself had no part.
(3) Unless otherwise provided, the penalty for participation in offenses that are not punishable more severely than with imprisonment for four months may be remitted where the accomplice only intended to give assistance of minor importance or to strengthen an intention already existing, or where his complicity is due to negligence.

The provision in Section 23(3) must be considered together with Section 21 of the Criminal Code, according to which attempts at offenses, which cannot be punished more severely than with imprisonment for four months, generally are not punished. It is further clearly presumed in the last part of Section 23(3), that the subjective element of intention is not required in order to punish for participation.

The rules of Section 23 of the Criminal Code make it possible to meter out less punishment than what is otherwise stipulated. The general rules for sentencing are included in Chapter 10 of the Criminal Code. These include possibilities both for a more severe and a more lenient decision in relation to different forms of participation. Below the rules are reproduced in an abridged version:

30. See further Komm. strl. (Annotated Criminal Code) I, pp. 218 ff. and 403 ff.; *Greve*, Straffene (The Penalties), pp. 231 ff.; *Toftegaard Nielsen*, Sanktionerne (The Sanctions), pp. 83 ff.

§ 80.
(1) In determining the penalty consideration shall, keeping with the principle of uniformity in sentencing, be given to the seriousness of the offense and to the information about the offender.
(2) In assessing the seriousness of the offense consideration shall be given to the harm, danger and violation involved, as well as to what the offender knew or should have known thereof. In assessing the information about the offender consideration shall be given to the offender's general personal and social circumstances, the offender's circumstances before and after the offense and the offender's motives for committing the offense.

§ 81.
In determining the penalty it shall, as a rule, be considered a circumstance in aggravation
1) …
2) that the offense is committed by several persons together;
3) that the offense is specifically planned or part of extensive crime;
4)–6) …
7) that the offense is committed during the execution of public service or duty or by abusing an official capacity or other special position of trust;
8) that the offender has caused another person to participate in the offense by use of force, deceit or by taking advantage of the other person's young age or considerable financial or personal troubles, lack of knowledge, irresponsibility or an existing state of dependence;
9)–11) …

§ 82.
In determining the penalty it shall, as a rule, be considered a circumstance in mitigation
1)–2) …
3) that the offense verges on grounds for impunity;
4) that the offender has acted in excusable ignorance or excusable misinterpretation of legal provisions, which prohibit or require the act;
5) that the act is committed in a state of agitation provoked by an unlawful attack or by a gross insult on the part of the injured party or individuals associated with the injured party;
6) that the offense results from use of force, deceit or from taking advantage of the offender's young age or considerable financial or personal troubles, lack of knowledge, irresponsibility or an existing state of dependence;
7)–9) …
10) that the offender has provided information that is crucial for solving punishable acts committed by others;
11)–14) …

§ 83.
The penalty may be reduced within the prescribed statutory range when information about the offense, the offender or other circumstances conclusively supports it. In particularly mitigating circumstances the penalty may be remitted.

About Section 81 No. 3, in particular, it is noted that it typically is applied in cases of systematic or professional criminal activities with several collaborating individuals, such as drug crimes, financial crimes or smuggling of people.

The rule can, however, also be applied to offenses committed single-handedly. The rule further applies, even if the person has not played a particularly important role in the planning or only fills a lower position in the criminal organization.

In addition, the offender's role can be decisive for whether the prosecuting authority dismisses the charges or the courts hand down a suspended sentence.

E. Specific issues

1. Participation in offenses that can only be committed by (statutorily) designated classes of persons; participation in offenses with special intent requirements[31]

a) Limitations of the class of persons subject to criminal liability

Several criminal offenses presume that one of the perpetrators has a special position or fulfills other particular prerequisites. They are called "specific offenses". For example, Section 158 of the Criminal Code, about giving false evidence before the court, requires that the evidence is given in court as testimony by a witness, a part in a civil case or by an expert witness. Other provisions require that the individual is a military person, seaman, medical doctor, etc. This does not necessarily mean that it is precluded to punish others *(extranei)* for participation. A person who contributes to the breach of a special duty knows, or should know, that he thereby becomes a co-perpetrator to an act, which is imposed with punishment by the legislature. A person, who has bought a witness to give false evidence to the court, can consequently be punished for (participation to) perjury, even if he never personally sets foot in the courtroom. This interpretation is presumed in Section 23(2) of the Criminal Code, which permits reduced punishment for any person, "who has contributed to the breach of a duty in a special relationship in which he himself had no part". In the area of the Military Criminal Code this only applies if the violation of the law can result in a punishment of imprisonment for four years or more; cf. Section 8(1) of the Military Criminal Code.

As mentioned several times, Danish law considers each person individually. In relation to the rules about false evidence this has the consequence that a person, who incites a defendant to give false evidence, can be punished for this incitement, even when the defendant himself enjoys absolute protection against a charge of perjury.[32]

31. See further *Greve*, Det strafferetlige ansvar (The Criminal Liability), pp. 165 ff.; *Toftegaard Nielsen*, Ansvaret (The Liability), pp. 228 ff.
32. See U.f.R. 1976.417 V.

At times it may, however, more or less distinctly follow from a criminal provision that the criminal liability only applies to a person, who explicitly is mentioned in the provision. Liability for participation is thereby impossible. The offense is then called a "single-handed offense". Very few examples of this kind exist in Danish law. The classical example is a mother's murder of her newborn.

b) Limitations based on special intent requirements

Each criminally liable person must, as mentioned above, individually have the necessary *mens rea* (intent or negligence) to all elements of the crime. If the crime elements include that the offense is committed against a victim of a special class, it is not sufficient that *mens rea* is present as for the remaining crime elements, e.g., the kind of act. The *mens rea* requirement must also be fulfilled as for the characteristics of the victim. If a violent offender does not know that it is a police officer on duty, he is assaulting, he can only be punished for assault pursuant to the general provisions; not for assault of a public servant. The same is true as for his friend, who has provided him with the tool used in the assault. If one of them – no matter who – has the necessary knowledge about the victim's status, he, but not the other, can be punished for assault of a public servant.

Since participants are considered as acting jointly it is of no importance whether one of them has a personal interest in the crime or simply wishes to support another's interest. If A and B commit extortion, both are guilty hereof even if it is agreed in advance that A shall receive all the money. The same applies if A has the necessary *mens rea* to commit genocide and B, having knowledge thereof, supports him.

2. Point in time of participatory act[33]

a) The commencement of the liability for participation

Danish law has an extremely wide concept of attempt. If the necessary intent is present, any given act can be sufficient to fulfill the requirements for attempt, pursuant to Section 21 of the Criminal Code. It is sufficient that two people enter into an agreement about committing a certain crime or that a person solicits another person to commit a certain crime. Such a situation constitutes participation in attempt. Incapable attempts are punished on equal

33. See further Komm. strl. (Annotated Criminal Code) I, pp. 225 ff.; *Greve*, Det strafferetlige ansvar (The Criminal Liability), pp. 165 ff.; *Toftegaard Nielsen*, Ansvaret (The Liability), pp. 231 ff.

terms with capable. Consequently, the possibility for imposing liability according to the participation rules sets in at a very early time.

If an individual in vain tries to be included in committing an offense, it is a case of attempted participation.

Both situations (participation in attempt and attempted participation) can be punished pursuant to Sections 21 and 23 of the Criminal Code.

b) The cessation of the liability for participation

Liability for participation pursuant to Section 23 is conditioned upon the individual having contributed to "the act". What "the act" is depends on the statutory elements of the crime. Traditionally the simple, but not exact, rule of thumb is that the cut-off time is the same as the time of consummation (compare Section 21 about the definition of attempt). Accordingly, the main rule is that the participation must have taken place prior to or simultaneously with the time of consummation.

Toftegaard Nielsen argues convincingly for changing the terminology so that the focus instead is on whether the criminal activity has been completed.[34] This linguistic adjustment does not, however, take away the real questions. It is still necessary to interpret the concrete crime elements, e.g., "carry away" in the section about theft (Section 276 of the Criminal Code), to find the cut-off time between participation to theft and handling of stolen property. The suggested terminology can further lead to the misconception that participation cannot take place between the act, which gets the crime underway, and the effectuation of the crime when an effect is required for consummation. (If A has placed a box of poisoned chocolates on the victim's table, the crime is underway. If B, fully aware of the chocolates' contents, encourages the victim to eat from it, then B can be punished for participation to homicide.) It is therefore probably more fitting, and in better agreement with the wording of Section 23, to express the thought by saying that the criminal act shall be completed.

If the consummation does not take place instantaneously, but over a (shorter) period of time, e.g., the landing of an illegal catch of fish, it is sufficient that the participant arrives at the scene and assists during the consummation. This, of course, also applies when the offense is characterized by a continuous unlawful state (e.g., false imprisonment).

A participation, which actually takes place after the consummation, but according to an agreement entered into before the consummation, is consid-

34. *Toftegaard Nielsen*, Ansvaret (The Liability), pp. 225 ff.

ered "prior". If A and B agree that B shall arrive by car at a certain time to fetch A and some stolen goods, which A by then will have taken in a burglary, then B's actual contribution is subsequent, but it is carried out according to a prior agreement. A and B shall therefore both be convicted for participation to theft.

If assistance is not given until after the completion of the criminal act (as described above) the behavior does not fall within the provision of participation in Section 23 of the Criminal Code. There is no rule in Denmark about criminal liability for "accessories after the fact". Further, there are only a few situations in which there is an obligation to report an offense or an offender to the police. Even if the acts or omissions cannot be punished as participation under Section 23, they do not necessarily go unpunished. There are some special provisions that authorize criminal liability for certain forms of subsequent "participation". The quotation marks are important. These are precisely not cases of participation in the criminal legal sense. The behaviors have evidently been criminalized in order to prevent the crimes that take place prior to them, but the criminalization should be justified based on an isolated evaluation of the "subsequent" behaviors' worthiness of punishment. Examples are handling stolen property, keeping smuggled goods and money laundering.

3. Special prohibitive norms: criminal organization/group, conspiracy

a) Concepts

Criminologically there is a gradual transition between the crime, which is committed in tightly organized groups with an actual defined goal, with a leader, delegation of tasks, status differences, clear separation between members and outsiders, i.e., by "gangs" in the classical sense; and the crime, which is committed by several individuals together, but lacking any real organization, a form for "group-crime". Gang crimes are in many regards comparable to the "organized crime" (e.g., the mafia), which also in concept and deed overlaps the "financial crime". These distinctions are of criminological and political interest, but have no significance worth mentioning in relation to the Danish criminal law.[35]

b) Membership of a criminal organization

As part of the complicity theory – or as an extension of it – some countries have different rules that are aimed, in particular, at groups of individuals, who

35. See, in this relation, for example *Cornils/Greve*, Rechtliche Initiativen, and *Cornils/Greve*, Denmark on the Road.

pursue unlawful aims. EU has repeatedly attempted to make the countries criminalize membership of a criminal organization. In the Palermo Convention against Transnational Organized Crime a similar duty can be found. Still, Denmark has not implemented such rules.[36]

Another situation is when the legislature directly criminalizes membership of a specific organization. Neither this is the case in current Danish law; the Nazi Party is, for example, completely legal in Denmark, just as pedophiles have had a lawful interest group.[37]

c) Dissolution of associations

The Danish Constitution Article 78(2) stipulates that "[a]ssociations that utilize or seek to attain their aim by utilizing violence, incite the use of violence or similar unlawful influence of those who think differently", must be dissolved. The provision is interpreted very strictly and such a case is brought about extremely rarely. It is, for example, not enough that several violent acts occur in connection with the organization, as was the case when *Hell's Angels* and *Bandidos* were in a war-like conflict resulting in many deaths. It was neither applied to an Islamic community that on its web-site replicated calls for the killings of infidels. Associations, which cannot be characterized in the mentioned manner, can be prohibited by law as long as such a prohibition is consistent with the fundamental and human rights, including EHRC Art. 11.[38] Neither this possibility is exercised at the time.

Participation in continued activities of an association that has been prohibited is punishable pursuant to Section 132 a of the Criminal Code.

36. See, further *Gade* et al., Det politimæssige og strafferetlige samarbejde (Police and Judicial Co-Operation), especially pp. 249 ff., 316 ff. and 330 ff.
37. Differently in the after-war trials of collaborators and war criminals after World War II, where membership of the uniformed Hipo (i.e., Hilfspolizei) Corps was punishable by a minimum penalty of ten years imprisonment. About this *Tamm* comments in Retsopgøret (The After-War Trials of Collaborators and War Criminals), pp. 311 ff.: "The fundamental idea behind this rule was that a gang or group, which commits criminal acts, is collectively responsible; a way of thinking that, for example, had been expressed in the previous Criminal Code from 1866 [which was in effect until 1933], the principles of which to a greater extent than the 1930 Criminal Code had been looked to for guidance during the after-war trials. The question was, however, whether it was a presumption for applying this notion that the Hipo members had participated in actions of an especially serious nature. This was the opinion of the majority of the Supreme Court Justices, … "
38. See further *Zahle* (ed.), Danmarks Riges Grundlov (The Constitution of the Kingdom of Denmark), pp. 459 ff.

d) Terrorism[39]

The general rules of participation also apply in relation to terror acts; see especially the Criminal Code Section 114 about terrorism. The general rules of participation are further considerably extended in this area by Sections 114 a–114 d of the Criminal Code, as follows:

§ 114 a.

Any person who

1) directly or indirectly provides financial support to;
2) directly or indirectly procures or collects means to; or
3) directly or indirectly places money, other assets or financial or other similar means at the disposal of a person, a group or an association, which commits or intends to commit acts of terrorism as included under Section 114 of this Act,

shall be liable to imprisonment for any term not exceeding ten years.

§ 114 b.

Any person who otherwise by instigation, advice or action contributes to advance the criminal activity or the common purpose of a group or an association, which commits one or more acts included under Section 114 or Section 114 a, No. 1 or 2 of this Act, when the activity or the purpose involves that one or more acts of this nature is committed, shall be liable to imprisonment for any term not exceeding six years.

§ 114 c.

Any person who, by any act other than those included under Sections 114–114 b of this Act, participates in or provides significant financial support or other significant support to any corps, group or association, which intends, by use of force, to exert influence on public affairs or give rise to disturbances of the public order, shall be liable to imprisonment for any term not exceeding six years.

§ 114 d.

Any person who, by any act other than those included under Sections 114–114 c of this Act, participates in an unlawful military organization or group, shall be liable to a fine or to imprisonment for any term not exceeding two years.

Section 114 a No. 1, is aimed at the contributor who, with his own means, financially supports a group that commits, or intends to commit, acts of terror. No. 2 concerns middlemen who collect or in other ways raise means. No. 3 concerns financial institutions and others who place money or other financial means at the disposal of a terror group. Also punishable is financing of the terror group's lawful activities, if the individual has sufficient knowledge about the fact that the group also, to a greater or lesser extent, commit terror

39. See, further Komm. strl. (Annotated Criminal Code) II, pp. 30 ff.; *Gade* et al., pp. 316 ff., 330 ff.

acts. The provision is a form for special participation rule; it is thus subsidiary to the common liability for participation pursuant to Section 23 in relation to Section 114. Section 114 a can hence be applied, e.g., if an intent is not sufficiently concretized to use Section 23 in relation to Section 114.

Also Section 114 b is an extended participation rule. It encompasses any support to a terror group, even if the support cannot be linked to specific terror acts. The decisive factor is whether the behavior is likely to advance the terroristic activity. This rule is also subsidiary to Section 23 in relation to Section 114. The legislative preliminary notes mention professional general advice as an example. Pure expressions of sympathy are not included under Section 114 b, but possibly under Section 136 as discussed next.

4. (Public) solicitation / incitement of crime

Solicitations to commit offenses can be punished as attempt to commit the offense in question, provided that the offense is sufficiently concretized and it is sufficiently concretized, who is going to commit it.

If these requirements are not met, criminal liability may still be imposed pursuant to Section 136 of the Criminal Code,[40] which reads:

(1) Any person who, without thereby having incurred a higher penalty, publicly incites others to an offense shall be liable to a fine or to imprisonment for any term not exceeding four years.

(2) Any person who, in public, expressly approves of any of the offenses dealt with in Chapters 12 or 13 of this Act [i.e., offenses against the independence and safety of the State, as well as offenses against the Constitution and the Supreme Authorities of the State] shall be liable to a fine or to imprisonment for any term not exceeding two years.

As it appears, the provision contains two parts. The first part relates to public incitements (Subsection 1); the second part relates to public approval (Subsection 2). The approval can be aimed towards already committed acts as well as towards a continued activity. If the act in question can be characterized as one of terror, then there is a special provision in Section 114 b of the Criminal Code, as cited above.

A solicitation can, depending on the circumstances, be a threat, in which case the general or special threat provisions can be applied. The general threat

40. See, further Komm. strl. (Annotated Criminal Code) II, pp. 92 ff.

provision in Section 266 of the Criminal Code[41] is supplemented by Section 266 a,[42] which reads:

> Any person who, in circumstances other than those covered by Sections 136 and 266 of this Act, makes public statements aimed at provoking acts of violence or destruction shall be liable to a fine or to imprisonment for any term not exceeding one year.

The provision was implemented in 1939 influenced by the political situation of the time. It has been applied to a case of a politician who, in a TV-program about an election, attempted to make people destroy a certain form for ceiling in pre-schools etc.

5. *Special national rules on participation in international criminal offenses (genocide, crimes against humanity, war crimes)*

Genocide is criminalized by Law No. 132 of 29 April 1955. This law refers directly to Chapter 4 of the Criminal Code, which means that the common rules of participation, discussed above, also apply in this legal area.

This would have been the case even if the law had not made a direct reference. Other rules of criminal liability, which are implemented in order to fulfill Denmark's international obligations, will, due to the rule of Section 2 of the Criminal Code about universal application of the Code's General Part, similarly be extended by the common participation rules.

The special rules about terrorism, which are discussed above, contain additional particular and particularly wide participation rules.

Special rules about crimes against humanity and war crimes do not exist in Danish law. (Offenses committed during World War II are here disregarded.) These crimes are presumed to be sufficiently regulated by the Criminal Code's general rules of homicide, etc.

41. According to the newspaper *Information*, 6 August 2005, a spokesman for Hizb ut-Tahrir has been charged pursuant to the threat provision. A leaflet had been handed out next to a Danish mosque; it included a solicitation to eliminate the regents who are in the way.
42. See, further Komm. strl. (Annotated Criminal Code) II, p. 397.

II. Case-scenarios

A. "Gang boss" case-scenario

1. Facts

A is the leader of a criminal group (active, for example, in the commission of economic, organized, terrorist, or international crime). B, C, D, E, F, G, and H belong to the group. A dominates all members of the group, and A's instructions are strictly followed by all members of the group. The *group structure* can be depicted as follows:

<table>
<tr><td colspan="7">A</td><td></td></tr>
<tr><td>B</td><td>C</td><td>D</td><td>E</td><td>F</td><td>G</td><td>H</td><td>X</td></tr>
</table>

A instructs group members B, C, D, E, and F to carry out certain serious crimes and assigns each group member a specific task in his precise criminal plan. B, by promising X money, recruits X – who does not belong to the group but who possesses essential expertise needed by the group – for the plan. C engages in preparatory activity long before the crimes are actually committed (e.g., procures the necessary tools for the crime). D drives the car that brings E and X to the crime scene. Together, E and X physically carry out the assigned offenses. F changes bank notes from the booty into foreign currency. G, the group's bookkeeper, is in charge of managing the group's assets and monetary transactions; G knows that the assets stem from criminal activity (e.g., that the assets stem from auto theft) but does not know the particulars of the individual crimes committed. H, chauffeur and bodyguard, is responsible for the transportation and security of group leader A; H knows that he chauffeurs and protects the leader of a group that commits serious crimes, but H does not know what kinds of crimes the group has committed and does not know any details about those crimes (i.e., H does not know that the group is involved in auto theft).

2. Case-based questions

a) Question 1.

How are the various participants punished for their contribution to the offense? Do the sentencing ranges for the various participants differ from the sentencing range that would apply to a solo perpetrator carrying out the underlying offense (and if so, how)? Are the various types of contributions to the offense accommodated for by means of special sentencing rules or by other sentencing mechanisms?

- Criminal liability of E

E (and X) commit the actual execution of the criminal act. As for the liability's commencement etc., the same applies as stated below in relation to B.

- Criminal liability of X

X takes his position in the group after the agreement with B. Together with E, X commits the actual execution of the criminal act. His liability is the same as B's; see further below.

- Criminal liability of D

D transports E and X to the scene of the crime. His liability is the same as B's; see further below. In the case law it has been debated whether such transport qualifies as a cause for reduced punishment pursuant to Section 23 of the Criminal Code about assistance of minor importance. This has generally been rejected.[43]

- Criminal liability of C

C procures the necessary tools, possibly weapons. His liability is the same as B's; see further below. It is noted that already the acquisition of the tools fulfill the requirements for punishment for attempt pursuant to Section 21 of the Criminal Code. Special areas of legislation may further apply, e.g., the regulations concerning weapons.

- Criminal liability of B

B recruits an outsider X by promising him money. This agreement is not in itself punishable. Since the agreement is entered into as part of the on-going planning of the crime, it has no significance for the criminal liability.

B is a part of the group and is punished as such for participation pursuant to Section 23 of the Criminal Code. He incurs liability for attempt already

43. In U.f.R. 1975.321 Ø, T had driven the murderer and the victim to a forest and lit up the homicide with the car's headlights; the rule of assistance of minor importance was not applied. In U.f.R. 1994.980 H, T had been the chauffeur for a bank robbery; the application of the rule of assistance of minor importance was also here rejected. On the other hand the rule was applied in U.f.R. 1976.235 Ø, to a person who had picked up a buyer of drugs at the railway station.

when he willingly accepts his assignment. There is no criminal provision that encompasses the membership of the group in itself.

He shall be convicted within the applicable sentencing range, i.e., the same sentencing range that would have been applied to a single-handedly committed offense.

When the sentence is being determined, it may be taken into consideration that the offense is committed by several persons together (Section 81 No. 2 of the Criminal Code), and that the offense is specifically planned and part of extensive crime (Section 81 No. 3 of the Criminal Code). Based on the available information there is only reason to believe that aggravating circumstances will be relevant.

- Criminal liability of F

F exchanges the money from the booty into foreign currency. Considering that this takes place according to the original plan, the exchange is encompassed by the common participation rules and not by the rules about handling stolen property, etc. F's liability is the same as B's.

- Criminal liability of G

G manages the group's assets; G knows that the assets stem from criminal activity but does not participate in carrying out the offenses and does not know the particulars hereof. This may constitute unlawful handling of stolen property. This will certainly be the case if G knows that all or most of A's income stems from criminal acts. It is questionable where this line should be drawn.[44] If the criminal activities follow a set pattern, e.g., car-thefts or drug dealing, the applicable provision will, after some time, possibly be the participation provision rather than the provision about handling stolen property.

44. Pursuant to Section 290 Subsection 1 of the Criminal Code: "Any person who unlawfully [...] by concealing, keeping, transporting, assisting in disposal or in a similar manner subsequently serves to ensure, for the benefit of another person, the profits of a punishable violation of the law, shall be guilty of receiving stolen goods and liable to a fine or imprisonment for any term not exceeding one year and six months." In the present example the increased sentencing range of Subsection 2 may be applied. The punishment can in that case be increased to imprisonment for up to six years, when "the receiving of stolen goods is of a particularly aggravated nature, especially due to the commercial nature of the offense, or due to the extent of the obtained or intended gain, or where a large number of offenses have been committed."

- Criminal liability of H

H, A's chauffeur and bodyguard, knows that A is a serious criminal but does not know anything about the kind of crimes committed or the details about those crimes. He cannot be punished pursuant to the participation rules, but he can be punished for receipt of stolen property by accepting payment stemming from crime.[45] There is a special rule, which in some cases gives cause for impunity in relation to receipt of unlawfully obtained profits,[46] however, this rule does not apply to a person such as H.

- Criminal liability of A

A plans the crime and gives out all instructions.

With that he incurs liability according to the relevant penal provision, even if he does not personally carry out the criminalized act; cf. Section 23 of the Criminal Code.

He is to be punished within the relevant sentencing range that also applies to single-handedly committed offenses.

In determining the punishment it is considered aggravating factors within the sentencing range, that the offense is committed by several persons together, pursuant to Section 81 No. 2 of the Criminal Code, and that the offense is specifically planned, pursuant to Section 81 No. 3 of the Criminal Code. It appears from the example that weapons possibly are used; if that is the case it will be considered an aggravating factor within the sentencing range and, depending on the circumstances, liability may be imposed pursuant to weapon regulations. (The latter also applies to the others.)

b) Question 2.

Is it relevant to B's criminal liability and/or B's punishment (i.e., sentencing range and actual sentence imposed) if X had previously made plans comparable to those made by A and thus had not been convinced to participate by B's promise of money but saw in B's offer only the opportunity to implement his own criminal intentions?

45. Pursuant to Section 290(1) of the Criminal Code: "Any person who unlawfully accepts or acquires for himself or for others a share in profits, which are obtained by a punishable violation of the law [...] shall be guilty of receiving stolen goods and liable to a fine or imprisonment for any term not exceeding one year and six months."
46. Section 290(3) of the Criminal Code: "Punishment pursuant to this provision [i.e., handling of stolen property] cannot be imposed on a person [...] who accepts profits as a normal payment for ordinary consumer goods, articles for everyday use, or services."

Based on the description of the course of events this will have no significance for B. Instigation is simply one form for participation and will not affect the criminal liability.

c) Question 3a.

Under what circumstances (paying special attention to intent requirements, mens rea) is the gang boss A criminally liable for excessive offenses committed by members of his gang at the crime scene if these offenses go beyond the scope of the offenses ordered by A, for example, if during the commission of the offense, E applies violence that was not part of the original offense plan (e.g., instead of simply stealing a car – i.e., simple theft, E employs physical violence to steal the car – i.e., robbery)?

In general the decisive question is whether the excessive acts were foreseeable for the others; see above I.C.3.

In this example E uses violence when taking possession of a car. Thereby, instead of the agreed upon theft, E now commits robbery (Section 288 of the Criminal Code). The other involved individuals can still be punished for participation to consummated theft (Section 23 of the Criminal Code in relation to Section 276), as the robbery contains an absorbed theft for E. Whether to hold them liable for robbery rather than for theft depends on whether it was foreseeable, that the course of events would develop as it did. This would especially be probable if a similar deviation had happened before and A and the others have not actively tried to prevent reoccurrences. On the other hand, if a great number of thefts had been committed up to that time without a single violent possession taking place, it would require some form for agreement to punish the others for participation to the robbery.

d) Question 3b.

Under what circumstances (paying special attention to intent requirements, mens rea) is the gang boss A criminally liable for excessive offenses committed by members of his gang at the crime scene if these offenses go beyond the scope of the offenses ordered by A, for example, if while committing the offense, E shoots an unexpected passer-by who tries to prevent the offense?

In this case E commits homicide as a means to complete the theft. The response will correspond entirely to the response given above to Question 3a. E shall, however, in this case be punished both for robbery and for homicide. Whether the others also can be punished for both robbery and homicide depends again on whether the homicide was foreseeable. Considering that homicide in this connection is a more abnormal crime than the simple violence, it will require more both in facts and in evidence to assume foreseeability in this question than it did in Question 3a.

In theory one can argue for liability based on negligence if A and the others should have realized that E's act was foreseeable. It is, however, quite unlikely that charges in this situation will be brought for negligently causing the death of another person. It is especially unlikely because the foreseeability assessment, which is performed to decide the presence of intent, overlaps greatly with the assessment of proximate cause, which must be performed to establish criminal liability for negligence.

e) Question 3c.

Under what circumstances (paying special attention to intent requirements, mens rea) is the gang boss A criminally liable for excessive offenses committed by members of his gang at the crime scene if these offenses go beyond the scope of the offenses ordered by A, for example, if E rapes someone who just happens to pass by the scene of the crime?

Here E commits rape of an arbitrary passerby. It is not known whether E also steals a car. Depending upon whether he actually steals a car or not, he and the others shall be punished for consummated theft or attempted theft. In addition, E shall obviously be punished for the rape. The rape is unrelated to the car-theft and there is not, based on the provided information, any basis for finding it to be an event foreseeable by the others. This further has the consequence that the punishment for rape shall be determined without taking into consideration any of the special mitigating or aggravating factors, which apply to participation cases.

f) Question 4a.

How does the law apply in the case of 3a if not only one member of the group exceeds the scope of the assigned offense but rather the entire group switches to more serious offenses (i.e., instead of simply stealing cars, as assigned, cars are obtained by means of violence) and A knows nothing about these excessive acts (i.e., robbery of cars)?

In this question it is not only E, but everybody except for A, who exceeds what was stipulated.

If A does not know of the excessive acts, then his liability will depend upon the foreseeability in exactly the same way as in Question 3 a.

g) Question 4b.

How does the law apply in the case of 3a if not only one member of the group exceeds the scope of the assigned offense but rather the entire group switches to more serious offenses (i.e., instead of simply stealing cars, as assigned, cars are obtained by means of violence) and A finds out about the excessive acts of his gang (e.g., from the press)? – However, he repeats his earlier instructions, does not make any comments to his gang members about their modus operandi, and the gang members continue to commit the more serious offense (i.e., robbery instead of theft) in the future. Whereas some of them feel encouraged in their actions by A's behavior, others do not reflect upon their actions at all.

If A knows nothing of the excessive acts at the time they are committed, then the answer may be found right above concerning Question 4a. If he subsequently becomes aware of the course of events, e.g., from the press, yet does nothing to prevent similar occurrences in the future, it is foreseeable for him that reoccurrences will take place, for which reason he can be punished pursuant to the common participation rules if it happens.

h) Question 5.

Is A criminally liable if it can be proven that an offense conforming to A's offense plan was committed by one of the gang members but it cannot be determined which gang member committed the offense?

A has made a plan that is carried out except that certain parts of the plan possibly are carried out by group members other than those, who were designated to do so. Such a deviation will have no significance for the criminal liability. A and the others may all still be punished for participation. It is hereby presumed that all had the sufficient intent in relation to the original plan.

B. "Network" case-scenario

1. Facts

A high-ranking military commander (A1), a high-ranking leader of the national police (A2), and a high-ranking national civilian political leader (A3) together develop an idea to commit crimes on a large scale (e.g., to attack a specific group of the population). They implement their criminal plan by using their authority over unit leaders B1, B2, and B3, persons at an intermediate level under their control (i.e., subordinate military and police commanders as well as subordinate members of civil organizations. The unit leaders achieve the crimes by having low-level members of the military and the police and civilians under their control (C1, D1, E1; C2, D2, E2; C3, D3, E3) physically carry out the plan. Those at this low level who carry out the *actus reus* of the crimes do not know the full extent of the scale of the crimes planned. The *network structure* can be depicted as follows:

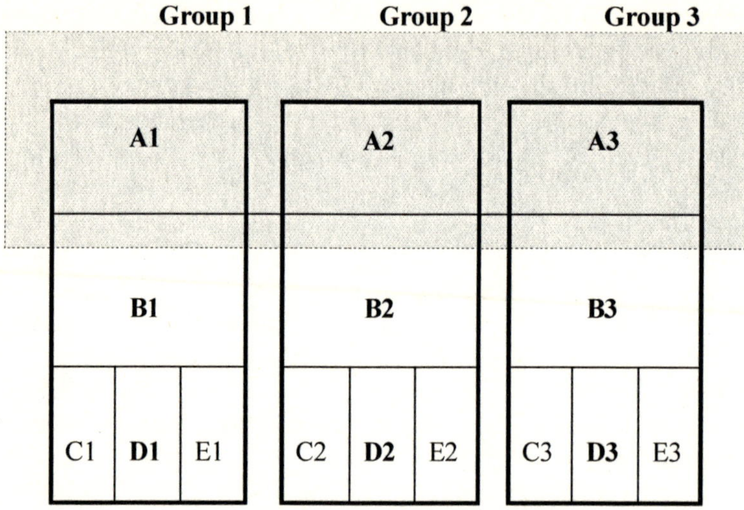

The leaders A1, A2, and A3 mutually agree upon the cooperation of their groups in a network with the common goal of committing certain serious crimes on a large scale. Leaders A1, A2, and A3 inform their unit leaders B1, B2, and B3 of the network's goal and instruct them to achieve this goal by means of their subgroups.

Thereupon, B1, B2, and B3 independently plan concrete offenses. B1 orders the commission of offenses by D1, B2 by D2, and B3 by D3. D1, D2, and D3 follow orders and kill numerous people. The members of the lowest level subgroups are unaware of the cooperation in a network and of the goals of A1, A2, and A3 (at least it is impossible to prove such knowledge).

2. Case-based questions

Introduction and overview

The example is hence designed so that it concerns a number of strictly organized groups. Within each of these groups the liability will be placed similarly to the example discussed above under II.A. However, the groups in this example are also part of a looser network, which raises the question of to which extent the common participation rules can be applied to committed offenses. The example concerns three groups, one of which is lead by a military person (A1), the second by a police chief (A2) and the third by a politician (A3). In spite of the fact that a military group is involved, the questions are to be answered entirely based on the ordinary participation rules, without getting into the special military criminal law. Then again it is noted that this probably would not make a difference under Danish law, as the military criminal law applies the same concept of participation as the civil criminal law. In the following it is presumed that the politician is not a member of the parliament nor is a minister, since special rules to some extent apply for these groups.

It is further assumed that the circumstances of the military group (1) are such that the subordinates are subject to very serious sanctions of the same kind facing soldiers, who commit insubordination during war; possibly including the death penalty. That the individuals in the police group (2) further are subject to a special system of sanctions, even if it is less severe than the military one. And that the subordinates in the civil group (3) can be subject to dismissal and other civil sanctions, if they refuse to follow orders.[47]

The three top leaders together develop a specific plan to commit mass-crimes. Such an agreement fulfills the requirements for an act of attempt under the Section 21 of the Criminal Code. It appears from the example that the plan includes homicides. The three top leaders (A1, A2 and A3) can consequently be punished for attempt to commit homicide. The same maximum penalty as for the consummated offense may be imposed, i.e., imprisonment for life (Section 21 of the Criminal Code in relation to Section 237). If the homicides are of such a nature that it constitutes genocide, then it will still amount to participation in attempt, although now attempt to commit genocide; the maximum penalty here as well is imprisonment for life (Section 21 of the Criminal Code in relation to the Law about Punishment for Genocide). It does not preclude punishment for attempt that the plan is relatively general or that the actual victims, methods of killing and times have not been established yet (compare below concerning Question 8). When the subordinates actually commit the killings, the attempt is consummated and the three top leaders can be convicted for homicide (or genocide). As long as only attempt is relevant, the penalty may be reduced pursuant to Section 21 of the Criminal Code. Both in case of attempt and consummated offenses there may be basis for penalty remittal, penalty reduction or mitigating or aggravating factors pursuant to Section 23 of the Criminal Code and Sections 80–83. Yet, based on the given description of the scenario it is extremely unlikely that penalty remittal, penalty reduction or mitigating factors would apply. The aggravating factors in the Section 81 of the Criminal Code, e.g., No. 2 (about several persons together), No. 7 (about the official capacity of the offender), and pos-

47. During the after-war trials of collaborators and war criminals following the German occupation the performance of police service was considered to belong to the very serious category; see *Tamm*, Retsopgøret (The After-War Trials of Collaborators and War Criminals), pp. 302 ff. There can thus be contradicting tendencies in relation to the worthiness of punishment within the three types.

sibly No. 6 (about acts stemming from others ethnical origins, religious beliefs, sexual orientation or similar) will, on the other hand, likely be applied so that the actually penalty – metered out within the sentencing range – will be higher than it otherwise would be.

The middle level (B1, B2, B3) is then involved in the plans and these unit leaders are instructed to implement and thereby concretize the plans. Since the unit leaders accept the task of achieving the goals, they become part of the collaboration, and it then follows from Section 23 of the Criminal Code that they also are criminally liable – first for attempt, then for consummated homicide. The actual homicides are committed by the lowest level individuals (D1, D2 and D3). They are obviously criminally liable for the homicides they themselves have committed. It is provided in the example that these subordinates are unaware of the cooperation in a network and of the leaders' goals. While the top and middle levels by means of the plan become liable for all the committed homicides, without regard to whether they are committed by military, police or civil persons, the individuals at the lowest level are only criminally liable according to their individual *mens rea*, i.e., in this example for the homicides, they themselves have committed. In determining the penalty it may, both at the middle and the lowest level, and based on the circumstances, be considered whether an individual's existing state of dependence was taken advantage of; see the last part of Section 82 No. 6 of the Criminal Code.

It is noted that only limited case law concerning such questions exists, but that the legislation, the existing case law and the criminal legal literature are in complete agreement about these outcomes.

a) Question 1.

Are A1 and B1 criminally liable for the actions of D1, A2 and B2 for the actions of D2, and A3 and B3 for the actions of D3? If so, how? Are the different acts of contribution accounted for by specific sentencing rules or specific aspects of sentencing? Is it relevant whether the leaders at A-level have direct contact with the persons at the executive level (C, D, E)?

The question is to what extent the top and middle levels become liable for the acts committed by the lowest level. According to Section 23 of the Criminal Code individuals are criminally liable for their "instigation, advice or action". It is reiterated that Danish law applies an *Einheitstäter*-system, so that everybody in the group are characterized as participants, i.e., also individuals who in other systems would be labeled as the "main perpetrator" or similar.[48] In this case the plan is made and put into action by the top level and realized by assistance from the middle level. In relation hereto it has no significance for the criminal liability whether the lower levels are influenced (D by B; B by A) through orders, incitement or other forms of instigation.

The highest level of pressure, i.e., an individual acting under the threat of being killed, will normally constitute a reason for impunity pursuant to the rules of necessity; however, it requires that the punishable act committed under pressure is "of relatively minor importance" (Section 14 of the Criminal Code); and that would never be the case with a homicide.

Neither is it a reason for impunity that an order has been given from A to B and from B to D. An order about committing an obvious and serious violation of the law is always void.[49]

Still, depending on the circumstances, it can affect the determination of the punishment that the acts are committed due to the influence of others. Pursuant to Section 82 No. 6 of the Criminal Code, it is a mitigating factor "that the offense results from use of force, deceit or from taking advantage of the offender's young age or considerable financial or personal troubles, lack of knowledge, irresponsibility or an existing state of dependence". This provision may apply to both B and D. Considering that the institutional structure is looser and the threatening reprisals are of less importance in the civil sector than in the military, it is possible that use of influence is more likely to be considered a mitigating factor within the military sector.

It is disregarded that the military group (1) may be subject to special military rules and sanctions; that the individuals in the police group (2) may be subject to special rules for police officers; and that the civil group (3) may be subject to special rules about duties of civil servants.

- Criminal liability of A1

A1 is, as mentioned above, fully liable, pursuant to Section 23 of the Criminal Code.

- Criminal liability of B1

B1 is, as mentioned above, fully liable, pursuant to Section 23 of the Criminal Code. Depending upon B1's circumstances the punishment may be increased

48. See above I.C.1.
49. See above I.C.5.

or decreased within the sentencing range pursuant to Sections 81–82 of the Criminal Code

- Criminal liability of A2

The liability is the same as A1's.

- Criminal liability of B2

The liability is the same as B1's.

- Criminal liability of A3

The liability is the same as A1's.

- Criminal liability of B3

The liability is the same as B1's.

b) Question 2.

Is it relevant to the criminal liability of A3 and B3 if their group is organized in a strict hierarchical fashion or if the group is loosely organized, i.e., a casual aggregation of civilians in which the mid-level (B3's level) has broad freedom of action? What criteria determine whether the persons "behind the scenes" are liable as perpetrators ("differential" system) or whether the sentencing ranges applicable to the persons "behind the scenes" are the same as for participants who physically carry out the offenses ("unitary" system)?

(a) The question here is whether it affects the criminal liability if the civilians' group (3) is strictly or loosely structured.

In both cases the criminal liability is, as a rule, decided pursuant to the same rule, i.e., Section 23 of the Criminal Code. This rule applies even if there is no real structure. Consequently, the structure has no significance for the criminal liability. On the other hand it may, similarly to the answer above to Question 1, in determining the penalty, possibly be taken into account that the civilians in reality have a greater freedom to choose whether they will carry out the criminal act. In light of this, the condemnation of their choice may be greater.

In addition, an order cannot be issued by a civilian in the strict sense of the word; hence the earlier discussion in this regard is irrelevant.

Finally it is noted that the special rules about the criminal liability of legal persons do not apply if the group of civilians is a casual aggregation.

(b) And what decides whether the person "behind the scenes" can be punished with the same penalty as a main perpetrator?

Danish law does not know the differentiation between "main perpetrators" and other categories of people. At the same moment the person "behind the scenes" meets the conditions for punishment, he also meets the conditions for punishment in full.

c) Question 3.

Is it relevant to the criminal liability of A3 and B3 if the only goal of the organizational units that make up the network is the organized commission of crime? What if the primary goal of the organizational units that make up the network is to carry out legal activities (e.g., fire department, administration)?

As a rule it has no significance for the criminal liability whether the group is created for the purposes of committing crime or if its primary purpose is lawful activities. In both cases it is the general conditions of Section 23 of the Criminal Code, which must be met.

Then again it can affect the sentence. Pursuant to Section 81 No. 3 of the Criminal Code, it is an aggravating factor if the offense is specifically planned. If a special organization is created solely for the purposes of criminal activities, it will indicate a particularly high degree of punishment worthiness.[50]

Membership of a criminal organization is not in itself criminalized in Denmark. However, certain special rules do exist; such as Sections 114 b–114 d of the Criminal Code (see above I.E.2.d).

d) Question 4a.

Can A1 be held liable under the following circumstances (modification of the original case scenario) and if yes for what form of participation (if relevant)? Upon the instruction of B1, C1 sets what he believes to be an empty building on fire. C1 does not know that people who have been locked inside the building upon the instruction of A1 will die in the fire. Is it relevant for the criminal liability of A1, if B1 knows that there are people inside the building?

Following B1's order ("instruction") C1 sets a building on fire. C1 believes it is empty, but in reality people are locked inside the building on A1's order ("instruction"). The people die.

50. During the after-war trials of collaborators and war criminals following the German occupation the Supreme Court found, in determining a sentence, that a person, who had been active in establishing a security guard, Schalburgkorpset, should not receive a lighter punishment than the privates, who had carried out the actual deeds, even if he personally had not been involved in the acts of violence; see *Tamm*, Retsopgøret (The After-War Trials of Collaborators and War Criminals), p. 309.

C1 only has the intention to set the building on fire. He can therefore not be punished for intentional homicide. If he should have realized that people were in the building, he can be punished for negligently causing the deaths. Setting the fire falls under Section 181 of the Criminal Code about simple arson.

If B1 also lacked the knowledge of the people inside, he shall be treated in the same way as C1. If B1 had knowledge of the people, he has committed homicide through a guiltless middleman. In that case he shall therefore be punished for intentional homicide as well as for arson.

If A1 has ordered the arson knowing about the trapped people, he shall be punished for homicide and arson. If A1 does not know about the arson, but knows that buildings in the area are being set on fire, then there may be a case of a lower degree of intention to letting the people perish in the fire or at least negligence in this regard. It is noted that criminal liability for intentional homicide, according to Danish law, can incur based on any degree of intent.

In all instances there is no differentiation between different types of offenders in placing the criminal liability.

e) Question 4b.

Can A1 be held liable under the following circumstances and if yes for what form of participation (if relevant)? Upon instructions received, C1 intentionally kills another person but does not have – in contrast to A1 – the specific intent necessary for the crime.

A1 instigates, with the necessary intent, a homicide of a particularly serious nature (e.g., genocide) and can be punished for that. It has no significance what kind of intent his tool C1 has, or if C1 has any intent at all.

C1 can be punished for intentional homicide as the order from A1 to commit homicide does not affect the criminal liability. However, C1 cannot be punished pursuant to special provisions about murder (e.g., genocide), which require a special intent. No person can be punished for acts that are not included by the individual's own *mens rea*. If he knows that his act constitutes a part of the network's genocide, e.g., if he knows that this is the reason for A1's order, then it is a part of his intent.

f) Question 5a.

Is it relevant to the criminal liability of A3 and B3 if it can be proven that the offenses were committed by a member of B3's subgroup (i.e., by C3, D3, or E3) but it cannot be proven which specific member committed the offenses?

It has no significance for neither A3 or B3 or the members C3, D3 and E3, who actually carries out the murderous act. Every one of them shall under all circumstances, pursuant to Section 23 of the Criminal Code, be punished for participation to commit homicide.

g) Question 5b.

Does it make a difference for the criminal liability of A3 as one of the three network leaders if it cannot be proven whether the individual who committed the offenses was a member of A3's group or a member of A1's group (but it is known that he was a member of one of these two groups)?

Considering that A1, A2 and A3 have entered into agreements that fulfill the requirements for participation according to Section 23 of the Criminal Code, they are all liable for what the persons of all three groups do to realize the leaders' agreements. Still, it must be assumed that it will require quite a high degree of concretization of the agreed upon offenses.[51] The requirement of concretization will probably to some degree depend on the type of offenses. It will take a higher degree of concretization to punish for (attempt to) murder a single person, than the degree of concretization, which is required in relation to genocide; genocide as a concept is aimed at a group of people, while homicide as a concept is aimed at a single person.

h) Question 6.

What requirements must be fulfilled in order to hold A1 criminally liable for crimes committed by D3? When (if ever) are these requirements fulfilled according to the (necessarily incomplete) facts given here?

To the extent D3 acts within the scope of the agreement that has been entered into by the three leaders, A1 can, for one, be liable together with D3 for the latter's acts. It presupposes, however, that D3's behavior to some extent is controlled by one of the individuals, who are part of the criminal agreement (here A3). If there is no such connection, and D3 single-handedly has decided and carried out an offense, then only D3 can be punished for the consummated offense. The three leaders have in that case, at the most, incurred liability for attempted participation.

i) Question 7.

What requirements would have to be fulfilled in order for D1 (member of another subgroup) to be held criminally liable for the offenses of D3 (would it suffice, for example, if D1 knew that he was part of a complex network

51. Compare case law from the after-war trials after World War II. See especially about acts of terror *Gade* et al., Det politimæssige og strafferetlige samarbejde (Police and Judicial Co-Operation), pp. 316 ff., 330 ff.

whose members commit homicides)? In what form (if relevant) would D1 be held liable for the offenses of D3?

As opposed to the three leaders (A1, A2 and A3) D1 has, as the case is presented, not entered into any agreement or in any other way acted in relation to D3 in this situation. Membership of a group does not in itself create liability for what members of other groups do – or, for that matter, for what members of one's own group do. While the leaders can incur liability through their general orders, the lower-level members must have a more concrete connection to the committed offense, before it can be said that they, as required by Section 23 of the Criminal Code, have given assistance in the form of "instigation, advice or action". This presumably applies even in the situations where a person volunteers to serve a certain corps, knowing that this corps is deeply involved in crimes.[52]

j) Question 8.

Would it make a difference if – in an alternate version of the case-scenario – A3 did not have authority over the others but acting alone pursuant to an agreement with A1 and A2, participated in achieving the network's goals by enacting legal instruments or by carrying out similar acts that are lawful as such? What requirements would have to be fulfilled in order to find A3 liable for D1's actions?

As a rule the means are not significant. A3 thus incurs liability, just the same, when he seeks to achieve an unlawful result with his act. This is especially clear in a legal system such as the Danish, in which very remote and ordinary day-to-day acts can incur liability for attempt. Many of the acts, which directly are parts of the implementation of the crime, would – lacking the criminal intent and motive – be lawful common acts. In this connection it is therefore also without importance whether A3, under other circumstances and with another motive, could issue general rules or concrete administrative decisions, which in content would be equivalent to unlawful acts, e.g., expropriation of real estate or administrative detention.

52. After World War II criminal provisions were implemented criminalizing membership of certain German and Danish corps. They were applied in practice. On the other hand, charges were not brought, e.g., for homicide, against other individuals than those, who were directly involved in them.

Annex

Bibliography

Betænkning nr. 1435 om den militære straffelov, retsplejelov og disciplinarlov [Report No. 1435 about the Military Criminal Code, Administration of Justice Act and Disciplinary Code]. Copenhagen 2004.

Biering-Sørensen, L.F./Gyde, V.E., Militær straffe- og retsplejelovgivning [Military Criminal Law and Administration of Justice]. Copenhagen 1988.

Christensen, Bent, Lydighedspligt, loyalitetspligt og centraladministrationens embedsmænd [Duty of Obedience, Duty of Loyalty, and the Civil Servants of the Central Administration]. U.f.R. 1992 B, p. 396 *et seq.*

Cornils, Karin/Greve, Vagn, Denmark on the Road to Organised Crime. In: Cyrille Fijnaut/Letizia Paoli (eds.), Organised Crime in Europe. Berlin 2004, pp. 853–878.

– Dänemark. In: Walter Gropp/Barbara Huber (Hrsg.), Rechtliche Initiativen gegen organisierte Kriminalität. Freiburg i.Br. 2001, pp. 3–68.

Frese Jensen, Malene/Greve, Vagn/Høyer, Gitte/Spencer, Martin, The Danish Criminal Code & The Danish Corrections Act. 2nd ed. Copenhagen 2003.

Gade, Ingeborg/Laulund, Rikke Freil/Schjønning, Katrine/Sørensen, Lykke, Det politimæssige og strafferetlige samarbejde i Den Europæiske Union [Police and Judicial Co-Operation in the European Union]. Copenhagen 2005.

Greve, Vagn, Strafzumessung im internationalen Strafrecht. In: Jörg Arnold et al. (Hrsg.), Menschengerechtes Strafrecht. Festschrift für Albin Eser. München 2005, pp. 751–763.

– Det strafferetlige ansvar [The Criminal Liability]. 2nd ed. Copenhagen 2004.

– Straffene [The Penalties]. 2nd ed. Copenhagen 2002.

– Collective Responsibility from a Danish point of view. In: Albin Eser/Barbara Huber/ Karin Cornils (Hrsg.), Einzelverantwortung und Mitverantwortung im Strafrecht. Freiburg i.Br. 1998, pp. 117–129 and pp. 406–408.

– Criminal responsibility of legal persons in Denmark. In: Bernd Schünemann/Carlos Suárez Gonzáles (Hrsg.), Bausteine des europäischen Wirtschaftsstrafrechts. Köln 1994, pp. 313–321.

Greve, Vagn/Jensen, Asbjørn/Toftegaard Nielsen, Gorm, Kommenteret straffelov, Almindelig del [Annotated Criminal Code, General Part]. 8th ed. Copenhagen 2005.

– Kommenteret straffelov, Speciel del [Annotated Criminal Code, Special Part]. 8th ed. Copenhagen 2005.

Hurwitz, Stephan, Den danske kriminalret, Almindelig del [The Danish Criminal Law, General Part]. 1st ed. Copenhagen 1952.

Karnovs lovsamling, Bo von Eyben/Jan Pedersen/Thomas Rørdam (eds.) (Annotated Law Collection). 20th ed. Copenhagen 2005.

Langsted, Lars Bo/Garde, Peter/Greve, Vagn, Criminal Law Denmark. In: International Encyclopedia of Laws, Kluwer Law International, vol. 2. The Hague 2003.

Lundgren, Kjeld, Lov om Tillæg til borgerlig Straffelov angaaende Forræderi og anden landsskadelig Virksomhed af 1. Juni 1945 [Law No. 259 of 1 June 1945 Augmenting the Criminal Code Concerning Treachery and Other Detrimental Acts Against the Country]. Copenhagen 1945.

Møller Sørensen, Annette Nørby, Hvor langt rækker ansvaret for den, der medvirker til kriminalitet? [How far does the liability extend for those who participate in crime?] Tidsskrift for Kriminalret 2005, pp. 282 *et seq.*

Revsbech, Carsten, Nyere tendenser i dansk forvaltningsretlig teori – systemhensyn eller retssikkerhed [Recent Tendencies in the Theory Regarding Danish Administrative Law – System Considerations or Due Process]. Copenhagen 1992.

Tamm, Ditlev, Retsopgøret efter besættelsen [The After-War Trials of Collaborators and War Criminals]. Copenhagen 1984.

Toftegaard Nielsen, Gorm, Strafferet 1, Ansvaret [Criminal Law 1, The Liability]. 2nd ed. Copenhagen 2004.

– Strafferet 2, Sanktionerne [Criminal Law 2, The Sanctions]. Copenhagen 2002.

Zahle, Henrik (ed.), Danmarks Riges Grundlov med kommentarer [Annotated Constitution of the Danish Kingdom]. Copenhagen 1999.

List of Abbreviations

DIK	Domme i kriminelle sager [Summaries of criminal judgments]
EHRC	European Human Rights Convention
FM	Fuldmægtigen [Law journal]
H	[Judgment by the] Supreme Court
ICC	International Criminal Court
Komm. strl. I	Greve, Vagn/Jensen, Asbjørn/Toftegaard Nielsen, Gorm, Kommenteret straffelov, Almindelig del [Annotated Criminal Code, General Part]. 8th ed. Copenhagen 2005
Komm. strl. II	Greve, Vagn/Jensen, Asbjørn/Toftegaard Nielsen, Gorm, Kommenteret straffelov, Speciel del [Annotated Criminal Code, Special Part], 8th ed. Copenhagen 2005
U.f.R.	Ugeskrift for Retsvæsen [Law journal].
V	[Judgment by the] Western High Court
Ø	[Judgment by the] Eastern High Court

Die Strafbarkeit des Inzests in Dänemark

I. Geschichtliche Entwicklung und rechtspolitische Begründung

A. Geschichtliche Entwicklung der strafrechtlichen Behandlung des Inzests

1. Danske Lov von 1683

Rechtshistorisch bildet das von *Christian V.* eingeführte große Gesetzbuch von 1683, das *Danske Lov*, die Trennlinie zwischen älterem und neuerem dänischen Recht. Noch älteres Recht soll daher hier außer Betracht bleiben. Dem dänischen folgte 1687 ein entsprechendes norwegisches Gesetzbuch mit in allen wesentlichen Punkten identischen Regelungen. Das Danske Lov war in Form und Inhalt davon geprägt, dass die lutherische Bibeltreue nach der Reformation von 1536 zum Fundament des Staates geworden war. Im Bereich der Sexualität führte die Reformation teilweise zu einem deutlich stärkeren Puritanismus, als man ihn aus der katholischen Zeit kannte. Das Gesetz sollte jegliche außereheliche Sexualität verhindern. Das Eherecht jener Zeit war zudem von weitgehenden Ehehindernissen geprägt. Vor diesem Hintergrund war es ganz natürlich, dass auch die strafrechtlichen Regeln über die Blutschande äußerst weit und streng gefasst wurden.

Die Inzestbestimmungen fanden sich im 6. Buch 13. Kapitel Danske Lov über „Unzucht". Die Hauptbestimmung war Art. 14, der in einer zeitgenössischen Übersetzung[1] lautet:

> Die sich im verbothenen Gliede wider Gottes Gesetz, entweder in der Blutfreundschafft oder Schwiegerschafft versündigen, die sollen am Leben gestrafft werden und wofern die Blutschande beydes mit Vater und Sohne, oder mit Mutter und Tochter, oder von dem Va-

1. *Weghorst*, Königs Christian des Fünfften Dänsches Gesetz.

ter mit der Tochter, oder von dem Sohn mit der Mutter begangen wäre, so sollen die Leiber, nach der Enthauptung, ins Feuer geworffen und verbrant werden.

Der Beischlaf mit Verwandten entfernteren Grades war in Art. 13 geregelt (in derselben Übersetzung):

Wann einige Personen, die einander im andern, oder im andern und dritten, oder im dritten Gliede gleicher Linie verwand oder beschwiegert seyn, in ärgerlichem Leben mit einander befunden, und Kinder mit einander zeugen würden, so soll der Amptmann oder wer sonst ihre Obrigkeit ist, die Sache mit ihnen nach äusserstem Vermögen abdingen, worauff sie des Landes sollen verwiesen werden; Räumen sie aber nicht, so werden sie am Leben gestrafft. Würde es aber zum andern mahl geschehen, so sollen sie es ohn alle Gnade mit dem Leben büssen.

Wie zu erkennen ist, wurde unterschieden zwischen Verstößen gegen Gottes Gesetz und anderen Straftaten gegen die Ehe. Bei ersteren sollte Gottes Strafe über das Land kommen, wenn die Behörden gegen Verstöße nicht vorgingen. Bei den anderen konnte die Staatsmacht insoweit frei wählen, ob sie bestrafte oder nicht. Die Strafen waren in Dänemark und Norwegen deutlich strenger als im angegliederten Herzogtum Holstein, wo deutsches Recht galt. In der Rechtsgeschichte wird angenommen, dass die nordischen Regeln insgesamt strenger waren als im übrigen Europa. Die meisten Verfahren wegen Blutschande gab es in Island und Norwegen. Schon frühzeitig begnadigte man den Deszendenten von der Todesstrafe, und dies wurde bald auch zur Praxis für den Aszendenten. Die letzte Hinrichtung wegen Blutschande fand in den damals verbundenen Königreichen Dänemark und Norwegen 1762 statt. Der Verurteilte war ein Isländer, der mit seiner Tochter vier Kinder gezeugt hatte. Die Entwicklung in Richtung milderer Strafen stieß von Seiten der theologischen Fakultät der Universität Kopenhagen, die eine solche Sentimentalität als Angriff auf Gottes Gesetz ansah, auf kräftigen Widerstand.[2]

2. Ende des 18./Beginn des 19. Jahrhunderts

Nach der Säkularisierung durch die Aufklärung konnte als Rechtsgrundlage für Kriminalisierungen nicht länger auf Gottes Gesetz verwiesen werden. Dies machte sich auch im Bereich des Sexualstrafrechts bemerkbar. Obwohl das Danske Lov so offensichtlich religiös fundiert war, suchte man den Rechtsgrund für die Blutschandebestimmungen nunmehr im Naturrecht. Es wurde zum Beispiel folgendermaßen argumentiert: „Die Natur selbst hat uns

2. Näheres hierzu bei *Krogh*, Oplysningstiden og det magiske, Henrettelser og korporlige straffe i 1700-tallets første halvdel, S. 151–190, 357.

eine natürliche Abscheu gegen den Beischlaf zwischen denen, die eng miteinander verwandt sind, mitgegeben; und sollte nicht dieser Wink heilig sein?" Von einem anderen Juristen jener Zeit wurde eingewandt, dies sei „eine wohlgemeinte Erdichtung; dass ein junger Mann nicht Zuneigung zu seiner alten Tante empfindet, ist nicht zu leugnen, aber liegt die Ursache in der Nähe der Verwandtschaft?". Unter dem Einfluss des Rationalismus gegen Ende des 18. Jahrhunderts wurde hervorgehoben, dass es wichtig sei zu untersuchen, ob mit der Kriminalisierung auf die Unmoralität der Handlung oder allein auf das Wohl des Staates abgestellt werde. Unter Hinweis auf Letzteres wurde auf die generelle Schädlichkeit unehelichen Beischlafs und des Beischlafs zwischen Partnern verschiedenen Alters sowie auf das Risiko von Verführungen verwiesen.[3]

Die Bestimmung im 6. Buch 13. Kapitel Art. 14 Danske Lov wurde indirekt aufgehoben, als die Eheverordnung von 1800 die Eheschließung in allen dort genannten familiären Beziehungen erlaubte; gleiches galt für einen Teil von Art. 13.[4]

Der absolut herausragende Jurist dieser Periode war *Anders Sandøe Ørsted.* Er trat im Allgemeinen für strenge Strafen ein und war auch im Hinblick auf seinen religiösen Glauben konservativ. Seine generell rigide Haltung tritt auch in diesem Zusammenhang klar hervor, wenn er sagt, die neueren Gesetze und Entwürfe (hier sind die neueren deutschen, österreichischen und schweizerischen Gesetze und Entwürfe gemeint) nähmen die Blutschande „äußerst leicht (wahrscheinlich zu leicht)".[5] Am deutlichsten wird dies in einer Besprechung und Kritik des Entwurfs von *Mittermaier:*

> „Noch überraschter ist man, wenn man liest, dass eine Strafe von ein bis zwei Monaten Arbeitshaus zu hart sei für Unzucht zwischen Geschwistern und dass gar keine Strafe verhängt werden solle, wenn entweder kein öffentliches Ärgernis vorliegt oder die Eltern keine Klage erheben, wobei ein Alter von 16 Jahren verlangt werden soll. Ich halte […] die vorgeschlagene Strafe für viel zu glimpflich. Es ist offensichtlich, dass sie in keinem Verhältnis steht zu der Verurteilung, die beinahe alle gesitteten, aber besonders alle christlichen Leute, über eine geschlechtliche Verbindung zwischen nahen Verwandten aussprechen würden. Und selbst wenn die festen Vorstellungen hierüber keine tieferen Wurzeln haben sollte als die, die Montesquieu ihnen zuschreibt (liv. 26, chap. 14), so wäre doch eine solche Bagatellstrafe in keinster Weise passend. Wie soll eine lebendige und wirksame Abscheu gegen eine solche Verbindung aufrechterhalten werden, wenn der Verstoß nur als eine wenig bedeutsame Übertretung betrachtet würde? Eine solche Bagatellstrafe würde

3. *Brorson*, Forsøg til den siette Bogs Fortolkning, S. 324 ff.
4. *Ørsted, Anders Sandøe*, Supplement til afdøde Generalauditør Nørregaards Forelæsninger, Bd. 1, S. 50.
5. *Ørsted*, in: NJA 1820 XXX, S. 39.

das Verbot gänzlich seiner bis jetzt bewahrten heiligen Prägung berauben, sei es, dass man sie heute aus der Vorstellung einer positiven gottesgerechten Sanktion oder aus den tiefstem sittlichen Überzeugungen der Menschheit herleitet."[6]

Diese Kritik kann man als direkte Fortsetzung der Diskrepanz zwischen dem harten nordischen Recht und dem milderen europäischen Recht sehen, die sich auf diesem Gebiet schon um das Jahr 1700 so deutlich zeigte.

T. Algreen-Ussing klassifizierte die Blutschande in der Mitte des 19. Jahrhunderts als ein ‚Sittlichkeitsdelikt', genauer als ein ‚Liederlichkeitsvergehen'. Solche wurden definiert als „jede vorsätzliche unrechtmäßige Befriedigung des Geschlechtstriebs". Die Begehung musste vorsätzlich sein, „da fahrlässige Blutschande [...] ein sich selbst widersprechender Begriff ist".[7]

Er hebt des Weiteren hervor,[8] dass die Bestimmungen über Blutschande nicht auf Adoptivverhältnisse angewandt werden können, dass in diesen Fällen aber wegen Verführung und Verlockung gemäß den Grundsätzen im 6. Buch 22. Kapitel Danske Lov über „Verlockung und Abspannung eines anderen Weibs, Kinder und Dienstbothen" (in der oben genannten Übersetzung) bestraft werden kann.

3. *Das Strafgesetz von 1866*

Nach mehr als 150 Jahren war das Danske Lov von 1683 stark veraltet. Dies galt ganz besonders für die Strafen,[9] aber auch in weitem Umfang für die Abgrenzung der Delikte. Darüber hinaus vermisste man einen Allgemeinen Teil; das Danske Lov war kasuistisch ausgeformt und beinhaltete nach heutiger Terminologie nur einen Besonderen Teil. 1849 – unmittelbar nach dem Ende des Absolutismus – wurde eine Strafgesetzkommission eingerichtet.

Der erste Entwurf der Kommission von 1859 behandelte in Kapitel 8 die ‚Sittlichkeitsdelikte' – oder ‚Liederlichkeitsdelikte', wie sie in den Motiven genannt wurden. Nach den Bestimmungen über Ehebruch (§§ 61–63) folgten fünf Paragrafen über Blutschande: § 64 über direkte Verwandtschaft in auf- oder absteigender Linie, § 65 über Stief- und Schwiegerkinder, § 66 über Schwäger, § 67 über Geschwister und Halbgeschwister sowie § 68 über ande-

6. *Ørsted*, in: JT 1828 XIV:2, S. 13 f.
7. *Algreen-Ussing*, Haandbog i den danske Kriminalret, S. 338.
8. *Algreen-Ussing*, Haandbog i den danske Kriminalret, S. 379.
9. Die wegen Blutschande Verurteilten wurden regelmäßig von der Todesstrafe begnadigt und diese in eine kurze Freiheitsstrafe umgewandelt, u.a. unter der Bedingung, dass sie nach der Entlassung mehr als vier dänische Meilen (ca. 28 km) voneinander entfernt wohnten, vgl. *Jensen*, En højesteretsdom om blodskam og dens følger, S. 27–32.

re Verwandtschafts- und Schwägerschaftsverhältnisse, die ein Eheverbot begründeten. Im darauf folgenden § 69 wurde der Beischlaf mit Pflegekindern und Mündeln behandelt. Darauf folgten Vorschriften über Vergewaltigung, Beischlaf mit Minderjährigen usw. Die Systematik zeigt deutlich, dass die Heiligkeit der Ehe der wichtigste Gesichtspunkt war. Rechtsgrund für die Kriminalisierung war die Sittlichkeit, also die Moral in der Gesellschaft. Die Kommission betonte: „was die Blutschande ausmacht, ist der Geschlechtsverkehr, sodass auf der einen Seite ein anderer leichtfertiger Umgang oder Unzucht nicht ausreichend ist und auf der anderen Seite eine Schwangerschaft nicht erforderlich ist". Es wurde darauf hingewiesen, dass Stiefkinder in einem besonderen Verhältnis zu den Eltern stehen und dass für sie die Strafe einer Milderung zugänglich sein muss. Auch für Halbgeschwister wurde die Möglichkeit einer niedrigeren Strafe eröffnet.[10]

Danach wurde eine neue Kommission eingesetzt, die ihren Entwurf 1864 vorlegte.[11] Die §§ 158–162 dieses Entwurfs folgen in allen wesentlichen Punkten dem früheren Vorschlag. In den Motiven wird auf die „Blutsverbindung" verwiesen. Die Begründung für eine niedrigere Strafe in Schwägerschaftsfällen wird in der „unterschiedlichen Beschaffenheit der Blutsverbindung" gesucht, ob sie „von größerer oder geringerer Innigkeit" ist, wie dies z.B. zwischen Schwägern oder bei unehelichen Verbindungen der Fall ist. Obwohl in den Motiven viel von ‚Blut' die Rede ist, gibt es keine Anzeichen dafür, dass dies biologisch aufzufassen sei. Es ist lediglich ein anderer Ausdruck für ein Verwandtschaftsverhältnis. Insgesamt ist mir nicht bekannt, dass vor der Zeit, die im nächsten Abschnitt behandelt werden soll, genetische Argumente vorgebracht wurden. Die Kommission wies weiter darauf hin, dass die Stellung des Deszendenten dessen Straftat weniger strafwürdig erscheinen lasse als die des Aszendenten.

Die vorgeschlagenen Bestimmungen wurden mit dem Strafgesetz von 1866 als §§ 161–166 erlassen. Auch dieses Gesetz war im internationalen Vergleich streng. So wurde in der Literatur darauf hingewiesen, dass das dänische Strafgesetz im Gegensatz zu § 173 des deutschen Strafgesetzbuchs unrechtmäßige Beziehungen zwischen Schwägern kriminalisiere und dass im dänischen, aber nicht im deutschen Recht eine Bestimmung existiere, die den Beischlaf zwischen Personen kriminalisiere, die die Ehe nur nach einer besonderen Befreiung eingehen konnten.[12]

10 Motiver til det foreløbige Udkast til Lov om Forbrydelser, S. 24.

11. Udkast til Straffelovbog for Danmark med tilhørende Motiver.

12. *Goos*, Den danske Strafferets specielle Del, Bd. 1, S. 465, Fn. 5.

Beischlaf zwischen dem Adoptierenden und dem Adoptivkind wurde nicht als Blutschande betrachtet. „Das durch die Adoption begründete künstliche Verwandtschaftsverhältnis ist nicht von dem Charakter, den die Blutschande voraussetzt.“[13]

4. *Rassenhygiene*

Näheres hierzu unter IV.2 über den Einfluss des biologistischen Menschenbildes auf andere Teile des Rechtssystems.

5. *Das Strafgesetz von 1930*

Um 1900 war das dänische Strafrecht gespalten in eine konservative und eine progressive Strömung. Letztere folgte den in der Internationalen Kriminalistischen Vereinigung vertretenen Ideen.

Als das Justizministerium 1906 eine *Kommission* zur Ausarbeitung eines neuen Strafgesetzes einsetzte, wurden hierfür hauptsächlich Vertreter der konservativen Ausrichtung gewählt. Die Kommission erstattete ihr Gutachten *1912*. Der Entwurf enthielt ein Kapitel 21 über Sittlichkeitsdelikte und ein Kapitel 22 über Straftaten gegen die Familie. Letzteres enthält § 235 über Blutschande, der den Beischlaf zwischen Verwandten in auf- und absteigender Linie und den Beischlaf zwischen Bruder und Schwester umfasst, sowie § 236 über den Beischlaf zwischen Personen, die durch Ehe gesetzlich in auf- oder absteigender Linie miteinander verschwägert sind. Straffrei sind Personen unter 18 Jahren, die von einer Person in aufsteigender Linie zum Geschlechtsverkehr verleitet wurden.

Die Kommission betonte, dass nur Schweden einen ebenso großen Bereich kriminalisiere und ebenso strenge Strafen vorsehe. Es bestand Einigkeit unter den Kommissionsmitgliedern darüber, dass die weitgehenden Regelungen im Gesetz von 1866 nicht aufrechterhalten werden sollten. Die Begründung für die fortgesetzte Bestrafung des Kernbereichs in § 235 lautete, dass „das allgemeine Empfinden Enthaltsamkeit verlangt“. Die Kriminalisierung von Beziehungen zwischen Schwägern in § 236 wurde „am ehesten auf den Wunsch gestützt, die moralische Bedeutung dieses Schwägerschaftsverhältnisses nicht zu schwächen“.[14]

Der Kommissionsentwurf traf auf harte Kritik, und 1914 bat das Justizministerium Professor *Carl Torp*, einen Vertreter der progressiven Richtung, um die Erstellung eines neuen Entwurfs. Diesen lieferte er *1917* ab.

13. *Goos*, Den danske Strafferets specielle Del, Bd. 1, S. 467.
14. Betænkning afgiven af Kommissionen nedsat til at foretage et Gennemsyn af den almindelige borgerlige Straffelovgivning, S. 220.

Torps Entwurf begrenzte in § 194 die Strafbarkeit auf den Beischlaf zwischen Aszendent und Deszendent sowie zwischen Bruder und Schwester, d.h. im Verhältnis zwischen Schwägern war keine Strafbarkeit mehr gegeben. „Das allgemeine Rechtsgefühl im Volke [...] steht gänzlich verständnislos vor einem solchen Verbot [...]. [Es ist] ein nicht zeitgemäßer Ausdruck für Auffassungen, die in veralteten, kirchlichen Geboten und in Familien- und Gesellschaftsverhältnissen wurzeln, die vollständig der Vergangenheit angehören."[15] Er betonte, dass Beziehungen solcher Art in den meisten Ländern straffrei seien. Darüber hinaus stellte Torp den Beischlaf zwischen Personen unter 16 bzw. 18 Jahren und mit einer verführten Person unter 21 Jahren von Strafe frei und begründete dies damit, dass „das Verständnis für die Strafbarkeit dieser Handlung in der Regel erst verhältnismäßig spät entwickelt wird".[16] Torps Begründung für die Kriminalisierung der Blutschande folge einer für ihn uncharakteristischen Argumentation:[17]

> „Über die richtige Begründung dieser Strafdrohung herrscht viel Zweifel. Einer Schädlichkeit der Inzucht, auf die früher oft das Hauptgewicht gelegt wurde, ist man heute kaum noch geneigt, so entscheidende Bedeutung beizumessen, wenn auch kaum bezweifelt werden kann, dass die nahe Verwandtschaft von Eltern eine Gefahr für die Gesundheit begründen kann. Der wichtigste Grund [...] liegt sicher in dem gesellschaftlichen Interesse, das darin besteht, eine geschlechtliche Verbindung gänzlich auszuschließen, weil dies die Bedingung ist, dass das Zusammenleben der Familie sich in den freien und natürlichen Formen abspielen kann, die hier üblich und erwünscht sind. Eine wirkliche Garantie für diese Reinheit der Familienverhältnisse wird jedoch nur dann erreicht, wenn der Unwillen gegen, ja man kann sagen das Grauen vor der geschlechtlichen Verbindung [...] seinen jetzigen angestammten instinktmäßigen Charakter bewahrt und folglich als ein kategorischer und unabänderlicher Imperativ betrachtet wird. Deshalb wäre es auch überhaupt nicht ratsam, dieses Erfordernis in den Ausnahmefällen aufzugeben, in denen die Betreffenden nicht derart zusammengelebt haben, sondern getrennt voneinander aufgewachsen sind. Denn verlöre das Verbot in der allgemeinen Vorstellung diesen seinen absoluten Charakter, wäre die Aussicht auf seine Einhaltung innerhalb der tatsächlich im Familienkreis Zusammenlebenden wesentlich verringert."

Daraufhin wurde eine neue *Strafgesetzkommission* eingesetzt, die ihr Gutachten *1923* erstattete. Der Entwurf dieses Ausschusses enthielt drei Bestimmungen. § 190 enthielt die Bestimmung über Beischlaf zwischen Verwandten in gerader Linie sowie zwischen Bruder und Schwester. In der ersten

15. *Torp*, Betænkning [...] indeholdende Udkast til Love vedrørende den borgerlige Straffelovgivning med Motiver, S. 184.
16. *Torp*, a.a.O. (Fn. 15), S. 187.
17. *Torp*, a.a.O. (Fn. 15), S. 183.

Gruppe blieb der Jüngere, wenn er unter 18 Jahre war, straffrei. Bei Beischlaf zwischen Geschwistern und Halbgeschwistern konnte die Strafe für denjenigen entfallen, der noch nicht 18 Jahre alt war. Die Kommission nahm die Strafdrohung für Schwäger wieder auf, wenn zwischen ihnen ein absolutes Eheverbot bestand (§ 191). Zuletzt sah § 192 eine Kriminalisierung von ‚anderem geschlechtlichem Umgang als Beischlaf' in den genannten Verhältnissen vor. Die Einschränkungen im Vergleich zum Strafgesetz von 1866 wurden damit begründet, dass „das allgemeine Rechtsempfinden in der heutigen Zeit […] vermutlich keine Strafanwendung in diesen Fällen verlangt".[18] In diesem Zusammenhang ist zu erwähnen, dass Ehebruch nicht länger bestraft werden sollte, „da Strafe schwerlich als ein geeignetes Mittel zum Schutz der Reinheit der Ehe angesehen werden kann".[19]

Auf der Grundlage dieser Gutachten erarbeitete die Regierung einen Gesetzesentwurf, der während der folgenden sieben Jahre im Reichstag behandelt wurde.

Der *Regierungsentwurf von 1924–25* ließ die Vorschrift über anderen geschlechtlichen Umgang als Beischlaf weg:

> „Auch wenn man sagen kann, dass es keinen prinzipiellen, sondern höchstens einen graduellen Unterschied gibt in der Beschmutzung der Reinheit des Familienlebens, die […] durch Beischlaf und anderen geschlechtlichen Umgang als Beischlaf in diesen Verhältnissen verursacht wird, so lässt sich doch praktisch die Strafbarkeit nicht soweit ausdehnen, dass sie auch anderes als Beischlaf umfasst. Es wird auch kein solches Bedürfnis gesehen, da anderer geschlechtlicher Umgang in diesen Verhältnissen vermutlich im erforderlichen Umfang nach den allgemeinen Bestimmungen in Kapitel 24 über die Straftaten gegen die sexuelle Sittlichkeit strafbar sein dürfte."[20]

Der *Regierungsentwurf von 1927–28* nahm erneut die Regelung über anderen geschlechtlichen Umgang (§ 212) mit der lakonischen Begründung auf, dass „man […] dies am gerechtesten finde".[21] Während der Behandlung im Reichstag wurde die Straffreistellungsregel für Jugendliche in eine Bestimmung über fakultatives Absehen von Strafe geändert.

Das *Strafgesetz von 1930* erhielt somit in Kapitel 23 über Straftaten gegen die Familie folgende Bestimmungen, die hier schematisch wiedergegeben werden. (Hier und im Folgenden sind alle Paragraphen solche des Strafgesetzes, soweit sich nicht aus dem Zusammenhang etwas anderes ergibt.)

18. Betænkning afgiven af Straffelovskommissionen af 9. November 1917, Sp. 310.
19. Betænkning afgiven af Straffelovskommissionen af 9. November 1917, Sp. 307.
20. Rigsdagstidende 1924–25 A.3368 f. zu §§ 213 und 214.
21. Rigsdagstidende 1927–28 A.5373.

§ 210
Beischlaf mit einem Deszendenten über 18 Jahren: 6 Monate bis 6 Jahre Gefängnis

Beischlaf mit einem Deszendenten unter 18 Jahren: 1 bis 10 Jahre Gefängnis

Beischlaf mit einem Aszendenten, wenn der Deszendent über 18 Jahre alt ist: bis zu zwei Jahren Gefängnis

Beischlaf mit einem Aszendenten, wenn der Deszendent unter 18 Jahre alt ist: straffrei

Beischlaf zwischen Bruder und Schwester: bis zu zwei Jahren Gefängnis, mit der Möglichkeit des Absehens von Strafe für denjenigen, der noch nicht 16 Jahre alt ist

§ 211
Beischlaf zwischen Verschwägerten bei absolutem Eheverbot: bis zu 2 Jahren Haft

Beischlaf zwischen Verschwägerten bei Eheverbot, von dem befreit werden kann: Geldstrafe

§ 212
Bei anderem geschlechtlichem Umgang als Beischlaf: „eine verhältnismäßig mildere Strafe“

Die Bestimmungen über Blutschande u.a. wurden ergänzt durch § 223, der im Strafgesetz von 1930 den Beischlaf mit Adoptiv- oder Pflegekindern unter 18 Jahren erfasste.

6. Die Entwicklung seit 1930

Die Entwicklung seit 1930 ist im Bereich der Sittlichkeitsdelikte besonders geprägt durch die Gleichstellung hetero- und homosexueller Beziehungen sowie durch die Ausformung von Bestimmungen, die im weitest möglichen Umfang geschlechtsneutral formuliert sind, sowohl was Täter als auch Opfer angeht. Terminologisch ist eine Bewegung von ‚Sittlichkeitsstraftaten' über ‚Sexualstraftaten' zu ‚Straftaten gegen die sexuelle Selbstbestimmung' zu beobachten. Das Strafgesetz und die Kriminalstatistik verwenden weiterhin den Ausdruck ‚Sittlichkeitsstraftaten', ältere Lehrbücher ‚Sexualstraftaten' und das neueste Lehrbuch ‚Straftaten gegen die sexuelle Selbstbestimmung'. Diese terminologische Entwicklung spiegelt gleichzeitig eine veränderte Haltung zu den geschützten Rechtsgütern wider. Auch wenn Blutschande gesetzestechnisch keine Straftat gegen die sexuelle Sittlichkeit (Kap. 24 Strafgesetz), sondern eine Straftat gegen die Familie (Kap. 23 Strafgesetz) ist, zeigt sich hier die gleiche Entwicklung. In der Strafrechtslehre ist es darüber hinaus üblich geworden, statt von ‚Blutschande' von ‚Inzest' zu sprechen. ‚Blutschande' ist ein außerordentlich kräftiger Ausdruck. Auf der anderen Seite wird ‚Inzest' oft in der nichtstrafrechtlichen Diskussion für alle sexuellen Übergriffe gegen Kinder benutzt. Dies gilt selbst für Fälle, in denen strafrechtlich gesehen nur eine Verletzung des Schamgefühls vorliegt und gelegentlich sogar dann, wenn nicht einmal von einer strafbaren Kränkung die

Rede sein kann. Dies führt oft zu einer gewissen Verwirrung in den Diskussionen über das Ausmaß des Phänomens und in den Untersuchungen hierüber.

Das Strafgesetz wurde in diesem Bereich seit 1930 vier Mal geändert.

1961 wurde im Rahmen einer generellen Überarbeitung des Strafgesetzes das *Mindeststrafmaß* entfernt.

1965 wurde § 211 über den *Beischlaf zwischen Verschwägerten* aufgehoben. Die Bestimmung war in der Praxis so gut wie immer zusammen mit § 223 in Fällen des Beischlafs mit Stieftöchtern angewandt worden. § 212 über anderen geschlechtlichen Umgang als Beischlaf wurde zu Absatz 3 des § 210. Die einzige Begründung, die für die Aufhebung des § 211 gegeben wurde, war die inhaltsleere Aussage, dass er „als überflüssig neben den Regeln über die Bestrafung der Blutschande (§ 210)" angesehen wurde. Realistischer wäre es gewesen, zu sagen, dass die strafwürdigen Beziehungen weiterhin von § 223 abgedeckt wurden.[22]

Im Jahr *1967* wurde § 210 neu formuliert und der *Deszendent generell straffrei gestellt*. Der Justizminister wies darauf hin, dass ein Strafverfahren gegen die Tochter eine „unangemessene Belastung für sie" darstellen würde und dass man in der Praxis immer von einer Anklage abgesehen habe. (In Dänemark gilt das Opportunitätsprinzip). Es wurde angeführt, dass dies in Norwegen, Schweden und vielen anderen Rechtssystemen bereits geltendes Recht sei. Bei dieser Gelegenheit wurde auch die Höchststrafe auf sechs Jahre Freiheitsstrafe reduziert. Endlich wurde das äußerst starke Wort ‚Blutschande' aus dem Gesetzestext entfernt.[23]

1997 wurde der Anwendungsbereich auf *homosexuelle Beziehungen* erweitert. Der Justizminister erklärte in den Anmerkungen zum Gesetzentwurf, dass eine Vater-Tochter-Beziehung unabhängig vom Alter der Tochter, eine Vater-Sohn-Beziehung hingegen nur nach den allgemeinen Regeln bestraft werden könne, also nicht, wenn der Sohn erwachsen war. „Nach Ansicht des Justizministeriums gibt es keinen realen Grund für diesen Unterschied. [...] Damit wird der Inzesttatbestand im Strafgesetz in diesem Punkt in Übereinstimmung mit den Bestimmungen über Straftaten gegen die sexuelle Sittlichkeit gebracht [...]." Gleichzeitig wurde die Strafdrohung für Beischlaf und für anderen geschlechtlichen Umgang als Beischlaf angeglichen. Der Justizminister wies darauf hin, dass für Kinder, Adoptivkinder, Stiefkinder und Pflegekinder unterschiedliche Regeln bestehen und stellte in Aussicht, dass sie harmonisiert würden.[24] Dies ist bisher jedoch nicht geschehen.

22. FT 1964–65 A.971.
23. FT 1966–67 A.2462 f.
24. FT 1996–97 A.3167 ff.

Damit wurde außerdem klargestellt, dass der Grund für die Kriminalisierung nicht oder jedenfalls nicht allein eugenisch sein kann.

Es ist offensichtlich, dass Inzest trotz der systematischen Regelung im 23. Kapitel des Strafgesetzes weder vom Gesetzgeber noch von der Rechtswissenschaft als eine Straftat gegen die Familie, sondern wie jede andere Straftat gegen die sexuelle Selbstbestimmung behandelt wird.

7. Geltendes Recht

Die heute geltende Bestimmung kriminalisiert den Beischlaf sowie anderen hetero- oder homosexuellen Umgang mit einem Verwandten absteigender Linie oder zwischen Geschwistern. Näheres hierzu unter II.

Im Folgenden wird die allgemeine Diskussion über die Bestimmung behandelt.

B. Ziele und Grund der Pönalisierung des Inzests

1. Die Behandlung in Gesetzgebung und Literatur

Aus dem historischen Überblick zur Entwicklung der Inzestregeln und aus den Hintergründen der jeweiligen Bestimmungen geht die bemerkenswerte Tatsache hervor, dass in den sehr ausführlichen Vorarbeiten zu den heutigen Regelungen keine entscheidende Begründung mit genetischen Argumenten zu finden ist. Die Argumentation stützt sich durchgehend auf das Rechtsgefühl und, soweit es die jetzt aufgehobenen Bestimmungen über Beischlaf zwischen Verschwägerten betrifft, den Schutz der Ehe.

In der führenden Strafrechtslehre[25] werden die Begründung und die Zielsetzung so zusammengefasst:

> „Mit der Befreiung des Strafrechts von religiösen Begründungen in der jüngeren Zeit musste für die Inzeststrafbestimmungen – in dem eher begrenzten Umfang, in dem sie aufrechterhalten wurden – eine neue Begründung gesucht werden. Man hat hier besonders die allgemeine Sittlichkeit, den Schutz des Familienlebens, das Bedürfnis, Kinder vor sexuellen Begehrlichkeiten zu schützen, sowie erbbiologische Belange als grundlegende Schutzinteressen hervorgehoben. Die einzelnen Belange können jeweils für sich allein den Inhalt der Strafbestimmungen nicht vollständig erklären, sondern deren Hintergrund muss in einem Zusammenwirken aller dieser Belange in Verbindung mit einem traditionell begründeten, gefühlsbestimmten Unwillen gegenüber zumindest bestimmten Formen von Inzest gesucht werden [...].“

Die Regelungen werden seit vielen Jahren stark kritisiert. Die Kritiker vertreten unterschiedliche Standpunkte, aber unabhängig vom jeweiligen Hinter-

25. *Hurwitz*, Den danske kriminalret, Speciel del, S. 215.

grund der Kritik wird durchgehend moniert, dass keine sachliche Begründung angegeben oder gesehen wird, die biologische Verwandtschaft anders als die soziale Verwandtschaft zu behandeln.

Das *Justizministerium* hat, wie oben erwähnt, 1997 in Aussicht gestellt, dass die Regelungen über Übergriffe gegen Kinder harmonisiert werden sollen.

Der frühere Professor für Strafrecht an der Universität Kopenhagen, *Knud Waaben*, hat in seiner Darstellung des Besonderen Teils des Strafrechts[26] geschrieben, dass einige Unsicherheit bestehe im Hinblick auf die Notwendigkeit einer besonderen Inzestbestimmung neben den allgemeinen Regelungen zum Schutz von Kindern und Jugendlichen. Er weist darauf hin, dass dänisches Recht in der Kriminalisierung von Beziehungen zwischen Halbgeschwistern weiter geht als schwedisches (dies ist weiterhin richtig, vgl. Kap. 6 § 7, Brottsbalken, schwedisches Kriminalgesetzbuch). Im Ergebnis schlägt er vor, § 210 Abs. 3 aufzuheben; auch hier zeigt er auf, dass die norwegischen und schwedischen Regelungen enger sind.

Der dänische Psychologe und Kriminologe, Universitätslektor *Berl Kutchinsky*, der sich am eingehendsten wissenschaftlich mit Sexualstraftaten befasst hat, trat dafür ein, die besonderen Inzestbestimmungen aufzuheben und stattdessen die allgemeinen Regelungen über Beischlaf mit Minderjährigen etc. anzuwenden.[27]

Die dänische Juristin und Kriminologin, die sich am eingehendsten mit Sexualdelikten gegen Kinder beschäftigt hat, Universitätslektorin *Beth Grothe Nielsen*, hat eine vollständige Gleichstellung von biologischen Kindern mit Stiefkindern vorgeschlagen.[28]

Der jetzige Professor für Strafrecht an der Universität Kopenhagen, *Vagn Greve*, Verfasser dieses Landesberichts, untersuchte 1996 in einem Aufsatz[29] vor dem Hintergrund der Anfrage zweier erwachsener Halbgeschwister die Begründung für die Aufrechterhaltung der besonderen Bestimmung über Blutschande. Die Argumente, das Strafrecht solle bestimmte Familienmuster schützen und ein eventuell erhöhtes Risiko verhindern, dass psychisch oder physisch abweichende Nachkommen gezeugt werden, werden zurückgewiesen. Das Schutzinteresse besteht darin und muss darin bestehen, Schwache vor sexuellem Missbrauch zu bewahren, und zwar gegenüber jedermann,

26. *Waaben*, Strafferettens specielle del, S. 74.

27. *Kutchinsky*, Blodskam/Incest.

28. *Nielsen*, Seksuelle overgreb mod børn i familien, S. 44 und S. 296; *dies*., Straffesystemet i børneperspektiv, S. 41 und S. 404.

29. *Greve*, Blodskam – en utidssvarende straffebestemmelse.

auch gegenüber den Mitgliedern der eigenen Familie, sei es die Familie im biologischen oder im sozialen Verständnis. Es ist deshalb wenig überzeugend, dass das Gesetz zwischen biologischen Kindern, Adoptiv-, Stief- und Pflegekindern unterscheidet. Es wird außerdem darauf hingewiesen, dass allgemeine Einigkeit darüber besteht, dass es nicht Aufgabe des Strafrechts ist, einverständliche sexuelle Beziehungen zwischen Erwachsenen zu kriminalisieren, also auch nicht zwischen Geschwistern oder Halbgeschwistern.

Es gibt in Dänemark einen besonderen *Strafgesetzrat*, der den Justizminister berät. Der Rat hat einen früheren Präsidenten des Obersten Gerichtshofs als Vorsitzenden und besteht darüber hinaus unter anderem aus dem Reichsstaatsanwalt, dem Direktor des Strafvollzugswesens, dem Reichspolizeichef, dem Leiter der Rechtsabteilung des Justizministeriums und einem Professor für Strafrecht. Der Strafgesetzrat hat sich mehrmals mit dem Inzesttatbestand beschäftigt. Einstimmig hielt der Rat 1987 fest:[30] „Es wäre naheliegend, eine Aufhebung des Absatzes 2 über Beziehungen zwischen Geschwistern zu erwägen. Es wird auch auf die Möglichkeit der Aufhebung des Absatzes 3 hingewiesen." Eine Mehrheit im Strafgesetzrat wollte die Höchststrafe auf drei Jahre herabsetzen. Im Jahr 2002 gab es Sympathien im Rat, den Erwägungen und dem Vorschlag zu folgen, die in *Vagn Greves* oben genanntem Aufsatz enthalten waren.[31]

2. Die Argumente im Einzelnen

Förderung der Moral

Nach allgemeiner kriminalpolitischer Ansicht ist es keine ausreichende Begründung für die Kriminalisierung eines Verhaltens, dass damit eine bestimmte Sexualmoral gefördert werden kann. Der Strafgesetzrat (vgl. oben unter I.B) hat dies so ausgedrückt:[32]

> [Es ist] ein Hauptprinzip der Strafgesetzgebung, dass eine Kriminalisierung nicht lediglich unter dem Hinweis erfolgen darf, dass damit eine moralische Auffassung unterstützt würde. Die Kriminalisierung muss auf die Annahme gestützt werden können, dass sie ein oder mehrere Ziele verfolgt, insbesondere indem sie solchen Handlungen entgegenwirkt, die zu Schaden oder Unheil für die Gesellschaft als Ganzes, für Bevölkerungsgruppen oder Einzelpersonen führen oder hierzu geeignet sind.

30. Straffelovrådets betænkning om strafferammer og prøveløsladelse, Nr. 1099, S. 205.
31. Straffelovrådets betænkning om straffastsættelse og strafferammer II, Nr. 1424, S. 692.
32. Straffelovrådets betænkning om straf for pornografi, Nr. 435, S. 48.

Schutz der Familie

Formal gesehen ist das Ziel der Inzestbestimmung, die Familie zu schützen, wie aus der Verortung in diesem Kapitel des Strafgesetzes zu ersehen ist. So wird die Norm jedoch nicht in den rechtswissenschaftlichen Analysen behandelt. Die Auffassungen lassen sich so zusammenfassen, dass die Aufgabe der Norm darin besteht, besonders gefährdete Personen vor sexuellen Begehrlichkeiten zu schützen. Das ist zumindest die durchgehende Haltung unter allen dänischen Sachkundigen. Aus der Gesetzgebung der letzten Jahre geht auch deutlich hervor, dass das Delikt genau auf die gleiche Art behandelt wird wie die Straftaten gegen die sexuelle Selbstbestimmung. Da der existierende Straftatbestand wesentlich weiter reicht und insbesondere auch einverständliche sexuelle Beziehungen zwischen Erwachsenen kriminalisiert, wird dieser Teil des § 210 von (vermutlich allen) denjenigen Sachverständigen kritisiert, die sich zu der Frage geäußert haben.

Der Schutz der Familie in früherer Zeit durch das Strafrecht und andere Teile des Rechtssystems ist auch im Übrigen überholt. Ehebruch ist nicht länger strafbar, nichteheliche Lebensgemeinschaften werden vermögens- und erbrechtlich in immer weiterem Umfang mit Ehepaaren gleichgestellt usw.

Eugenische Aspekte

Die dänischen Regeln über Inzest sind weder jetzt noch waren sie früher mit eugenischen Gesichtspunkten begründet, auch wenn es Versuche gibt, genetische Begründungen ergänzend heranzuziehen. Heute sind diese Argumente nicht akzeptabel.

Erstens ist das Risiko von erblichen Behinderungen u.ä. äußerst gering.

Zweitens baut das Argument darauf auf, dass Kinder mit Behinderung nicht den gleichen menschlichen Wert haben wie Kinder ohne Behinderung.

Drittens würde dies eine ungerechtfertigte Ungleichbehandlung darstellen. Für einige sexuelle Beziehungen besteht statistisch ein weit höheres Risiko, Kinder mit Behinderungen hervorzubringen, als für Beischlaf zwischen Verwandten. Dies gilt sowohl dann, wenn die Kombination der Sexualpartner eine erhöhte Wahrscheinlichkeit von Behinderungen mit sich bringt, als auch dann, wenn diese erhöhte Wahrscheinlichkeit unabhängig von der genetischen Veranlagung der Partner gegeben ist. Wenn solche Beziehungen nicht kriminalisiert werden und auch nicht länger Ehehindernisse sind, muss man von einer ungerechtfertigten Ungleichbehandlung von Geschwistern sprechen.

Schlussfolgerung
Wie bereits mehrfach ausgeführt spricht dies nicht für eine Entkriminalisierung aller inzestuösen Beziehungen, aber für eine Entkriminalisierung des Inzests zwischen Erwachsenen und hierunter auch zwischen erwachsenen Geschwistern.

II. Aktuelle Rechtslage

A. Überblick und Systematik

In Kapitel 23 des Strafgesetzes über Straftaten gegen die Familie findet sich in § 210 die eigentliche Inzestbestimmung. Sie lautet:

§ 210
(1) Wer mit einem Verwandten absteigender Linie den Beischlaf vollzieht, wird mit Gefängnis bis zu 6 Jahren bestraft.
(2) Wer mit seinem Bruder oder seiner Schwester den Beischlaf vollzieht, wird mit Gefängnis bis zu 2 Jahren bestraft. Gegenüber demjenigen, der das 18. Lebensjahr noch nicht vollendet hat, kann von Strafe abgesehen werden.
(3) Die Vorschriften der Abs. 1 und 2 finden entsprechende Anwendung bei geschlechtlichem Umgang mit einer Person gleichen Geschlechts sowie bei anderem geschlechtlichem Umgang als Beischlaf.

Wie aus dem oben Gezeigten deutlich wird, ist die Bestimmung im Hinblick auf das geschützte Rechtsgut etc. äußerst eng mit mehreren Straftaten in Kapitel 24 über Straftaten gegen die sexuelle Sittlichkeit verbunden. Dies gilt besonders für

§ 223
(1) Wer den Beischlaf mit einer Person unter 18 Jahren vollzieht, die sein eigenes Adoptivkind, Stiefkind oder Pflegekind ist oder ihm zur Ausbildung oder Erziehung anvertraut ist, wird mit Gefängnis bis zu vier Jahren bestraft.
(2) Mit der gleichen Strafe wird bestraft, wer unter grobem Missbrauch einer auf Alter und Erfahrung beruhenden Überlegenheit eine Person unter 18 Jahren zum Beischlaf verführt.

Grunddelikt in § 210 Abs. 1 und 2 und in § 223 ist der gesetzwidrige Beischlaf. In § 210 Abs. 3 wird der Tatbestand erweitert, sodass er auch anderen geschlechtlichen Umgang als Beischlaf und homosexuelle Beziehungen umfasst. Entsprechende Erweiterungen des § 223 finden sich in § 224 über anderen geschlechtlichen Umgang als Beischlaf und in § 225 über homosexuelle Beziehungen.

Hinsichtlich beider Delikte kann eine gleichzeitige Strafbarkeit wegen z.B. Vergewaltigung (§ 216) und Beischlaf mit Minderjährigen (§ 222) gegeben sein.

B. Inhalt der Strafnorm zur Erfassung des Inzests

1. Erfasster Personenkreis

§ 210 unterscheidet zwischen Beischlaf mit einem Verwandten in auf- und absteigender Linie (Abs. 1) und Beischlaf zwischen Geschwistern (Abs. 2). Es ist jedoch nur der Aszendent, der in Situationen des Absatzes 1 bestraft werden kann. In beiden Absätzen wird ein biologisches Kriterium angewandt. Beruht die Verwandtschaft auf einer Adoption oder anderem, so wird § 223 angewandt. Umgekehrt kann § 210 angewandt werden, selbst wenn einer der Beteiligten (Abs. 1 und 2) oder beide (Abs. 2) durch Dritte adoptiert worden sind. Geschwister im Sinne von Abs. 2 sind sowohl Voll- als auch Halbgeschwister. Sind die beiden Personen von gleichem Geschlecht, kommt Abs. 3 zur Anwendung.

2. Tathandlung

§ 210 Abs. 1 und 2 verlangen einen vollendeten Beischlaf. Unter Beischlaf wird verstanden, dass das Glied des Mannes in die Scheide der Frau ganz oder teilweise eingeführt wird. ‚Anderer geschlechtlicher Umgang als Beischlaf' wird in Abs. 3 mit demselben Strafrahmen kriminalisiert. Bei ‚anderem geschlechtlichem Umgang als Beischlaf' muss die Handlung einen beischlafähnlichen Charakter haben, als Ersatz für den Beischlaf fungieren oder im Übrigen für das Opfer den Charakter eines Übergriffs haben, der gleichwertig oder fast gleichwertig mit dem Beischlaf ist (§ 210 Abs. 3 i.V.m. § 224). Als Beispiele können Oral- oder Analverkehr oder das Einführen eines Fingers in die Scheide genannt werden. Geschlechtlicher Umgang mit einer Person des gleichen Geschlechts wird in den Fällen bestraft, in denen die Handlung gegenüber einer Person des anderen Geschlechts einen ‚anderen geschlechtlichen Umgang als Beischlaf' darstellen würde (§ 210 Abs. 3 i.V.m. § 225). Ist der Übergriff nicht von einer solchen Art, sondern besteht z.B. aus einem Betasten des Oberkörpers oder einem Kuss auf den Mund, so greifen die allgemeinen Regelungen über die Verletzung des Schamgefühls in § 232, eventuell in Tateinheit mit Nötigung in § 260 ein.

In Bezug auf die Tathandlung werden keine weiteren Bedingungen gestellt, also beispielsweise auch nicht, dass die Beziehung öffentliches Ärgernis hervorruft.

3. Erschwerungsgründe und mildernde Umstände für die Straftat des Inzests
Im Gesetz sind keine besonderen Strafschärfungs- oder Strafmilderungsgründe angegeben. Die Strafzumessung erfolgt demgemäß nach den allgemeinen Strafzumessungsgrundsätzen. Danach ist es ein erschwerender Umstand, dass der Täter eine wehrlose Situation des Opfers ausgenutzt hat (§ 81 Nr. 10).

Bei der Festsetzung der Strafe wird u.a. die Anzahl der Vorfälle, das Alter des Verletzten, bei Geschwisterinzest das Alter beider Beteiligten berücksichtigt.

4. Vorsatz
Vorsatz ist bezüglich aller Tatbestandsmerkmale des § 210 erforderlich (§ 19). Das bedeutet, dass auch Kenntnis des Verwandtschaftsverhältnisses verlangt wird. (Wie unten unter 7. dargestellt, kann eine Strafbarkeit in Tateinheit mit § 222, Beischlaf mit Minderjährigen, gegeben sein; in diesem Zusammenhang ist fahrlässige Unkenntnis der Minderjährigkeit ausreichend, § 226). Es wird der allgemeine Vorsatzbegriff des dänischen Strafrechts (Absicht, Wahrscheinlichkeitsvorsatz und *dolus eventualis*) angewandt.

5. Strafrahmen und Strafzumessung
Höchststrafe sind sechs Jahre Gefängnis nach Abs. 1 und zwei Jahre nach Abs. 2, die Mindeststrafe beträgt in beiden Fällen sieben Tage. In Fällen der Konkurrenz mit anderen Delikten kann sich die Höchststrafe erhöhen. In der Praxis gibt es nur wenige Inzestverfahren.[33] Vor allem, weil Fälle des § 210 Abs. 2 so selten sind, kann man hier keine Standardstrafe ausmachen. Auch unter den veröffentlichten Entscheidungen finden sich nur sehr wenige Urteile über Inzest zwischen Geschwistern.

Urteil des Østre Landret (Obergericht Ost) vom 16. September 1992, veröffentlicht in UfR 1993, S. 93: Der 32-jährige T war angeklagt wegen Vergewaltigung und § 210 Abs. 2 gegenüber seiner 15-jährigen Halbschwester. Zudem wurde ihm vorgeworfen, in dem darauf folgenden halben Jahr viele Male mit ihr geschlafen zu haben und auch damit § 210 Abs. 2 erfüllt zu haben. Er wurde vom Vorwurf der Vergewaltigung freigesprochen, aber wegen Inzests zu einer Freiheitsstrafe von sechs Monaten und einem Schmerzensgeld an seine Halbschwester in Höhe von 20 000 Kronen (ca. 2700 €) verurteilt. Das Landgericht hob den großen Altersunterschied und den langen Zeitraum der Tatbegehung hervor.

Nach § 210 Abs. 2 S. 2 besteht die Möglichkeit, gegenüber demjenigen von Strafe abzusehen, der das 18. Lebensjahr noch nicht vollendet hat. Im Straf-

33. Siehe näher dazu unten IV.1.

gesetzkommentar wird angenommen, dass bei Personen unter 18 Jahren dann von einer Anklage abgesehen wird, wenn der Andere ungefähr gleichaltrig war.[34] Ich habe bei der Reichsstaatsanwaltschaft nachgefragt, ob man sagen könne, wie eine Sache behandelt würde, in der beide Geschwister volljährig sind und völlig freiwillig handeln. Es gibt keine Regeln hierzu und niemand konnte sich erinnern, einen solchen Fall bearbeitet zu haben.

Es kann Tateinheit zwischen Inzest (§ 210) und beispielsweise Vergewaltigung (§ 216 mit einer Höchststrafe von zwölf Jahren) oder Beischlaf mit Minderjährigen (§ 222 mit einer Höchststrafe von zwölf Jahren) vorliegen. Im Falle der Konkurrenz kann die Höchststrafe des strengsten Strafrahmens um die Hälfte erhöht werden (§ 88 Abs. 1).

Sowohl für § 210 (Inzest) als auch für § 223 (Beischlaf mit Adoptiv-, Stief- und Pflegekindern) gilt eine besondere Verjährungsregel. Danach beginnt die Verjährungsfrist frühestens, wenn der Verletzte das 18. Lebensjahr vollendet hat (§ 94 Abs. 4).

6. Sonstige Gesichtspunkte, die im Hinblick auf die Rechtfertigung oder Begründung des Tatbestandes Aufschluss geben könnten

Es besteht allgemeine Einigkeit darüber, dass Kinder vor sexuellen Übergriffen geschützt werden müssen. Allseitige Einigkeit besteht auch darüber, dass die allgemeine Altersgrenze (in Dänemark 15 Jahre, § 222) zu niedrig ist in Fällen, in denen ein Vater sein Kind missbraucht, sei es ein biologisches oder nichtbiologisches Kind. Es gibt deshalb im dänischen Recht eine Grenze von 18 Jahren für Adoptiv-, Stief- und Pflegekinder, § 223. In der jüngeren Zeit besteht auch Einigkeit darüber, dass das Strafrecht sexuelle Handlungen zwischen erwachsenen, einwilligenden Personen nicht zu regulieren hat. Es widerspricht deshalb den ansonsten allgemein anerkannten rechtspolitischen Prinzipien, dass § 210 den Inzest mit Kindern über 18 Jahren und den Inzest zwischen erwachsenen Geschwistern unter Strafe stellt. Diese Kriminalisierungen können nicht begründet werden, weder mit dem Schutz der Familie (die im Übrigen mindestens genau so stark durch sexuelle Beziehungen mit Stief- oder Adoptivkindern beeinträchtigt wird, die straffrei sind, wenn das Kind über 18 Jahre alt ist), noch mit eugenischen Gesichtspunkten.

7. Konsequenzen aus der Tatbestandsanalyse für die Rechtsgutbestimmung

Geschütztes Rechtsgut ist nicht mehr wie im älteren Recht die Ehe und die familiären Beziehungen, sondern die sexuelle Selbstbestimmung. Das bedeu-

34. *Greve/Jensen/Nielsen*, Kommenteret straffelov, Speciel del, S. 253.

tet, dass der Tatbestand im Kapitel des Strafgesetzes über Straftaten gegen die Familie fehlplaziert ist und dass er richtigerweise in das Kapitel über Sittlichkeitsstraftaten gehört. Darüber hinaus bedeutet es, wie bereits mehrfach erwähnt, dass die existierende Kriminalisierung von sexuellen Beziehungen zwischen Erwachsenen sich nicht zufriedenstellend begründen lässt. Im älteren Recht gab es eine Reihe strafrechtlicher Begrenzungen der sexuellen Selbstbestimmung, z.B. im Hinblick auf Ehebruch, auf Formen der sexuellen Befriedigung (analer und oraler Geschlechtsverkehr) und auf homosexuelle Beziehungen. Diese wurden alle aufgrund der Erkenntnis aufgehoben, dass es dem Staat nicht zusteht, sich einzumischen, wenn die Beziehung freiwillig ist und zwischen Erwachsenen stattfindet. Die Inzestregeln stellen insofern ein Relikt dar.

III. Qualifizierte Straftatbestände im Umfeld des Inzests

Das Strafgesetz enthält eine Reihe von Tatbeständen der Verletzung sexueller Selbstbestimmung, z.B. Vergewaltigung, Beischlaf mit Minderjährigen, Erschleichung des Beischlafs, Ausnutzung einer übergeordneten Stellung, Verführung von Minderjährigen zum Beischlaf unter Missbrauch einer auf Alter oder Erfahrung beruhenden Überlegenheit, Kauf sexueller Dienste von minderjährigen Prostituierten und Verletzungen des Schamgefühls.

§ 216
(1) Wer sich durch Gewalt oder Drohung mit Gewalt den Beischlaf erzwingt, wird wegen Vergewaltigung mit Gefängnis bis zu acht Jahren bestraft. Mit Gewalt gleichgestellt ist die Versetzung in einen Zustand, in welchem die betreffende Person außerstande ist, sich der Handlung zu widersetzen.
(2) Die Strafe kann auf Gefängnis bis zu 12 Jahren erhöht werden, wenn die Vergewaltigung von besonders gefährlicher Art gewesen ist oder im Übrigen besonders erschwerende Umstände vorliegen.

§ 217
Wer anstatt durch Gewalt oder Drohung mit Gewalt sich den Beischlaf durch andere Nötigung gemäß § 260 verschafft, wird mit Gefängnis bis zu 4 Jahren bestraft.

§ 218
(1) Wer sich den außerehelichen Beischlaf mit einer Person durch Ausnutzung ihrer Geisteskrankheit oder geistigen Behinderung verschafft, wird mit Gefängnis bis zu 4 Jahren bestraft.
(2) Wer sich den außerehelichen Beischlaf mit einer Person verschafft, die sich in einem Zustand befindet, in dem sie außerstande ist, sich der Handlung zu widersetzen, wird mit Gefängnis bis zu 4 Jahren bestraft, sofern nicht ein Fall des § 216 vorliegt.

§ 220
Wer sich den außerehelichen Beischlaf mit einer Person durch groben Missbrauch ihrer dienstlichen oder wirtschaftlichen Abhängigkeit verschafft, wird mit Gefängnis bis zu einem Jahr oder, wenn die Person noch nicht 21 Jahre alt ist, mit Gefängnis bis zu 3 Jahren bestraft.

§ 221
Mit Gefängnis bis zu 6 Jahren wird bestraft, wer sich den Beischlaf mit einer Person erschleicht, die den Beischlaf irrtümlich für ehelich hält oder den Täter mit einem anderen verwechselt.

§ 222
(1) Wer mit einem Kind unter 15 Jahren den Beischlaf vollzieht, wird mit Gefängnis bis zu 8 Jahren bestraft.
(2) War das Kind noch nicht 12 Jahre alt oder hat sich der Täter den Beischlaf durch Zwang oder Drohungen verschafft, so kann die Strafe auf Gefängnis bis zu 12 Jahren erhöht werden.

§ 223
(1) Wer den Beischlaf mit einer Person unter 18 Jahren vollzieht, die sein eigenes Adoptivkind, Stiefkind oder Pflegekind ist oder ihm zur Ausbildung oder Erziehung anvertraut ist, wird mit Gefängnis bis zu 4 Jahren bestraft.
(2) Mit der gleichen Strafe wird bestraft, wer unter grobem Missbrauch einer auf Alter und Erfahrung beruhenden Überlegenheit eine Person unter 18 Jahren zum Beischlaf verführt.

§ 224
Die Vorschriften der §§ 216–223 a finden entsprechende Anwendung bei anderem geschlechtlichem Umgang als Beischlaf.

§ 225
Die Vorschriften der §§ 216–220 und 222–223 a finden entsprechende Anwendung bei geschlechtlichem Umgang mit einer Person gleichen Geschlechts.

Inzeststraftaten nach § 210 werden oft gegen minderjährige Personen begangen. In einem solchen Fall erfolgt die Verurteilung in Tateinheit mit § 222, unter Umständen in Verbindung mit § 224, sofern die Tathandlung in anderem sexuellem Umgang als Beischlaf bestand, beziehungsweise in Verbindung mit § 225, wenn es sich um eine homosexuelle Beziehung handelt. Wird der Beischlaf durch Gewalt, Drohung oder Ähnliches erzwungen, so wird der Täter in Tateinheit mit den einschlägigen Bestimmungen des Kapitels über Sexualstraftaten verurteilt.

Es besteht Einigkeit darüber, dass im Fall einer Aufhebung der existierenden Inzestbestimmung (§ 210) auch die Regelung über den Beischlaf mit Adoptiv-, Stief- und Pflegekindern (§ 223) dahingehend geändert werden müsste, dass sie auch biologische Kinder unter 18 Jahren umfasst. Eine Entfernung der besonderen Inzestbestimmung hätte selbstverständlich keine Auswirkungen auf die übrigen Straftatbestände.

IV. Tabuisierung und Durchsetzung des Inzestverbots

1. Inzest in der heutigen dänischen Gesellschaft

Unzweifelhaft gibt es in der dänischen Gesellschaft eine sehr weit verbreitete und sehr starke Ablehnung von inzestuösen Beziehungen. In welchem Umfang diese Moral in früheren kirchlichen Einflüssen wurzelt oder unabhängig davon besteht, lässt sich kaum sagen. Das heutige Dänemark ist stark säkularisiert und die Moralvorstellungen haben sich verselbstständigt.

Bereits aus Gründen der Gesellschaftsmoral sind inzestuöse Beziehungen selten. In einer dänischen Untersuchung zum faktischen Vorkommen hatten beispielsweise nur zwei von 1325 Personen (1,5 ‰), die einen entsprechenden Fragebogen beantworteten, Geschlechtsverkehr mit einem Bruder bzw. einer Schwester gehabt (beide waren Frauen).[35] Deshalb gibt es in der Praxis auch nur wenige Inzestverfahren. So wurden 2006 insgesamt 84 Fälle von „Blutschande u.ä." (wie es in der Kriminalstatistik bezeichnet wird) angezeigt. In den vorausgegangenen Jahren lag die Zahl der Anzeigen in gleicher oder ähnlicher Höhe.[36] Die statistische Angabe umfasst sowohl Fälle des § 210 (Inzest) als auch solche des § 223 Abs. 1 (Beischlaf mit einem Adoptiv- oder Stiefkind o.ä.). Dabei handelt es sich um die Zahl der angezeigten Taten, nicht die der Täter. Fälle des Geschwisterinzests (§ 210 Abs. 2) werden in der Statistik nicht gesondert ausgewiesen.

2. Inzest und Rassenhygiene im neueren dänischen Recht außerhalb des Strafrechts

Mit dem (sozial-)darwinistischen Menschenbild und der lombrosianischen Kriminologie erhielt das Strafrecht und das sonstige Recht im 20. Jahrhundert in einer Reihe von Punkten eine biologische Orientierung. In Dänemark waren die führenden Fürsprecher Sozialdemokraten, aber die rassenhygienischen Auffassungen erhielten breite politische und wissenschaftliche Unterstützung.[37]

35. *Stenvig*, in: Nordisk Tidsskrift for Kriminalvidenskab, S. 192, 201.
36. 2000: 92; 2001: 84; 2002: 90; 2003: 81; 2004: 82; 2005: 84.
37. *Koch*, Racehygiejne i Danmark 1920–56.

Das *Ehegesetz von 1922* enthielt eine Reihe absoluter oder bedingter Eheverbote, z.B. auch zwischen Personen, von denen die eine mit einem Verwandten der anderen in auf- oder absteigender Linie geschlafen hatte. Die Vorschriften über die Ehe zwischen nahen Verwandten wurden durch dieses neue Gesetz verschärft. Die dänischen Regeln waren im internationalen Vergleich äußerst restriktiv.[38] Die Verbote wurden mit der Rassenhygiene begründet;[39] sie wurden als Fortpflanzungskontrolle angewandt.[40] Ab 1938 war für Psychopaten, Alkoholiker, Epileptiker u.a. eine Genehmigung erforderlich, um die Ehe eingehen zu können. Diese Genehmigung hing unter anderem von einer ärztlichen Erklärung ab, dass die Gefahr der Übertragung auf den Nachwuchs gering sei. Man erwog in den 1930er Jahren auch Eheverbote für Blinde, Taube und Sprachbehinderte.

Die Begründung des Verbots der Eheschließung zwischen Schwägern lautete, dass „es zweckmäßig [sei], um bestehende Ehen davor zu schützen, dass erotische Gefühle auf Abwege geraten".[41] Dies ist zum einen sehr optimistisch und basiert zum anderen auf der Voraussetzung, dass es Abwege gibt.

1989 wurden die meisten dieser Ehehindernisse aufgehoben. Die weiterhin existierenden Ehevoraussetzungen, z.B. das Verbot der Eheschließung zwischen Voll- und Halbgeschwistern,[42] werden teilweise immer noch mit dem Risiko erblich bedingter Defekte begründet.[43] Diese Regelungen sind kritisiert worden. Es wurde darauf hingewiesen, dass die Nachkommen von Geschwistern kein höheres Risiko der Behinderung haben als die Nachkommen von Vettern und Cousinen.[44] In jüngerer Zeit wurde mehrfach von Eherechtsexperten vorgeschlagen, dass Halbgeschwistern die Möglichkeit einer Befreiung eingeräumt werden sollte, um die Ehe miteinander einzugehen.[45]

38. *Andersen*, Ægteskabsret, S. 40.
39. *Lund-Andersen* et al., Familieret, S. 167, Fn. 5.
40. *Koch*, Racehygiejne i Danmark 1920–56, S. 35 ff.
41. *Andersen*, Ægteskabsret, S. 41.
42. Daneben gibt es ein absolutes Eheverbot für verheiratete Personen (§ 9 Ehegesetz), für Verwandte in direkt auf- und absteigender Linie (§ 6 Ehegesetz) sowie für Adoptiveltern und -kinder, solange das Adoptivverhältnis besteht (§ 8 Ehegesetz). Die Eheschließung zwischen Personen, von denen eine mit einem Verwandten in direkt auf- oder absteigender Linie der anderen verheiratet war, bedarf der ministeriellen Erlaubnis (§ 7 Ehegesetz). Erlaubnis- beziehungsweise einwilligungsbedürftig ist die Eheschließung auch für Minderjährige und für Personen, die unter Pflegschaft stehen (§§ 1–4 Ehegesetz).
43. *Lund-Andersen* et al., Familieret, S. 167 ff.
44. *Andersen*, Ægteskabsret, S. 40.
45. *Danielsen* et al., Ægteskabsloven, S. 40, mit weiteren Nachweisen.

Bereits 1929 wurde in Dänemark ein *Gesetz über die Zwangssterilisation und -kastration von Geistesschwachen und Anderen* eingeführt. Das deutsche Gesetz zur Verhütung erbkranken Nachwuchses von 1933 wurde verhältnismäßig positiv von dänischen Politikern und Wissenschaftlern aufgenommen und beeinflusste die dänische Gesetzgebung der Jahre 1934–35.[46] In Dänemark war der Untergang des Nationalsozialismus in dieser Hinsicht kein Wendepunkt; erst in den 1960er Jahren verloren die eugenischen Gesichtspunkte an Gewicht. In der Praxis wurde großer Wert auf das Vorliegen einer mehr oder weniger freiwilligen Einwilligung in die Sterilisation und Kastration gelegt. Zwischen 1935 und 1950 waren von Sterilisierungen mehrheitlich psychisch Abnorme und geistig Zurückgebliebene betroffen; nach 1951 waren es überforderte Mütter.[47]

In das *Schwangerschaftsgesetz* von 1937 wurde eine eugenische Indikation für den Schwangerschaftsabbruch aufgenommen.[48]

Die Rigidität, die historisch das dänische Strafrecht auf dem Gebiet der Blutschande geprägt hat, findet sich also auch in diesem in gewisser Weise angrenzenden Bereich wieder.

46. *Koch*, Racehygiejne i Danmark 1920–56.
47. *Koch*, Tvangssterilisation i Danmark 1929–67, S. 148, 207 und 311.
48. *Koch*, Racehygiejne i Danmark 1920–56, S. 122 ff.

Literaturverzeichnis

Algreen-Ussing, T., Haandbog i den danske Kriminalret. 3. Aufl. Kopenhagen 1841.

Andersen, Ernst, Ægteskabsret I. Kopenhagen 1954.

Betænkning afgiven af Kommissionen nedsat til at foretage et Gennemsyn af den almindelige borgerlige Straffelovgivning. Kopenhagen 1912.

Betænkning afgiven af Straffelovskommissionen af 9. November 1917. Kopenhagen 1923.

Brorson, Christian, Forsøg til den siette Bogs Fortolkning [...]. Sorøe 1797.

Cornils, Karin/Greve, Vagn, Das dänische Strafgesetz, Straffeloven. 2. Aufl. Freiburg im Breisgau 2001.

Danielsen, Svend et al., Ægteskabsloven. 2. Aufl. Kopenhagen 1984.

Foreløbigt Udkast til Lov om Forbrydelser. [Kopenhagen 1859].

Goos, C. Den danske Strafferets specielle Del, Band I. Kopenhagen 1895.

Greve, Vagn, Blodskam – en utidssvarende straffebestemmelse. In: Lene Ravn (Red.), Kriminalistisk Årbog 1996, S. 161 ff.

Greve, Vagn/Jensen, Asbjørn/Nielsen, Gorm Toftegaard, Kommenteret straffelov, Speciel del. 8. Aufl. Kopenhagen 2005.

Grothe Nielsen, Beth, Seksuelle overgreb mod børn i familien, Et offerperspektiv på straffesystemet. Århus 1991.

– Straffesystemet i børneperspektiv – seksuelle overgreb mod børn i familien. 2. Aufl. Kopenhagen 2001.

Hurwitz, Stephan, Den danske kriminalret, Speciel del. Kopenhagen 1955.

Jensen, Sv. Gram, En højesteretsdom om blodskam (1862) og dens følger, Fra Himmerland og Kjær Herred 1990, S. 27–32.

Jónsson, Már, Blóðskömm Á Íslandi 1270–1870. Reykjavik 1993.

Koch, Lene, Racehygiejne i Danmark 1920–56. Kopenhagen 1996.

– Tvangssterilisation i Danmark 1929–67. Kopenhagen 2000.

Königs Christians Des Fünfften, Dänsches Gesetz [...] übersetzet [...] Durch H[enr.] W[eghorst]. Kopenhagen 1699.

Krogh, Tyge, Oplysningstiden og det magiske, Henrettelser og korporlige straffe i 1700-tallets første halvdel. Kopenhagen 2000.

Kutchinsky, Berl, Blodskam/Incest. Kopenhagen 1980.

Lund-Andersen, Ingrid et al., Familieret. 4. Aufl. Kopenhagen 1996.

Motiver til det foreløbige Udkast til Lov om Forbrydelser. [Kopenhagen 1859].

Stenvig, Bodil, Seksuelle overgreb på børn, definition og omfang – en analyse af datamaterialet fra den danske undersøgelse i 1987. Nordisk Tidsskrift for Kriminalvidenskab 1990, S. 192 ff.

Straffelovrådets betænkning om straf for pornografi, Nr. 435. Kopenhagen 1966.

Straffelovrådets betænkning om strafferammer og prøveløsladelse, Nr. 1099. Kopenhagen, 1987.

Straffelovrådets betænkning om straffastsættelse og strafferammer II, Nr. 1424. Kopenhagen 2002.

Torp, Carl, Betænkning [...] indeholdende Udkast til Love vedrørende den borgerlige Straffelovgivning med Motiver. Kopenhagen 1917.

Udkast til Straffelovbog for Danmark med tilhørende Motiver. Kopenhagen 1864.

Waaben, Knud, Strafferettens specielle del. 5. Aufl. Kopenhagen 1999.

Ørsted, Anders Sandøe, Supplement til afdøde Generalauditør Nørregaards Forelæsninger [...]. Kopenhagen 1804.

– Eunomia [...], Kopenhagen 1817.

Abkürzungsverzeichnis

FT	Folketingstidende
JT	Juridisk Tidsskrift
NJA	Nyt Juridisk Arkiv
UfR	Ugeskrift for Retsvæsen